MEANING AND METHOD IN INFORMATION STUDIES

Information Management, Policy, and Services

Peter Hernon, series editor

Technology and Library Information Services
  Carol Anderson and Robert Hauptman
Information Policies
  Robert H. Burger
Organizational Decision Making and Information Use
  Mairéad Browne
Meaning and Method in Information Studies
  Ian Cornelius
Library Performance Accountability and Responsiveness: Essays in Honor of Ernest R. DeProspo
  Charles C. Curran and F. William Summers
Curriculum Initiative: An Agenda and Strategy for Library Media Programs
  Michael B. Eisenberg and Robert E. Berkowitz
Resource Companion to Curriculum Initiative: An Agenda and Strategy for Library Media Programs
  Michael B. Eisenberg and Robert E. Berkowitz
Information Problem-Solving: The Big Six Skills Approach to Library & Information Skills Instruction
  Michael B. Eisenberg and Robert E. Berkowitz
Research for School Library Media Specialists
  Kent R. Gustafson and Jane Bandy Smith
The Role and Importance of Managing Information for Competitive Positions in Economic Development
  Keith Harman
A Practical Guide to Managing Information for Competitive Positioning to Economic Development
  Roma Harris
Service Quality in Academic Libraries
  Peter Hernon and Ellen Altman
Microcomputer Software for Performing Statistical Analysis: A Handbook for Supporting Library Decision Making
  Peter Hernon and John V. Richardson (editors)
Public Access to Government Information, Second Edition
  Peter Hernon and Charles R. McClure
Statistics for Library Decision Making: A Handbook
  Peter Hernon, et al.
Reclaiming the American Library Past: Writing the Women In
  Suzanne Hildenbrand (editor)

Libraries: Partners in Adult Literacy
   Deborah Johnson, Jane Robbins, and Douglas L. Zweizig
Information Seeking as a Process of Construction
   Carol Kuhlthau
Library and Information Science Research: Perspective and Strategies for Improvement
   Charles R. McClure and Peter Hernon (editors)
U.S. Government Information Policies: Views and Perspectives
   Charles R. McClure, Peter Hernon, and Harold C. Relyea
U.S. Scientific and Technical Information Policies: Views and Perspectives
   Charles R. McClure and Peter Hernon
Gatekeepers in Ethnolinguistic Communities
   Cheryl Metoyer-Duran
Assessing the Public Library Planning Process
   Annabel K. Stephens
For Information Specialists
   Howard White, Marcia Bates, and Patrick Wilson
Public Library Youth Services: A Public Policy Approach
   Holly G. Willet

In Preparation:
Knowledge Diffusion in the U.S. Aerospace Industry
   Thomas E. Pinelli, et al.
Federal Information Policies in the 1990s: Views and Perspectives
   Peter Hernon, Charles McClure, and Harold C. Relyea

MEANING AND METHOD IN INFORMATION STUDIES

by

Ian Cornelius

Ablex Publishing Corporation
Norwood, New Jersey

Copyright © 1996 by Ian V. Cornelius

All rights reserved. No part of this publication may be reproduced, stored in a retrieval system, or transmitted, in any form, or by any means, electronic, mechanical, photocopying, microfilming, recording or otherwise, without permission of the author.

Printed in the United States of America

Library of Congress Cataloging-in-Publication Data

Cornelius, Ian V.
    Meaning and method in information studies / Ian V. Cornelius.
      p. cm. — (Information management, policy, and services)
    Includes bibliographical references and indexes.
    ISBN 1-56750-227-X (cloth). — ISBN 1-56750-228-8
    1. Information science—Methodology. 2. Hermeneutics.
3. Information science—United States—Methodology. I. Title.
II. Series.
Z665.C7565   1996
020—dc20   96-17290
                                                                                   CIP

Ablex Publishing Corporation
355 Chestnut Street
Norwood, New Jersey 07648

Acknowledgments

This work began in 1986 when I was on sabbatical leave from University College Dublin (UCD). I wish to thank University College Dublin for granting me leave. Columbia University in New York, the University of California at Berkeley, St. Andrews University, and the European University Institute (EUI) in Florence all at various times kindly allowed me the use of their facilities and access to the stimulating company of their faculty and students.

Over the years this book has been in preparation I have greatly benefited from discussions with several generations of students at UCD. I wish to thank them and also my colleagues Mary Burke, Michael Casey, John Dean, Bob Pearce, Allan Ramsay, and Barbara Traxler-Brown who gave me good collegiate support and enhanced my understanding of our discipline with their own insights and practice. Noreen Hayes relieved me of a great burden by transforming much of the material from manuscript to electronic form, and the Computing Services staff at UCD made life much easier by facilitating my use of computer resources. I thank the Library staff at UCD for easing the path of study and helping with access to printed material. I also wish to thank Robert Wedgeworth and the faculty of the Columbia University School of Library Service for a rewarding semester while I was their colleague in the fall of 1986. Monash University Graduate School of Librarianship, in Melbourne, and the Departments of Library and Information Studies in what are now the University of South Australia in Adelaide, and Curtin University in Perth, Western Australia, kindly let me try out some of my early ideas for this book in papers read to them in early 1987. I must also record a special thanks to Professor Klaus Eder and the Department of Social and Political Science at the EUI for welcoming me as a visiting research fellow for a most fruitful year in 1993–1994.

For sustained encouragement and general intellectual support, I gratefully acknowledge the important contributions at various times of other colleagues and friends, particularly Maria Baghramian, John Baker, John Brewer, Michael Koenig, Michael Walsh, and especially Keith van Rijsbergen. I also owe special debts to Tom Wilson for reading a complete early draft and offering much needed comment and criticism, and also to Norman Roberts for patiently reading and rereading several later drafts, and for his acute and constructive criticism that guided me past several minefields.

My warmest and sincerest thanks are due to Attracta Ingram who has been my most stimulating critic, and whose constructive reading has helped this book into its final form, pulling me out of various theoretical ditches on the way. Her intellectual companionship is my most treasured reward.

Vivienne and Melissa Dunlop bore the burdens of a preoccupied academic family with fortitude and goodwill. My mother was attentive and steadfast in her encouragement for many years, and my son Alec was patient and understanding about my unavailability for play on so many occasions; they both have my affection and gratitude.

For the errors and failings that remain, responsibility lies with me alone.

—Ian Cornelius

*For my mother and to the memory of my father,
and for Attracta and Alec*

Contents

Part One: Introduction and Background *1*

1 Introduction *5*
2 The Art of Interpretation *21*
3 Interpretation in Politics and Law *37*
4 The Context of Meaning and the Concept of the Information Culture *55*

Part Two: Preparations and Objections *83*

5 Interpretation in Library and Information Studies *85*
6 Objections to the Interpretive Position *97*
7 Practice and Theories *121*

Part Three: Conceptions of Information Studies *137*

8 Bibliography *139*
9 Information Science *155*
10 Information Management *187*
11 Summary and Conclusion *203*

References *217*

Author Index *225*

Subject Index *229*

Part I

Introduction and Background

This book is about the development of meaning and the interpretation of practice in information studies, and how we badly need an overall view of the field that gives an understanding of what the field is, how it develops, and how we identify our place within it when it is changing so rapidly. Over the last 30 years the library and information profession has been pulled in several conflicting directions by theoretical disputes about what the field is. As a consequence there has been a loss of a sense of central coherence in the field. Succeeding versions of what the field "is" and what its practitioners "do" have left us unsure of where legitimacy lies—and how our own future can be reconciled to prevailing trends and impending changes.

At the same time there has been a long movement to get away from positivist, or "scientific," models of research practice. Qualitative methods have frequently been used and advocated, but their status has never quite matched that of the scientific paradigm. I argue that positivist models of what the field is should be rejected because they take no account of how human sciences work or how people in service professions actually construct theory and make sense of the practice they are in. Instead, it is proposed, the tradition of hermeneutics, in the form known as interpretation, can supply a better basis for building an account of the field and constructing theory in and for the field.

Much of current attention in this field focuses on the influence of new information technology and the overall social impact of the "information society." The book considers this to be the cultural context within which the field currently operates, and to be the context of meaning for practitioners in the field.

The implication of accepting an interpretive account of the field is that many versions of what the field is and what practitioners in it do can flourish at one time, so there can be parallel legitimate discourses or languages in and of the field. The book examines what these parallel conceptions of the field might be and dismisses alternative incompatible views of how the field should be viewed.

I argue that the interpretive account and approach has a powerful validity because it is the way we intuitively view the field anyway: It is only that prevailing orthodoxies have not allowed this to surface, and that we would all benefit from formally recognizing what our natural practice is and making the most of its possibilities. An interpretive approach gives practice an enhanced role in theory construction for the field by binding practice and theory into a closer and more complex relationship. This also gives due attention to the way all practitioners form their own sense of professional identity by their involvement in the creation of meaning for the field, which is formed with and shared by others in the field.

The reconceptualization I propose addresses current theoretical and epistemological debates within the field. Although older positivist approaches have been under strong attack for some time, there is no clear indication of how to construct an alternative approach. Hitherto, writers have emphasized the field's need to construct itself as a true science or as a social science conforming to the scientific paradigm. Many writers have observed that this has not been achieved, and may not be achievable. The field must therefore fail in its desire to achieve any kind of scientific respectability. However, alternative approaches are available, and I want to show how, by keeping in step with new currents in the social sciences, a new methodology and theoretical base of the field can be constructed. This book works through the theoretical argument and shows how it can be applied in three key areas.

The work is divided into three parts. In Part One the problem is introduced and two critical components for discussion are identified: what is meant by interpretation, and within what context of meaning it is currently applied.

The field of information studies is seen as including, *inter alia*, librarianship, library science, documentation, information management, information science, and bibliography. At times I use the broader phrase *library and information studies*. In my view, theory development and research allow all these areas to be seen as part of a common tradition. Chapter 1 shows how there has been a desire for an epistemological grounding that copes with some of the problems not resolved by current approaches to research. In Chapter 2, the hermeneutic background to interpretation and some of the arguments used for the particular technical application of interpretation in the social sciences are reviewed. In Chapter 3 the application of the interpretive method in two other social science disciplines is examined, and the way similar arguments can be used in the field of library and information studies is demonstrated. Chapter 4 introduces the idea of a "context of meaning" for interpretation and shows how the so-called information age can be seen as the current context of meaning for the field.

INTRODUCTION AND BACKGROUND

In Part Two, objections to the application of interpretation to library and information studies are considered, and in Part Three there is an examination of various representations of practice in the field as conceptions of what the field "is." Here the relation of theory to practice is discussed.

1
Introduction

What is a librarian, one may ask and possibly not stay for an answer. It may be that the great days of librarianship are over. That the total operation has become such a rabbit warren that no longer can a single man put his impress on the whole complex of operations. Indeed, one wonders whether the specialization required to staff the different sections of a large institutional library these days must not necessarily produce men and women trained in such various skills that there can be as little identification, or communication, among them as there is in a university faculty between, say, the engineers and the art historians.
—Fredson Bowers (1975, p. 75)[1]

Bowers speaks with immense authority in his own area of bibliography, but today he will be known only to a small part of the community of librarians. Yet his remarks of 1966, as true now as they were then, pose questions for all people engaged in what is now broadly called library and information studies. How do we all talk to one another across our increasing range of specialisms? How do we describe to one another or to outsiders what we do? How do we maintain a vocabulary that enables us, so long after Bowers' observation, to speak to one another at all?

In answer to the question "What do you do?" most of us would reply by saying "I am an information manager," or "I am a librarian," and this would satisfy the questioner's curiosity at a simple level. The reply would convey some meaning to the questioner, who might then interpret the question to augment his own, unrevealed background state of knowledge. The interpretation might not be one we would like, but as long as questioner and respondent shared enough common cultural inheritance, the exchange would be meaningful.

Of course such a simple exchange conveys too little information. If a

---

[1] First delivered May 9, 1966, as the Leitlin-Verbrugge Lecture in Bibliography at UCLA and on May 10 as the Howell Lecture at the University of California, Berkeley, printed by the University of California, 1966.

persistent questioner pursued the issue and wanted to know *exactly* what it was that we did, we could embellish our answer in various ways: We could describe the various tasks that make up our daily practice, we could enumerate the objectives our daily activity was meant to attain, or the objectives of supplying library and information services in society in general, or we could attempt to convey a sense of what all these activities actually mean, either to ourselves and our own lives, or to some other person, or to "society" or its intellectual life. In colloquial speech, we need an answer to the question "What are you up to?" or "What are you playing at?" More formally, we need to be able to say what the purposive strategy of our actions is (see Pocock, 1985, p. 5).

This last is rather more difficult. In this work I attempt to uncover a way of describing the practice of library and information studies that both reveals its meaning, and allows us to answer Bowers' question and confound his speculation about identification. Describing a practice and all its entailments, especially in a time of rapid social, technological, and professional change, is a theoretical task, and requires that we employ and explore the language of theory (Pocock, 1985, p. 1).

There is then a theoretical task in seeking a way of developing an understanding, and uncovering meaning, for and within information studies. The discussion is about a "high-level" theory of the field, within which competing but mutually acceptable middle-range theories of what the field is can be developed (is it information management, for example, or is it bibliography?). Below these middle-range theories there are, within the higher levels of understanding, theories about everyday tasks and purposes, which help give effect to and are given structure by the middle and higher level theory. This book is primarily concerned with high-level theory and the way it affects the development of middle-range theories.

Without a clear and conscious high-level theory, there is no basis for a clear understanding either of where the field presently stands or where it is going. The myriad inputs from a range of other strong disciplines, the burgeoning range of information-handling professions, and the increasing pace of technological change make it increasingly difficult to state simply and with confidence what it is that librarians or other information workers *do* in a way that makes sense for those practicing in all aspects of the field, including research and education.

This question of practice, of what librarians or information managers do, has become a matter of constant concern. The relationship between theory, research, and practice has also come into focus in the professional literature. (See, e.g., Allen & Exon, 1986; DuMont, 1989; Exon, 1989.)

The issue in part centers on a perception of some rupture between practice and research. Long ago Batty and Bearman (1983) complained of what they saw as the excessive emphasis on scientific research and demanded an increased emphasis on the problems of practice, saying that "The profession may do itself a disservice if it seeks to emphasize only 'respectable' research. . . . Like medicine and law, we are a profession with a job to do. We hope to improve by learning from research, but we can also improve through carefully considered practice" (p. 369).

It is not only that there is a job to be done. Our enthusiasm for doing the job is something we bring to it or take from it according to how much we feel the job is worthwhile or rewarding, either a single task or the whole job. Our whole sense of identity is bound up with our work, and as we evaluate our relationship to our work we do so with our own self-definition in mind. We are careful about what we do in relation to our sense of ourselves, but careful consideration of practice is rare: Certainly it is most unusual to find any examination of the meaning of practice. Senior commentators in the field commonly skip over difficult questions about the nature of the profession, and the most sophisticated analyses rarely reach below the surface description of technical performance. This situation has arisen because the world in which we live and work has changed, and our work has changed with it. At one level we have been happy to change the names of professional institutions, of library schools, curricula, and job titles, but we have been reluctant to look at a broader world that has experienced the same traumatic upheavals that we have and has produced some credible new forms of explanation. These newer explanations could be used, but so far have not been put to use, to build more satisfactory pictures of our own discipline and practice. In the past there have been attempts to build on the then-dominant epistemological approach in the social sciences, taken wholesale from the natural sciences. Attempts to hold on to this ultimately unsuccessful scientific model of true inquiry have merely obscured the unpleasant facts that such a model never did work for the whole profession and now applies even less in a world in which "scientific" models are being rejected and replaced throughout the social sciences.

The uncertainty this situation has produced has existed for a long time, and has added to the problems of securing a clear self-identity for ourselves, for our profession and its discipline, in fact, for the whole realm of practice and for the outside world to accept. Several authors have alluded to this problem: Meadow (1979) observed of information science that:

> An aspect of today's information science is that we lack a self definition that covers all of us. For any given researcher or practitioner

that is of no consequence—we can do our jobs without the definition. It becomes a problem when we convene in meetings such as this and try to decide whose future we are looking into. (p. 219)

Similarly Wilkinson (1983), concerned about the future of librarians and librarianship rather than information science, was skeptical of continued existence, although he seemed sure of the identity, when he wondered "whether *librarianship* as an academic discipline will develop or even survive" (p. 37).

Other writers have also drawn attention to uncomfortable aspects of the epistemological situation of library and information studies in general: Beagle (1988), for example, concluded forcefully that "Library and information science research, then, has developed in this uneasy middle ground between inadequate definitions and an outmoded world-view" (p. 28).

What we need is an alternative view of library and information studies that has the advantage of being both consonant with other strands of theorizing in the humanities and social sciences and consistent with the experience of practice, and the relationship between practice and theory, in all aspects of library and information studies. Any view of the field must be one that accommodates not only analysis of the matter and objects in the field, but also the relationship all participants in the field experience between their life overall and their professional life. As we reflect on ourselves and think about the kind of people we are, we are theorizing about our situation, and we carry this over to our work, not merely in relation to how it affects us, but also in respect to the business we are in at work, the practice. In this work the term *practice* is taken to cover all aspects of work undertaken by all involved in the information field: Therefore, researchers, educators, and theorists are all considered as part of the practice, alongside those more commonly assumed to be "in practice." The activities of researching, teaching, and theorizing may also be considered a legitimate part of the work of any other practitioner. For convenience, the term *practitioner* is not normally used in this work to describe those employed as theorists or researchers or educators, except where the term is explicitly meant to be more inclusive.

What I want to show, then, is how, by basing our work within the tradition known as hermeneutics, or *Verstehen*, or *interpretation*, or *understanding*, we can identify the grounds for building a theory for the library and information field that shows how the powerful intellectual and professional influences that have strongly affected the recent development of the field can be accommodated within the information studies tradition, even when they seem to be in conflict. This will also show how professional practice gradually replaces one model of the field by another but still accommodates all models within the tradition. How practice involves a more inclusive approach to theory that includes the processes of research and theorizing within practice will emerge from this study. In doing this I discuss how the information culture now acts as a context of meaning for the field.

The immediate task is to outline the precise nature of the problem and show the kind of solution that can be offered by the interpretive method, and to indicate the direction I am taking.

THE PROBLEM

Writers in our field have been unable to develop a sufficiently comprehensive theory that can offer adequate support for all in practice within it. Some authorities have pursued a rigorous scientific method, others have sought unsuccessfully to apply the scientific method in certain areas, and in some parts of the discipline that method has been rejected as inappropriate, or has been ignored. However, the lure of science remains strong. Few writers have attempted to provide alternative theoretical frameworks, despite frequent calls in the literature for a new theory, and increasingly frequent examinations of alternative methods of approaching the field and its problems. (See especially Bradley, 1993; Bradley & Sutton, 1993; Sutton, 1993.) Any practitioner requires a way of working out how to understand the practice he or she is engaged in: As we reflect on our practice and situation we need some means of explaining all the processes that contribute to the definition of them and changes in them.

The Lure of Science

The dominance of the scientific method in both the natural and the social sciences has proved irresistible for those intent on establishing the status of library and information studies. Busha and Harter (1980), for example, claimed that:

> If librarianship is to merit the coveted designation "science," a significant number of scholars and research workers must regularly apply scientific method . . . Moreover, the study of library science can attain recognition as a true science only when a general body of theory is developed. . . .Thus, the major thesis of this book is that scientific method *can be used* effectively in the study of library and information science, allowing the derivation of system-

atized knowledge from observation, experimentation, and other productive research methods. (p. 4)

Bibliometrics and experimental computerized information retrieval are two areas within the field that obviously seem to reflect and lend support to this notion. In contrast, this book denies that scientific method can be used effectively across the whole field of library and information studies, and (following Winch, Suppe, and others) contests the claim that neutral observation is possible in a social science. A general body of theory can only come from a different perspective, and the theory that scientific method can produce is of limited application.

Other writers have shown some confusion about the applicability of scientific method. Vickery and Vickery (1987) claimed in the preface to their work to present "a scientific understanding of the processes of information transfer. This transfer is a human, social activity: it is the transfer of meaning from one person to another" (p. v). They did not explain how the transfer of meaning is to be analyzed by their preferred method, and soon conceded that "It is unlikely that an analysis confined to the unit act (of communication) itself will give us full understanding. It is necessary to explore what social influences affect information resources and wants, . . . we may expect to find a continually evolving pattern of informative communication within society" (p. 14). In other words, their objectively observed fact (the communication event or act) cannot be explained without reference to a constantly changing external world.

The strong orientation toward science has been critically observed by Olaisen (1985), who claimed that "The field has developed in a quantitative way where easily accessible facts have been collected . . . and the statistical methods have been overemphasized to attain 'scientific' respectability" (p. 129). The powerful influence of science on method has been challenged from within the profession. Olaisen (1985) called for a movement away from the scientific and quantitative model and suggested a different focus that would

> support the shift in focus from quantitative methods to more qualitative methods by insisting upon the use of qualitative social research methods for the development of concepts and theories from the point of view of the philosophy of the social sciences and humanities rather than the physical sciences. (p. 147)

Natoli (1982) also objected to the neglect of the tradition of the humanities in the conduct of research and inquiry in the field. He argued:

Since librarianship has very much to do with the "human factor," with subjectivity, in the form of librarian, patron, and administrator, it is conceivable that its problems and attendant research could be well served by a subjective approach. This subjective approach is based on a phenomenological, rather than a behavioural, perspective. It is my contention that research in librarianship cannot be modeled to any great extent on an objective approach, not without producing conclusions far removed from the reality of librarianship as readily perceived by every librarian in the field. Nor can such an approach take into account the diverse nature of librarianship itself, one in which the purely technical objective exists side by side with the conceptual—the bureaucratic with the professional. (p. 164)

Recent literature shows a burgeoning acceptance of research methods that offer an alternative to the scientific paradigm, but it is also apparent that the debate has been framed in terms of quantitative and nonquantitative methods for particular inquiries, rather than in terms of general theory.

The Information Culture

The variously named phenomenon, identified from the 1960s onward, and commonly called the *Information Age* or the *Information Society* has quickly become axiomatic for writers in the field, and is rarely given anything more than mention or crude description. Rarely is the real relationship between this phenomenon and the field analyzed, and rarely is the phenomenon given a description other than that of its protagonists. Thus Vickery and Vickery (1987) had as the very first sentence of their preface, "It is nowadays a commonplace that we are living in an 'information society.' The practical importance of information to problem solving, decision making, and just plain coping with life is clear to all" (p. v). And in the Butterworths series *Guides to Information Sources*, Foskett and Hill, the series editors, have as the first sentence of their preface, "Daniel Bell has made it clear in his book *The Post-Industrial Society* that we now live in an age in which information has succeeded raw materials and energy as the primary commodity" (see, e.g., Vernon, 1984, p. v).

Other examples can be found, and in Chapter 4 some are discussed. In this work the term *information culture* is used to cover all approaches to the phenomenon, and the term is used to refer to a point of view that is prepared to believe in the supreme importance of information and the various theories that have been associated with it. The analysis of information culture presented here considers that culture as the context of meaning for the current age and for any meaning that can be generated for the library and information field.

Our ideas about the information culture come from outside the profession. The idea is general in society, and has attracted comment from philosophers and other social theorists who have no interest in the particular problems of the field of library and information studies, but who do write about the general human condition. It is clear, therefore, that the information culture cannot be ignored if a body of theory consonant with the current age, and with current thinking in the social sciences, is to be developed.

The Problem Restated

The problem is to find a method that will offer a means to understanding developments across the broad range of library and information studies, and that will fit in with current interpretations of the information age. The next section examines the reasons for choosing interpretation as that method.

METHODS

This is a study of theory and practice. It has already been indicated that the intention is to show that interpretive approaches closely linked to hermeneutics are the most appropriate for a social science discipline like library and information studies. The historical and theoretical background to the development of this method are discussed in the next chapter, and its application is discussed in succeeding chapters. Hermeneutics is the *koine* of the current age and it is used here as a response, more consonant with our own times, to the unsolved problems and unsatisfactory situations left by alternative methods that have proven inadequate. Those methods, particularly the scientific method known better as logical positivism or logical empiricism, are based on a view of the world and an epistemology that is, ultimately, unsuitable and almost unusable for most practitioners in the field. Librarianship and information science have had differing approaches to the problem of relating their respective disciplinary traditions to the broader framework of epistemology in the social sciences and humanities. In information science, or rather in that part of it most easily identified from the literature as a self-aware empirical research subject, there has been no hesitation in associating, almost implicitly, with the general tradition of scientific research. This association has been sought partly of necessity because of the close association with computer science and partly by default as so many of the researchers themselves come from backgrounds in the hard sciences. The result has been a mirror of science that has been reinforced by its own success. Those who come from the humanities and who are familiar only with the traditional research methods and interests of the humanities may feel excluded from much of the research enterprise and may conclude that the scope of legitimate inquiry is, for them, severely limited.

In consequence, a large body of practitioners both in librarianship and in information science could feel either that published research is inaccessible, if it is "properly" scientific, or that it is, literally, academic if it concerns only the construction of a library or bibliographic history.

In between these positions, which have been deliberately painted as extremes, lies the work that is of major and immediate practical interest to the bulk of practicing professionals. Such work, which is most typically concerned with examinations of the social nature of library or information use, the behavior of library or information workers, and the sociolinguistic problems of catalog use, classification, indexing, and information retrieval, most typically falls within the field of the broadly defined social sciences, and has most frequently attracted the research methods of those sciences. These social sciences reflect, to a heightened degree, that concern to conform to the scientific research paradigm (although inroads on that position have been made in increasing strength in recent years), and the less precisely that paradigm seems to fit, the greater the concern with the results, and the greater the uncertainty about their applicability. These epistemological problems in the social sciences have in recent years aroused renewed interest in the possibility of discovering alternatives to the scientific paradigm: One such alternative has been sought in the rediscovery of Grand Theory.

Theory and Grand Theory

The mood of the 1960s and 1970s, which by and large despised general social philosophies and aspired to some positivist exactitude, has been questioned if not actually replaced, or everywhere discarded. A new mood, most obviously exemplified by *The Return of Grand Theory* (Skinner, 1985) is due largely to a recovery of confidence by social philosophers, a recovery closely linked to a new interest and understanding in "continental" European philosophy. For decades the European tradition in social philosophy had been neglected in Anglo-American circles. Now, the works of Dilthey, Gadamer, Habermas, Foucault, and others are being discussed not as replacements for Kuhn and Popper, but alongside them.

Skinner (1985) identified two significant components of the older tradition: first, a belief that "human action should . . . be viewed and explained in exactly the same way as natural events" (p. 5) and thus that—as A. J. Ayer put it, "man is a suitable subject for science"; second, a belief that rationalist assumptions about the practice of science were the only correct ones. These tendencies have both been evident in librarianship and information science and have colored and sometimes dictated the character of research, even when the results seem barren or the criteria seem inapplicable to the subject matter.

The assumptions that are now questioned have posed serious barriers to the development of a satisfactory research confidence in, and theory construction in, library and information studies. If library and information studies can be placed *in toto* among the social sciences and humanities, then new movements in social philosophy can be used both to discover a better epistemology for the subject and to improve the profession's sense of itself by offering an alternative, and comprehensible, framework of explanation. Social philosophers have not simply rejected the positivist account most closely associated by the library and information studies research community with Popper. There has instead been a joining of traditions: Linguistic philosophy, particularly the work of Wittgenstein as interpreted by Winch, has been joined to the continental tradition that can be traced through Dilthey, Weber, Shutz, Gadamer, and Habermas. This tradition claims that theories of social explanation must take account of both the meanings and the causes of social phenomena, and that meaning is a matter of use (Skinner, 1985).

Use is a matter for personal interpretation, and the immediate positivist response to such stances is that it makes impossible any "objective" knowledge—knowledge that is evidently true to all who approach it, whatever their point of departure, providing they are rigorous and rational in their approach. This objection in turn has encouraged the development of two stances within the antipositivist debate. First, there is the anarchic claim that there can be no objective knowledge and no true method (associated with Feyerabend) and that even the reading of texts cannot allow the imputation of any authorial meaning in many cases (associated with Derrida). An alternative approach that rejects such anarchic views (which make almost impossible any knowledge at all) has been that of Gadamer, who talked of the "fusing of horizons" in an interpretative world of shared meanings. In sum, recent social thought offers two alternatives to an unattainable scientific exactitude—a rejection of any method, and one associated with the broad continental tradition of hermeneutics and most recently made available under the heading *Verstehen* or *interpretation*. In this work I normally use the term *interpretation* or *interpretive*.

Philosophical Reaction in Library and Information Studies

Such considerations have not yet permeated far into our professional consciousness, but there has been unease for some time with the limited possibilities that "normal" scientific method offers. In particular, two reactions stand out: an interest in Thomas Kuhn and an interest in phenomenological approaches to library and information studies.[2]

Thomas Kuhn. Kuhn's work has been of interest to the library and information community primarily for its descriptive power in relation to the subject literature handled. He advanced the view that the rationalist claims of science are not in themselves sufficient to justify much of the research that is accepted by the scientific community and published with authority. He claimed that in fact much of this work reflects a scientific consensus about what is "good" or "bad" research—and, in consequence, knowledge, and that this consensus will change at various times as alternative frameworks of explanation offer better or more complete explanations. He advanced a sociological claim about the nature of acceptable scientific research—that good research is a matter of agreement within scientific communities, rather than something determined by rationality alone. In this respect, Kuhn is close to an interpretive explanation, although he does not adopt that approach. Reasoning, in effect, is a conventional activity (Barnes, 1985), and the process of controlling what counts as scientific knowledge is seen as scientific practice—a social activity (Skinner, 1985).

The Phenomenological Approach to Information Studies. In the United Kingdom, Young and Oldman both drew attention to the phenomenological tradition from the standpoint of sociology, and they both emphasized the need to escape from the positivist paradigm. Oldman (1981)

---

[2] I have discovered only two recent hermeneutic approaches to the problems in this field: Bennett (1988) and Benediktsson (1989). Bennett's question is different from mine, and he takes his hermeneutics from a different source (for reasons he does not make clear), but I make use of some of the same source material. Benediktsson's study is very useful as a descriptive framework of the various hermeneutic approaches, but his preference for the approach of Betti and Ricoeur, and his own concentration on the process of finding texts (and his acceptance of texts as "objectivations of mind") means that his work is based on different premises and has different objectives to mine.

observed that "We are constantly worrying as a profession about the gap between research and practice. A phenomenological methodology is more likely than a positivist one to bridge that gap" (p. 27). Young (1981) enjoined more explicitly the use of interpretative methods without spelling them out:

> To conclude, this paper has attempted to provide an analysis of the underlying taken for granteds of sociological perspectives which might be employed when considering the questions of access and control of knowledge in librarianship and information work. Underlying this were the conceptions of the very nature of knowledge. An approach involving both structural and interpretative levels of analysis was suggested in an hermeneutical tradition, with an emphasis on understanding rather than explanation. (p. 38)

Even more explicitly, Bennett found when examining the problem of professional identity that hermeneutics offered the most promising method. Commenting on the move from an identity of library science to the more recent library and information science, Bennett (1988) noted, "the important matters . . . were the interpretations of library science and library-and-information-science, it seemed to me that hermeneutics or the theory of interpretation was the appropriate theoretical framework from which to hang my inquiry" (p. 174).

Capurro (1992) recently observed, in respect to information science, that "With the rise of philosophical Hermeneutics and Analytical Philosophy we have gained new paths of thinking which are, I believe, relevant to the foundations of information science" (p. 83). Hoel (1992) also recommended the application of hermeneutics to information science.

The Problems With Positivism

As Kuhn showed, the problem with positivism was that as an account of scientific method, it was not true of scientific practice. Positivists claim that meaningful statements are of two categories: statements of logic and mathematics on the one hand, and statements of fact on the other. Putative scientific statements are statements of fact and as such must be empirically verifiable (or, in some views, falsifiable). Those that cannot satisfy this test are properly, if anything, in the realm of metaphysical speculation, but strictly speaking, meaningless. A serious theoretical flaw with this position is the assumption that the facts that are to provide empirical verification or falsification are theory neutral. Suppe (1985) criticized the main positivist claim about observation: "Today there is widespread consensus among philosophers of science that observation is theory-laden—influenced by beliefs, theories, linguistic abilities and cognitive states—and that the Positivist's dream of theory-neutral observation fails" (188–189).

The work of Kuhn on the history of science showed the dependence of observation on theory and the role of "acceptability to a relevant scientific community" in establishing claims to scientific validity (Kuhn 1957, 1970). This "acceptability" means the ability to solve problems, and fruitfulness in formulating and resolving further research questions. In science, this means, in part, the ability to make predictions. The claim of theory-neutral observation is inconvenient for most inquiries into human subjects, and although it might work well for natural science, it does not always work in a practical discipline.

Yet belief in "scientific method" as understood by positivism has continued to dominate the basis of much work in information science, especially in areas such as experimental information retrieval. However, there has been some movement away from the purely scientific tradition by researchers. One of the first to make this move was van Rijsbergen (1986), who in a telling admission stated that:

> In the last few years, I have become increasingly dissatisfied with the state-of-the-art in information retrieval. I have reluctantly concluded that the fundamental basis of all the previous work is wrong. Almost all of the previous work in Information Retrieval (including my own) has been based on the assumption that a formal notion of *meaning* is not required to solve the information retrieval problems. (p. 194)

Similarly, Winograd and Flores (1986) concluded about the same time that rationalist assumptions about computer design and artificial intelligence were misplaced and that alternative, hermeneutic approaches could be more fruitful, saying that "we need to replace the rationalistic orientation if we want to understand human thought, language, and action, or to design effective computer tools" (p. 26).[3]

There has also been some recognition from within library and information studies that the field has for too long pursued one particular paradigm. Olaisen (1985), for example, claimed that "the library field has limited itself to a functionalist orientation (i.e., logical empiricism) and has in this way remained a one-dimensional science concerned with technology and problem solving" (p. 148).

---

[3] Fidel (1993) showed that qualitative research methods are now widely applicable in information retrieval.

Without pointing to any new theoretical approach, Hollnagel (1980) earlier observed that information science research needed to shift from a narrowly scientific base, and to incorporate the experience of the practitioner:

> The basis for information science is therefore to be found in our experience of using and searching for information, and my guess is that any significant progress in information science will be the result of the analysis of the experiences of information scientists, rather than of formally deduced hypotheses. (p. 184)

In more sociologically oriented research within library and information studies, awareness of the shortcoming of scientific method and the search for an alternative came at about the same time. Hounsell and Winn (1981), introducing papers from a symposium on qualitative research, stated:

> Our starting point was an awareness that the dominant methodology in information science has been the "hypothetico-deductive" model of research. . . . The appropriateness to the social sciences of this model of research is now being widely challenged, and a number of new models are emerging which question both the premises and the procedures of the conventional approach. (p. 204)

These statements have found increasingly insistent support in more recent years. However, the move to qualitative research, although important, is only part of a more radical shift in methodology that has been urged by theorists of social science for some time. Library and information studies is perhaps one of the most difficult areas to bring under the sway of the new methodology. In what follows, I try to explain the new approach and to show how a particular version of it can provide theoretical unity for our field.

Hermeneutics

What then is this hermeneutical tradition of interpretation, and how can it be applied? This approach is described in greater detail in the following chapters. Hermeneutics denies the existence of objective facts in the humanities or social sciences, and claims that in gaining understanding of our situation, of one another, and of "foreign" societies, we are constantly in dialogue, and our position becomes transformed by the process of understanding as we develop shared meanings. As a method, an epistemology, and an environment it offers the comfort of sustained meaning, even as a relativist and local phenomenon, and does not require agreement to universal statements or conformity to a rigid and possibly unattainable logic. It is firmly rooted in our interpretation of experience.

EVIDENCE AND TECHNIQUE

If the paradigm of "scientific" method is being rejected, there must be not only another method, but also data collection techniques and evidence that is appropriate to the new method. Two comments need to be made here. First, the new method, being new, requires an approach to evidence that will strike many as a retreat from any basis in fact. The interpretive approach is founded on experience, and the basis of its argument is what can commonly be agreed on as experience. There are no "facts" in the sense of aggregated statistics or survey responses to uncover; there is no realm of discovery that the researcher can reveal to a reader. The power of the interpretive method lies in its appeal to what is a shared understanding, and its authority is in what, in its descriptions and explanations, is experientially true. The character of evidence can be extended beyond what would commonly be regarded as typical everyday experience by including within that experience the body of descriptions and interpretations that are ever present in the minds of practitioners. Thus, it is legitimate to include as evidence statements culled from serious, seminal, or influential literature, or observations on the behavior of leading figures, or the actions of central or leading professional institutions. This material will be presented much in the way that a literary critic might use evidence: selectively, with selective emphasis, and without obligation to use all information available from one source or any at all from another. In collecting and organizing the evidence, the task is to build and present a "text," or account, which can be the basis of or the informant of the interpretation.

The second observation that should be made about the evidence, especially that selected from published texts, is that in many cases it joins no existing debate but instead constructs another. The material used will have been presented initially with another purpose in mind, and the task is to build the interpretive case from materials from disparate sources, occasionally by imposing a new construction on the meaning. It is analogous to driving across country rather than following well-established arterial routes. The evidence is the evidence of shared meaning in the field of library and information studies. The need for this approach to evidence and its collection is made apparent in Chapter 3 where the interpretive approach is discussed in greater detail.

CONTEXT

The context is the information age. For the field of library and information studies this may be called an information culture, an environment in which claims about the role of information in economic and social life, and the consequences for our professional life, are readily and uncritically accepted. However, the context extends beyond arguments about economic and social change. As this work uses a method that emphasizes meaning, it is essential that the sense of context be broadened to include some idea of how meanings, at least for a thinking community, have been generated for society at large. Additionally, it is part of my claim that library and information studies suffers from not following more closely the general movements in theory in the social sciences, and therefore the current intellectual context in the humanities and social sciences should be considered part of our context.

The discussion of context is limited to examination of the information culture as the context of meaning for the field of library and information studies. The implications of this are examined in Chapter 4 and in the discussion on practice. The immediate task is to build up a picture of the hermeneutic or interpretive method and its position within the changing theoretical currents of the social sciences.

2
The Art of Interpretation

In this chapter I give an overview of the interpretive approach before filling in some of the detail in the following chapter by showing the case made for it in two key social science disciplines, politics and law. In chapter 5, I examine how interpretation could be applied to information studies (broadly defined), looking at the conditions required for its application, the manner of application, and the benefits for the discipline and the profession which might ensue. All this lays the groundwork for later chapters in which various conceptions of library and information studies are themselves examined in turn to see if they are suitable candidates for interpretive treatment. It is a high-level theory that is being considered here, to see what role it can play in developing understanding of the phenomena that form the subject matter of the social sciences. The particular approach to interpretation considered in the next chapter is one appropriate to the social sciences that has never been applied to the field of information studies. Other writers have preferred alternative, more schematic, versions of the hermeneutic tradition. The reasons for choosing the approach introduced here are made apparent later.

INTERPRETATION/UNDERSTANDING/*VERSTEHEN*

The sense in which the terms interpretation, understanding, and *Verstehen* have been used by the phenomenological tradition in history and sociology is really the "common" sense of everyday understanding and language. There is a need to distinguish this kind of hermeneutic understanding from the psychological understanding that is common in scientific research.

What people are doing can be distinguished from what motivates them to do it. What people do can be described in terms of simple actions and words (filing catalog cards, directing a user to a book), but these are obviously different from and more elementary than a more complex judgment about the real import of what people do or say. In the example given just now it is clear that the real import of filing cards in a drawer demands a far more complex set of understandings than an uninformed observer of the action would have. These actions and words and their real significance are to be distinguished from any determination of motive about why people file catalog cards. Clearly, we can distinguish causal explanations of individual acts, the conscious purpose of individuals, which is the psychological level of understanding, from a more general understanding that interprets actions in terms of the broader context, so that we can say we understand the situation in which the words used or actions make sense (Outhwaite, 1971).

The observable data about human behavior, even the words people use to describe their actions, are in fact already interpretations of the situation. The observable data of human life are not like the observable data of natural phenomena. Outhwaite (1971) followed Habermas in claiming that:

> Human actions are not "given" to the investigator in the same way as natural phenomena. The social scientist must begin with data which are already partially interpreted in the ordinary language of everyday life. Moreover, social scientists cannot coherently aim to provide a natural science of human life, but rather to deepen, systematise and often qualify, by means of empirical and conceptual investigations, an "understanding" which is already present. (p. 16)

My claim is that we can only really understand what librarians and information managers do if we follow this approach, and I suggest that in much of our theorizing and in our research and practice, we partly do that anyway. A clearer conceptualization—or understanding—of the process will clarify the profession's sense of itself and its actions and will bring theory and research into closer relationship with practice. I am not concerned with examination of theories of *verstehen* or interpretation: That is the province of philosophers. The task is to take the work they make available and to apply it in our own arena, to see if it helps our understanding. My claim, implicitly, is that it does. In the following chapter the techniques of interpretation are examined. This chapter paints its background.

BACKGROUND

The 19th-century tradition of hermeneutics grew out of biblical scholarship, and the more rigorous exponents of that tradition were concerned quite explicitly to render biblical texts to the reader by reading meaning out of, rather than into, the text. This served a theological requirement to render an exact authorial intention. It has now become clear that the same sort of textual analysis, when applied to a broader field of social life (which can be construed as a special sort of text), will often offer a variety of readings, all of which may be more or less plausible. Even if such readings are contradictory there is no process for deciding between them analogous to scientific methods of verification. It is also clear that hermeneutics is no longer solely concerned with restoring the "original" meaning of the text—especially older literary or historical texts (Outhwaite, 1971).

The process is really one of constructing a text that is interpreted for contemporary use. Any librarian who has wrestled with the latest version of international catalog codes, classification schedules, or online manuals will have been through a process of interpretation when deciding how to apply these international products to local requirements and conditions. The interpreter is a partner in dialogue with the original text.

If individuals are left to a simple atomized personal experience of interpretation, of re-experiencing some event, there is still a difficulty in resolving how social life with its shared sets of meaning can possibly develop. The response of Habermas to this "psychological" danger was to suggest, following Gadamer, that we learn to interpret through dialogue in all forms of social life, by participation in communication that has been learned in interaction, and that only by melting our individual horizons in with those of others can we get beyond the subjectivity of the individual viewpoint (Outhwaite, 1971).

There remains a problem about the relationship of phenomenological sociology to the hermeneutic, or, more precisely, *Verstehen* tradition. This is an important point. The strict interpretation of phenomenological sociology is rather different from *Verstehen*, although it can illuminate the latter (Outhwaite, 1971). The world is actually more complex than the way an agglomeration of individuals might perceive it. The limitations of personal language must be overcome if shared meanings are to be generated, and this is a critical problem for the phenomenologist, except in circumstances where the language defining a situation is employed solely in the interests of one interest group. For example, the ideal of a library is that of an institution used and usable both by librarians and by readers. If readers and librarians are to enjoy any shared world or view about the library they must in part use the same language. Outhwaite's (1971) final position on *Verstehen* and its relation to social objects of study is worth quoting at length:

> Few people would deny, though some would consider it uninteresting, that the *starting point* of social inquiry is some sort of intersubjective understanding. This is not merely to affirm that ordi-

nary language is the ultimate meta-language of any science (a claim that might be questioned in the case of some of the more highly mathematised natural sciences); it is rather that we begin in the *Lebenswelt*, talking "everyday language", and using "everyday accounting procedures". This initial situation, I would argue, has a different significance for the social than for the natural sciences; the former take their concepts from everyday life from the language which is common to them and their objects of investigation, and their explanatory principles remain extremely close to those of everyday life. Where social scientists have strayed too far from "common-sense" constructs, the result has been not greater sophistication, but trivialisation. (pp. 111–112)

One task for this work is to show how we can develop a language of library and information studies that avoids trivialization and gives us increased sophistication. Toward that end we must now turn to an examination of the techniques of interpretation and their application in some other social sciences. The experience of applying interpretation in other disciplines can give a measure of the level of confidence that will be obtained when it is applied to information studies.

HERMENEUTICS AND INTERPRETATION: A NOTE

Before that can be done, the relationship between interpretation and the more general tradition of hermeneutics requires elaboration. There is under consideration here a relatively low-level theory, taking as sources work by Outhwaite, Taylor, and Dworkin, and occasionally referring to higher level theories of hermeneutics.

The relationship is not quite so straightforward, as there are competing strands of hermeneutics, and the picture is confused by my choice of a different account of the hermeneutic tradition than that chosen by Bennett and Benediktsson, the authors of the other published interpretive studies of library and information studies. The obvious question to answer is: "Why have I not chosen that method too?" This section makes clear why I do not follow Bennett and Benediktsson.[1]

Luckily, the task is simplified by Benediktsson, who clearly laid out the map of hermeneutics and who also gave the grounds for following the approach of Ricoeur, which both he and Bennett prefer. Benediktsson identified a hermeneutic theory, associated with the work of Betti, and a

---

[1] I do not use the work of Capurro or Hoel. Although both these authors favor the use of a hermeneutic approach, their subject is *information*, rather than the practice of library and information studies. See Capurro (1992) and Hoel (1992).

hermeneutic philosophy, which he connected with the work of Heidegger and Gadamer (Benediktsson, 1989). He also identified the work of Ricoeur as something that integrates the other strands. According to Benediktsson, Ricoeur did this by "bringing in the structuralist analysis of sign systems in relation to the hermeneutical interpretation of texts" (Benediktsson, 1989, p. 210). Broadly speaking, whereas Benediktsson followed Betti and Ricoeur, I follow a tradition built on the same grounds as the work of Gadamer. Benediktsson's reason for his choice is connected both to his own focus, which is on the relationship of the librarian (and it seems to be an isolated atomistic librarian) to the text of the items he stocks, and also to Betti's belief in the "objectivation of mind" in the intellectual product, the book. Benediktsson rejected the tradition of Heidegger and Gadamer because it "rejects methodological procedures and chooses to proceed through a dialogical mediation of the subject and object" (Benediktsson, 1989, p. 210). He accepted that this approach "implies that the social scientist as interpreter already had a pre-understanding of his object as he approaches it, because they are linked by a context of tradition" (p. 210).

I believe that, whatever the rejection of the Gadamer approach may mean for the projects of Bennett and Benediktsson, it is misplaced for my inquiry because the concern here is with the way groups of people, working in shared contexts and environments, come to understand what they do. How each person sees himself or herself in practice, and how interpretation is established, is discussed in the following sections. I firmly reject the idea of objectivation of mind, if that means that there is only one way of regarding a particular text. Similarly, the concentration that Benediktsson and Bennett saw in Ricoeur on constructing an analysis of text to discover authorial intention or original meaning must also be rejected, because my concern is not to recreate a past state of mind but to discover and describe a current, shared, intersubjective environment.

Finally, there are two other important observations about the high theory, top-down approach to method taken by Bennett and Benediktsson. First, the preferred sources for my inquiry are accessible—in English—and they work practical examples. Second, unlike the high theory of all hermeneutic philosophers, Taylor and Dworkin are not programmatic; they work from what they find in practice, from the bottom up rather than the top down.

BUILDING KNOWLEDGE

In the preceding chapter two explicit claims about the inadequacy of the positivist tradition were made. These were, first, that contrary to the earlier accepted view, human behavior is not a suitable subject for scientific treatment, and second, that claims for the supremacy of rationalist explanations were misplaced.

A basic claim of interpretation is that some meaning that is unclear can be clarified, that it can be made available in a clearer form that offers a better interpretation than that previously available. A clearer interpretation is one that makes more coherent sense of a particular practice, pulling together more of its history and data than does another interpretation. There remains a question about how one can know that this new, clearer interpretation is correct. The efforts to break out of this hermeneutic circle are, at least within the human sciences, bound to fail, and the requirements they impose on us in the attempt to achieve some objectivity themselves lead to impossible conditions (Taylor, 1978).

The interpretive approach claims that it is possible to construct clearer meanings than those currently available. The appeal to a clearer meaning is through the language of expression. This requirement to see through the language itself requires that the language is a shared set of meanings. This language can only be availed of if it is available to us. Our recourse if it fails is to other attempts to explain, or to "read" the phenomenon or text whose meaning is unclear, by widening the framework to include other readings, ad infinitum. There must be an appeal to some common understanding, and it is within this hermeneutic circle that we must exist and seek all our meanings. A further complication arises from a problem of self-reflection. If you cannot convince someone else of your views, if you experience failure in expressing some meaning, how can you continue to be convinced of it yourself? This point will be keenly felt in many circles where expression of "information studies" has been problematic, for professors and practitioners, and also for the public.

The positivist response to this position is an empiricist one. The empirical attempt to escape from the hermeneutic circle is to use a construct that is, it is claimed, open only to one interpretation—that is, beyond any subjectivity and always understood by all observers in the same way. These "objective" facts are the building blocks of scientific knowledge and it has been a task of the social sciences to find or construct similar objective facts. Taylor (1978) called these facts "brute data": "By 'brute data' I mean here and throughout data whose validity cannot be questioned by offering another interpretation or reading, data whose credibility cannot be founded or undermined by further reasoning" (p. 160). It is on the foundation of brute data that the empiricist bases science. Reality must be explainable by the process of nonarbitrary verification and by the use of induction—the weapons of mathematical and logical inference added to the verifiable brute data produce a brand of science that offers unquestionable certainty (Taylor, 1978).

Taylor's objection to this approach centers on questions of whether there can be brute data that are beyond any question for the social sciences. (There is no question here about the position for the natural sciences.) The interpretive position is that brute data in the social sciences should really be seen as a different category, primitive data, which are in themselves already interpreted, and which may be open to a variety of interpretations of equal validity.

The problem revolves around the question of meaning. In the hermeneutic and interpretive tradition, various meanings, or readings, of a text or text analogue are accepted, and this plurality of possible meanings is fundamentally objectionable to the empiricist. How does the interpretive tradition use the notion of meaning, and how does this in turn affect the construction of any science?

Meaning for Taylor has three principal components. First, it is meaning for a subject—there is no "meaning" of any situation independent of the (usually human) subject or subjects who experience it. Second, meaning is about something; that is, we can separate the meaning of an event from the event itself—the two are not identical; the event can be described in itself, or described in terms of its meaning. An event or phenomenon may have only one meaning, but we must keep open the possibility of there being other meanings for the same object. Third, meaning is only available to us in relation to other meanings. We define meanings in contrast to other meanings, so things have meaning in a field, such as a discipline (Taylor, 1978). Ultimately of course all the meanings in any field are, within the hermeneutic circle, defined by relation to each other, so each part of a discipline is defined by relation to the whole.

Such a stance about the circle of meaning can be related to the basic culture within which we live or to specialized overlays within that culture, where special languages are employed. The full sense of the meaning of law or politics, for example, can only be grasped by someone who experiences the meanings within either of those fields and grasps their expression. The reality of, say, information studies, is available to us only if we understand the set of meanings that exist for that discipline.

Such a position has been advocated in the later writing of Shera, but not always in the sense of a hermeneutic science. Shera called for librarians and information scientists to use the methods of symbolic interactionism—a phenomenological social psychology—to improve their grasp on the nature of their discipline. However, such a position is not compatible with an interpretive approach, partly because it vests meaning in individual subjects.

A hermeneutic science requires three conditions to be met. First, there must be a field of objects about which we have some sense and which have some coherence. Second, it must be possible to distinguish between various expressions of the meaning or sense. This must be so, because otherwise we cannot say that one particular expression makes more sense than another. Third, there must be a subject (human) for whom the meanings exist (Taylor, 1978). This point is obviously completely at odds with empiricist claims, for in that tradition, the meaning must be the same for all subjects.[2] The point of an interpretive science is that we interpret the practice for particular individuals who are the subjects within a particular environment.

So what is it that is interpreted, and how is this done? In a field like sociology it may be that for each subject there is a different sense of what counts as sociology. A process of interpretation has already taken place. I cannot say that sociology is what all the libraries jointly contain under that subject heading, because what is currently available internationally or locally in documentary form ignores all other information bearing signal sources. In short, the "text" of sociology is not merely a text to interpret as early hermeneutic scholars interpreted the Bible. It is more of a text analogue, which might as an account of some event or process or discipline in its turn become a text, which we construct from all our interpretations of texts and discourse and practice. However, in making these interpretations of text or text analogue, we confront problems about language.[3]

> The range of human desires, feelings, emotions, and hence meanings is bound up with the level and type of culture, which in turn is inseparable from the distinctions and categories marked by the language people speak. The field of meanings in which a given situation can find its place is bound up with the semantic field of the terms characterizing these meanings and the related feelings, desires, predicaments. (Taylor, 1978, p. 167)

The consequence of this is that the structure of meaning is not independent of the interpretation of meaning. Thus it must be accepted that any human subject is in fact a self-interpreting animal (Taylor, 1978). There are then two interwoven meshes of experience and meanings. On

---

[2] Where there are conflicting claims in science they are usually between competing theories: there is rarely disagreement about what the objects are. In an interpretive science we can admit disagreement, and allow two conflicting theories equal validity. In 'hard' science, usually, one must win.

[3] For a good example of some problems of this nature in bibliography, see McKenzie (1985). It is worth saying that semiological or linguistic interpretations as meanings are similarly for subjects and in a field, but are also about the world of referents and the meaning of signifiers, whereas hermeneutic science is concerned with only three dimensions—for a subject, of something, in a field (see Taylor, 1978).

the one hand, the subject is bound up in some self-interpretation; on the other, the field of objects that he or she might be trying to grasp the sense of is being interpreted or reinterpreted by the same human subject using the same set of meanings. This can be seen as three interrelated layers of interpretation. First, simply being alive is to experience life in terms of meanings, which are (as the second level) themselves "interpreted and shaped by the language in which the agent lives these meanings. This whole is then at a third level interpreted by the explanation we proffer of his actions" (Taylor, 1978, p. 168).

If some interpretation proffered is clearer, or is felt to be clearer, than the understanding the interpreting human subject currently has, then, if this improved clarity is fully assimilated by the subject, it will alter the behavior of the subject. So when we feel we understand better, we may amend our behavior—in respect to, say, catalog use, or even of the whole field of information studies. In this latter case there may be problems with the concept of the subject, as it may be that everyone engaged in or concerned with information studies (the object) may be an interpreting subject. However, certainly there is a process of interpretation whereby we make sense of some experience—we generate experiential meaning that shows a coherence of meaning. As we make sense of something, we are offering an interpretation that improves coherence and, by expressing the interpretation—which will be in some other form than the expression of what is being interpreted—we make clearer what is only implicit in what is interpreted. Bernstein (1983) made the point that this art of interpretation does not follow deterministic rules, except insofar as the rules operate as heuristic guides, appealing to exemplars of interpretation. However, the interpreter "must have the insight, imagination, openness, and patience to acquire this art—an art achieved through practice" (Bernstein, 1983, p. 135). Interpretation, then, is a practice in itself, in which the interpreter is engaged along with the practice being interpreted.

INTERPRETATION AND VALIDATION

All this is rather strange to those familiar only with the logical empiricist tradition, where attempts are made to reconstruct social reality from brute data alone (Taylor 1978). What is it about brute data that is so unacceptable? What is it that makes it impossible to accept the idea of brute data in the social sciences? The logical positivist might also ask what a hermeneutic science will supply by way of verification.

To speak of verification is to use the language of positivism: Although verification is very important for positivism, it does not follow that other methods must employ a similar device. Hermeneutics cannot offer any substitute for the empiricist's verification, but it can appeal to another factor, insight, as a resource beyond differences of interpretation. (Brute data is limited as it cannot supply insight or intention.) The ultimate situation is that the hermeneutic scientist claims that, through his improved insight into a situation, he can understand both his own position and that of his opponent, but that the opponent, lacking this insight, cannot have the broader understanding (Taylor, 1978). The consequence of this is that the opponent has to not only develop his intuitions but also, through this, to admit that he has been deluded about his interpretation of the situation he is in. A psychotherapist, for example, will work on the dysfunctional behavior patterns of the patient and work with the patient to construct a view of the patient's life that makes that life seem more comprehensible, and enables the patient to gain insight into his or her life and to dispel any illusions that the patient's previous, inadequate interpretation would have created. Or take the case of the librarian who believes people need more information. Mental modeling may posit that we make decisions by processing information, and endless surveys may apparently support the notion that more information would improve our decision making, but it is certainly impossible to find brute data that can prove beyond doubt that people need more information. The conviction in the librarian is sustained by some belief in the current situation and in turn is part of that librarian's self-identity.

This idea of self-identity is quite critical in the interpretive account of basic material of the social sciences. Self-identity needs to be considered in two special respects. First, because of self-identity and the interpretation by human subjects of their environment or some component of it, there is a process of validation within the interpretive approach. Consider what the social sciences are for: It is quickly apparent that they are substantially different from the natural sciences. The latter are constructed to offer an enhanced understanding of the natural world, but, except in a very indirect sense, the knowledge so gained, although offering a base for more effective planning of social life, does not offer insights into the nature of that life. The social sciences do not (although there have been many attempts to make them) explain underlying mechanisms and processes in life. The social science account tends to be historical, to be ex post facto, and to offer some account of what has happened—or what is still happening. Social theory offers us a better explanation of our own lives and cultures than any pretheoretical understanding or common sense can do. Social theory, therefore, can offer insight into our living of our lives and can thus inform and change our practice (Taylor, 1983). The validation of social theory in the hermeneutic account lies in its ability to change social practice for the better. A good or better theory will challenge self-understandings about practices and may lead to an improved practice:

> Put tersely, our social theories can be validated because they can be tested in practice. If theory can transform practice then it can be tested in the quality of the practice it informs. What makes a theory right is that it brings practice out in the clear; that its adoption makes possible what is in some sense a more effective practice. (Taylor, 1983, pp. 15–16)

In a later note, Taylor amended or qualified this claim slightly by emphasizing that good theory allows "clairvoyant" practice rather than more successful practice—the practice becomes more clearly understood by the practitioner (Taylor, 1983). He was suggesting that the theory transforms our view of our practices, and if we then feel those to be inadequate or wrong, we can change them to more successful practices, but that the theory alone does not determine the character of the change. The theory provides the understanding of practice previously absent or incomplete. Applying theory in practice and using theory to clarify our view of our practice obviously has attractions in a practical profession. Thus the interpretive approach can be employed to find and define what librarians do: The approach involves recognition of the need for individuals to give a coherent account to themselves of the practices they are in, and that account becomes a validation of the practice.

The second problem already mentioned in connection with self-identity and self-definition is what Taylor (1983) identified as a false ally (logical positivism being the original enemy), the view that misconstrues interpretation as adopting the agent's point of view. Obviously, the claim of interpretation to offer better understanding or clearer theory about the situation of another becomes impossible if the viewpoint of a human agent is accepted wholesale. That agent's view then becomes the only view possible. At a slightly different level, it would also make impossible the description of any culture or subculture in any terms other than those of its own members. There would be a danger here for subcultures, too, so that library science (and any individual library) could only be described in the terms of its own membership. Interpretation strives to offer improved theoretical understanding by developing shared meanings, and aspires to be normative and critical, and not merely descriptive of the internal view of a practice.

The idea of shared meanings is important both because it touches on a point of interest for the library and information community and because it is also technically important to distinguish shared from common meanings in the interpretive argument (Taylor, 1983). Taking the point made earlier that the interpretive account rejects the idea of uncritically taking the agent's point of view, it might be argued, particularly by those who favor an atomist analysis of the constitution of society, that we can only take our own views or the expressed views of other agents. There are two points to make here. First, society does recognize common and shared goods and meanings. The much used example of a common interest is that of people living in a valley with a dam at its head. They all have a common interest in the dam not breaking, although they may have no other interests that coincide. Shared meanings arise when institutions in a society are interpreted by all in a way that defines that society and that might be represented in some ceremony or ritual—saluting the flag, singing the anthem, marching in a commemorative parade. Similarly, the interpretation of law in a community is a shaping and defining interpretation that shows what a community feels it is, what characterizes it. It could be argued that a library is a shared good in society and is also a shared meaning, alike at the local, institutional, and global levels. The idea of the library is something that, for educated people at least, is one of the marks of our civilization, and also of other civilizations. This is not incompatible with the trenchant defense of every individual's right to use the library for his or her own purposes and to be treated atomistically, as an individual pursuing individual ends that are not necessarily related to those of anyone else in the society. For it is a shared meaning of liberal society that individuals may pursue their own ends provided they do not harm others similarly pursuing their ends. The library, and other information resources, participate in such shared social meaning. This paradox will be left for the moment: The significance of the idea of shared meanings remains a key component of the interpretive idea.

However, another question remains. Can we bridge the gap between our own interpretations and those of others, at either the individual or the community level? In answer to this point, Taylor (1983) called for the development of a "language of perspicuous contrast" that would illuminate interpretations of each of two standpoints by expressing in a common language contrasting stances adopted in relation to some human constants. Taylor saw this as close to Gadamer's call for a "fusion of horizons," whereby we, as interpreters, will seek some means of gradually fusing our own meanings and expectations with that of the text, the other agent, or some other culture (Outhwaite, 1985). It can be argued that this is precisely what the reference librarian attempts to do when interrogating a reader to determine the real, underlying question that has not been articulated by the initial inquiry. The interpreter will also reject the claim that neutral scientific languages can be developed that can analyze any and every culture or individual position. This rejected claim is, of course, fundamental to the development of a universal empiricist social science and is closely associated with functionalist approaches. Taylor (1983) argued that such languages are in fact ethnocentric and visit the norms of our own culture or society onto others, with consequent confusion of meaning when those norms do not fit. He concluded:

> Understanding another society can make us challenge our self-definitions. It can force us to do this, because we cannot get an adequate explanatory account of them until we understand their self-definitions, and these may be different enough from ours to force us to extend our language of human possibilities.
>
> But what this also shows is the way in which explanatory sciences of society are logically and historically dependent on our self-definitions . . . because a valid account . . . must take the subject as an agent . . . within any given culture, the languages of social science are developed out of and nourished by the languages of self-definition which have grown within it. (p. 44)

HERMENEUTICS AND LOGICAL POSITIVISM: THE IMPOSSIBILITY OF FUSION

It has been suggested that hermeneutic insights can be incorporated into the general method, the logic of discovery, of the positivist, and familiar brute data can then be used to test the hypotheses that the insight will have produced. This attractive approach would allow the incorporation of intersubjective meanings into the formation of hypotheses but would not lose the exactitude of empiricism.

In respect to the social sciences, two immediate objections are that human events cannot be isolated from external interference (nor can reproducible experiments be carried out on human subjects), and that the exactitude associated with the brute data of the natural sciences is unobtainable because different interpretations may produce different predictions and, in turn, widely varying futures, so the data cannot be used in the same way as it would be by the natural scientist (Taylor, 1978).

It is probably worth reminding ourselves here that the normal empiricist rendering of the logical positivist position is one that claims that "scientific" predictions are of the kind that "all As are Bs," or that "A will always lead to B." This is called *hypothetico-deductive logical positivism*. Philosophers of the social sciences have had to qualify such claims. In an attempt to retain some version of this, an alternative, known as *statistical-*

probabilistic-logical positivism, is proposed (Lessnoff, 1974). The social science alternative proposes that, whereas in the hard sciences 100% certainty is attached (as in the phrase "all As are Bs"), in the social sciences we can only talk in terms of tendencies, so that "all As tend to be Bs," with a percentage attached that will vary according to the material under discussion.

With such reduced certainty about the utility of the so-called brute data, the claims of the empiricists to offer the best or the only truly scientific method for the social sciences are considerably reduced. There is also the additional claim of the interpretive position that the so-called facts or brute data are really not objective facts as the logical positivist requires but are actually themselves interpretations, and that, as suggested earlier, humans are self-defining beings, defining themselves through their language and through their interpretation of the objects and institutions around them. This renders the use of brute data more difficult. The interpretation, for example, of the *meaning* of the Information Age is not a question that can be resolved by accumulations of brute data. The claim that to understand the information age requires a shift in patterns of thinking also seems to support the notion that there is a need for a hermeneutic, interpretive method within information studies, and that the older methods used in the social sciences are, for questions of this nature, inadequate.

According to Giddens (1985), Habermas attempted to reconcile the hermeneutic and positivist traditions within the social sciences by suggesting that there are social forces that resemble the forces of nature and that condition human life in a way that makes the claims of the natural science model for the social sciences seem more reasonable. However, as Giddens made clear, Habermas did not concede that such forces are immutable like the laws of nature: "The more human beings understand about the springs of their own behaviour, and the social institutions in which that behaviour is involved, the more they are likely to be able to escape from constraints to which previously they were subject" (Giddens, 1985, p. 126).

Thus, the positivist claims about social facts are only tenable in a world where people are not interpreting their environment, and claims for a natural science model or for brute data are not supported by the case advanced by Habermas. Indeed, the claim that increased understanding of our environment destroys the case for viewing some social forces as being like forces of nature seems to underline the impossibility of reconciling the two different traditions. As much of information work is dedicated to bringing more information, and presumably understanding through information, to the attention of clients, it would seem in this field in particular that there are important reasons associated with our own sense of identity to reject claims that describe social forces or conditions as immutable. We have a professional investment in the possibility of change. The claim that improved understanding confounds the natural science model seems to echo Taylor's argument that improved understanding results in more clairvoyant practice.

Practice has received increased attention in the professional literature, but as an idea it has been poorly treated, concentrating more on the performance of tasks than on the problem of what practice in the profession means for the self-identity of each practitioner. As the interpretive account builds on the meaning generated for each participant in any activity by the experience of participation, there must be a picture of what practice means. This task will be tackled in chapter 7, in Part II, where the framework for examining various conceptions of the field is considered.

The more immediate task is to fill in the broad picture by showing the case for the interpretive method made by two leading exponents in the areas of politics and law.

3
Interpretation in Politics and Law

I now turn from the general case for interpretation in the social sciences to a brief account of the role of interpretation in two important social sciences, politics and law.[1] These two fields are convenient examples because for different reasons they seem to be relevant to the library and information field. Politics has been selected because Taylor, whose account of interpretation is one of the clearest and most accessible for those of us working in the Anglo-American tradition, used it as his main example in his account of interpretation, which I have relied on heavily, and because it is a discipline whose interpretation is quite critical for the discussion of some aspects of information work. Law has been chosen as an example of a practical profession with a theoretical base—rather a good parallel for library and information work.

INTERPRETATION IN POLITICS: TAYLOR'S ACCOUNT

Politics, or rather the account rendered by Taylor, I have found useful for two reasons. First, as a discipline, politics has experienced many of the same features that beset information studies. Politics as a field includes a wide variety of studies, ranging from the philosophical studies of political theorists through historical and narrative studies of political conditions to behaviorist studies of aspects of voting behavior. It is a field that has been subjected to strenuous attempts to make it conform to the scientific, logical positivist paradigm. Second, Taylor showed how the empiricist case breaks down in discussing political behavior in certain quite critical and fundamental tests. I first sketch his attack on positivism in political science.

---

[1] The hermeneutic examination of library science by Bennett is ignored in this chapter because Bennett did not consider the state of the discipline except insofar as it relates to his prime concern with professional identity (Bennett, 1988).

The Assault on "Brute Data"

The core of Taylor's objection is that reconstruction of social reality on the basis of brute data, even when such a reconstruction allows the inclusion of a subjective reality of individuals' beliefs, attitudes, and values, does not consider social reality as characterized by intersubjective and common meanings (Taylor, 1978). He widened his argument to attack the ethnocentrism of Western political science—even in its most enlightened modern form. These intercultural considerations are of course relevant to certain aspects of the study of comparative library science and information studies, but here I concentrate on the identification of what constitutes the core of his attack on the empiricist construction of political science's universalist character.

First, he made clear that politics is a social science and is closely concerned with the broadly understood social sciences: The epistemology of the social sciences will be applied here and there, but there should be no divorce between the overall group of social sciences and individual disciplines. This point, obvious perhaps to an epistemologist, is worth reiterating with respect to information studies.

Second, by carefully chosen examples, he destroyed the empiricist case with respect to the meanings that can attach to the empiricist's brute data. At first sight:

> It would appear that there are actions which can be identified beyond fear of interpretative dispute; and this is what gives the foundation for the category of "political behaviour." Thus there are some acts of obvious political relevance which can be specified . . . from physical acts by institutional rules, such as voting for instance.
>
> But of course a science of politics confined to such acts would be much too narrow. For on another level these actions also have meaning for the agents which is not exhausted in the brute data descriptions, and which is often crucial to understanding why they were done. Thus, in voting for the motion I am also saving the honour of my party, or defending the value of free speech, or vindicating public morality, or saving civilization from breakdown. It is in such terms that the agents talk about the motivation of much of their political action, and it is difficult to conceive a science of politics which does not come to grips with it. (Taylor, 1978, p. 170)

In empirical science, beliefs and values, as attested by concurrence with a certain form of words, are also reduced to brute data. So, through the opinion poll or survey, meanings are reduced to data.[2] Taylor's immediate objection is that the process of selecting questions for the questionnaire must surely reveal some preunderstanding (perhaps a challengeable one) about the goals and beliefs of the questionnaire subjects—in other words, there is (in a good questionnaire presumably) already some interpretation and some set of shared meanings that allow it to work, and that the empiricist ignores. He also pointed out that the process of political science lies in the analysis of the questionnaire responses, correlating certain acts with certain beliefs in individuals. For this kind of social science, social reality is what can be reduced to, or identified as, brute data. Taylor's objection is that this kind of analysis does not allow for intersubjective meanings, a point that he emphasized by claiming that in a political society (or indeed we may say in any constituted society) social reality is actually constructed from these intersubjective meanings, both common and shared.

> The situation . . . is one in which the vocabulary of a given social dimension is grounded in the shape of social practice in this dimension; that is, the vocabulary would not make sense, could not be applied sensibly, where this range of practices did not prevail. And yet this range of practices could not exist without the prevalence of this or some related vocabulary. There is no simple one way dependence here. We can speak of mutual dependence if we like, but really what this points up is the artificiality of the distinction between social reality and the language of description of that social reality. The language is constitutive of reality, is essential to its being the kind of reality it is. . . . (Taylor, 1978, p. 175)

Voting can be seen as an example of this. There is a certain language in use about the processes of voting that are the rules that constitute the practice of voting.

Voting is not voting without these shared intersubjective rules. For example, putting marks on bits of paper only counts as voting in the context of a shared understanding of such marks as *voting*. To use a frivolous example, the presence of 22 men in a field does not have meaning to us until we can see from their actual behavior that they are playing football or hockey; the practice reveals the constitutive rules, which are understood and shared by observers who share that meaning

---

[2] There are, of course, innumerable library parallels for this, and clever questionnaires have allegedly captured meaning in responses to questions like "how important is the library to you?"

and reality. Similarly, it can be said of the process of cataloging, for example, that possession of a set of cataloging rules does not reveal how to catalog: experience in cataloging alongside people who catalog will alone reveal that.

In another example, used by Taylor (the previous example is mine), he discussed the concepts of bargaining and negotiation in Western society and used the differing usages of traditional Japanese villagers to develop a language of "perspicuous contrast"—both to assail the ethnocentrism of Western political epistemology, and to show how the technique of using such a language can elucidate the underlying shared meanings in Western life that empiricism does not reveal. In the Japanese village, Taylor (1978) told us, social life was founded on a powerful form of consensus that put a high premium on unanimous decisions. The consensus would dissolve if Western patterns of bargaining were to be followed, where the distinct identity of the contracting parties would be respected: Our Western recognition of autonomous parties entering into contractual relationships through a recognized process of negotiation is outside the range of language available to the villagers. They live in a different social reality, but not an objective reality that can be described independently of the language or vocabulary used by that society. Their social realities are practices, and cannot be identified independently from the language context in which they are lived. This suggests that we cannot use our terms to describe their practices, and that any comparison is impossible. However, Taylor (1983) got around this problem:

> It will almost always be the case that the adequate language in which we can understand another society is not our language of understanding, or theirs, but rather what one could call a language of perspicuous contrast. This would be a language in which we could formulate both their way of life and ours as alternative possibilities in relation to some human constants at work in both. (p. 38)

Individuals and Societies

A further assault on the empiricist construction of social science concerns the treatment of individuals and societies. It can be objected that mainstream social (and political) science is unable to describe societies except in terms of the aggregation of individual responses (*vide supra*), and thus retreats to "forcing the psycho-historical facts of identity into the grid of an individual psychology, in short, by re-interpreting all meanings as subjective" (Taylor, 1978, p. 173). From this, Taylor claimed that political science, in search of a universalist base, has seized on one aspect of modern social life (the civilization of work), just one little, but significant cluster of intersubjective meanings, and has treated it not for what it is, but as the "inescapable background of social action as such" (Taylor, 1978, p. 188). Taylor's complaint was that this aspect then becomes a universal framework within which "actions and structures will be brute-data identifiable." From this starting point, analysis of all societies proceeds. Whatever advantages may flow from this, and Taylor was doubtful if there are any, there are severe disadvantages that invalidate the study based on such a foundation. Grounded in just one view of Western society, the epistemology of political science is unable to explain (and was certainly unable to predict) the breakdown of that model of Western society. He claimed that long-term developments, like the Puritan Revolution, can only be subjected to satisfactory empiricist account after the event.

There are obvious parallels in the library and information field. Is there a satisfactory account of the Information Age? Do we have a discipline and profession whose self-images reveal, historically, successive waves of interpretation that are contradictory and incompatible, as "library science as management" succeeds "librarianship as scholarship," or whatever? These parallels are discussed later: Currently they are adduced to show that an interpretive approach to similar problems in another discipline can both show some of the shortcomings of mainstream empiricist methods, and, according to Taylor, redefine our past in order to make our present and future intelligible.

Taylor's final complaint against mainstream political science was that the treatment of certain beliefs and attitudes in a society as a consensus, or rather as Taylor preferred to say, as a convergence of beliefs, is misplaced. Taylor (1978) denied that the convergence of beliefs is a consensus, but what he particularly wanted to explain was the idea that the "convergence of belief or attitude or its absence presupposes a common language in which these beliefs can be formulated, and in which these formulations can be opposed" (p. 178).

To develop a hypothetical library example, we may say that a bibliographer who asserts the distinction of bibliography from librarianship and who adduces as an example the difference of a bibliographic description from cataloging, is in fact demonstrating that he or she shares a common language with the librarian from whom he or she wishes to distance himself or herself, and we may infer that the two do in some way constitute a kind of society, as they share at least some of the same language. Taylor's claim would be that the recognition of diversity reveals a set of intersubjective meanings that can still allow cleavage between various groups: Intersubjective meaning does not mean convergence.

Taylor's review of political science is in fact a gloss on mainstream empiricist renderings of that subject, showing how interpretive epistemology based on a reading of meaning can offer better access to important political problems of our time, rather than a reconstitution of the discipline. His comments are good for any science of society, and it is in that respect that I have chosen them for exposure here. His use of a language of contrast, his rejection of atomist interpretations of questionnaire-style brute data, his rejection of brute data based on a limited model of political life, and his rejection of psychological readings of individuals' beliefs and actions are all relevant to the development of understanding of the library and information field. Similarly, the development of a realm of primitive data, based on readings of meanings seen through the use of a shared language, offers a critical tool for the construction of an interpretation of library and information studies that encompasses the very disparate conceptions of the field that are described in Part III of this volume.

INTERPRETATION AND LAW

Law was the subject of an interpretive account by Dworkin (1986). His construction of an interpretive account is rather different from Taylor's. Dworkin's work is used here because law offers some very striking parallels for information studies. Law is both a discipline and a profession, and can make serious claims to be a knowledge-based construction, rather like information studies. By this I mean that their practices are based on the accumulation of knowledge and the application of some intellectual analysis to that knowledge base. The legal profession comprises a large number of practitioners from whom clients usually want practical advice rather than theoretical speculation. If someone has a claim about a neighbor's negligence, they want a lawyer who will get redress for their grievance, not one who can tell them that the law on this matter is good or bad. We use lawyers to get the law on our side. Similarly, when we want to find a book in a library, we just want the book: We are usually happy to remain ignorant about any niceties or problems of library organization, classification, or information retrieval systems. In both cases the practitioners use in their work a body of theory representing some understanding of the state of knowledge in the field. In law there is a group of people, varying in number and membership, who by constant discussion through the formal and informal communication channels of the profession determine what view is to be taken about the law and the character of its interpretation. The information field lacks a formal body such as judges or legislators who must be among that group, but there is an extensive community that might perform a similar function. Whether information studies needs such a formal interpretive body as the judiciary is an interesting question, but one that is only tangential to the current inquiry. The general parallel of two professions with a large scattered body of practitioners applying a body of knowledge, the attitude toward which is determined by the actions and beliefs of a smaller, more centralized (although in some senses internationally scattered) coterie is a good one, and information studies can benefit from the example of law.

Dworkin's account is phrased in different language than Taylor's. His readership is more general and his language is correspondingly less philosophical. This different expression of the interpretive approach is an aid to understanding its application. There is not a direct correspondence between the two accounts, and Dworkin's is a useful corrective from a more pragmatic standpoint.

There are two significant aspects of Dworkin's book, which are conveniently separated. First is his account of interpretation; second, his interpretive account of law. His general conclusion shows that there are intuitively direct comparisons to be made between law and information studies:

> Law is an interpretive concept. Judges should decide what the law is by interpreting the practice of other judges deciding what the law is. General theories of law, for us, are general interpretations of our own judicial practice ... I urged ... law as integrity, which unites jurisprudence and adjudication. It makes the content of law depend not on special conventions or independent crusades but on more refined and concrete interpretations of the same legal practice it has begun to interpret. (Dworkin, 1986, p. 410)

Dworkin was plainly making an appeal to an understanding of law on the basis of shared meanings—intersubjectivities—and he was also committed to the notion of the possibility of alternative expressions and accounts of law—his process of "refinement" being the development of a more meaningful interpretation of practice, with the aim of improving that practice. Dworkin's (1986) hyperbole in his final paragraph is again strongly illustrative of the point:

> Law's attitude is constructive: it aims, in the interpretive spirit, to lay principle over practice to show the best route to a better future,

keeping the right faith with the past. It is, finally, a fraternal attitude, an expression of how we are united in community though divided in project, interest, and conviction. That is, anyway, what law is for us: for the people we want to be and the community we aim to have. (p. 413)

Dworkin here echoed Taylor's claims about shared meanings not necessarily meaning a convergence of views, and also Taylor's claim that the interpretive approach finds its primitive (not brute) data in the meanings expressed by the community.

Dworkin's Interpretive Attitude

It should be noted how Dworkin (1986) built up his version of the interpretive attitude.

The constructive account of creative interpretation, therefore, could perhaps provide a more general account of interpretation in all its forms. We would then say that all interpretation strives to make an object the best it can be, as an instance of some assumed enterprise, and that interpretation takes different forms in different contexts only because different enterprises engage in different standards of value or success. (p. 53).

Dworkin built up this picture in two stages. First, he described the history and interpretive development of a social practice, courtesy, taking the example of how a social practice like removing hats before social superiors can come to be interpreted. The interpretation is in two stages. First, it becomes assumed by everyone that the practice of courtesy is not merely an action but also has value, serving some purpose. Second, given this understanding of value, courtesy, or rather the practice of it, will require actions that serve that purpose. Dworkin claimed that by this stage, courtesy is not merely a practice but has meaning and becomes reconstructed by that meaning. Change in the practices of courtesy arise as people begin to demand more or different practices and actions to serve the point of courtesy. Dworkin claimed that the first and second stages are independent, and mentioned games as an example where argument exists about how rules should be changed (which implies a reference to some purpose or value) but where there is little discussion of what the rules currently are. A similar exercise takes place in discussions about the revision of classification schemes or catalog codes.

Forms of Interpretation

Dworkin cited courtesy as an example of a social practice that is interpreted. He then refined his review of interpretation to suggest that there are several kinds of interpretation, and that the interpretation of social practices or works of art, which he together called "creative interpretation," can stand as a general model of interpretation. He distinguished these two forms because they "both aim to interpret something created by people as an entity distinct from them" (Dworkin, 1986, p. 50). He identified conversational (what people say) and scientific (natural objects) interpretation as other forms. He then stepped further with creative interpretation to differentiate the rediscovery of authorial intentions (as was the case with Biblical hermeneutics) from what he called constructive interpretation, which is concerned not with cause but with purpose: "Constructive interpretation is a matter of imposing purpose on an object or practice in order to make of it the best possible example of the form or guise to which it is taken to belong" (Dworkin, 1986, p. 52).

Dworkin limited the freedom of the constructing interpreter by insisting that the history of a practice constrains the range of available interpretations. From this point, Dworkin (1986) suggested that anyone (a participant) interpreting a social practice "proposes value for the practice by describing some scheme of interests or goals or principles the practice can be taken to serve or express or exemplify" (p. 52). It is obvious why these stances are relevant and interesting to a lawyer (and perhaps more particularly a judge). Dworkin also rejected both the counterclaims that interpretation is only concerned with accurate portrayal of the author's intentions, and that the interpretation of social practices can be determined only by questioning individuals, one by one, who use that practice. He also placed one severe restriction on any interpreter: "It follows that a social scientist must participate in a social practice if he hopes to understand it, as distinguished from understanding its members" (p. 55). Intuitively this claim seems to be true. It might well be claimed that people who have not done research cannot understand it, or that people who are not information managers, or bibliographers, cannot understand those practices. It is a claim that Shera implicitly supported in his call for more participant research based on the phenomenological method known as symbolic interactionism. Yet we can question the limitation. How narrowly is the term *participation* to be defined? It could be argued that anyone using a library participates in the library, or anyone who (maybe unknowingly) obeys the law also participates in law. However, Dworkin (1986) explicitly stated elsewhere that any social scientist must join the practice he proposes to understand. Just as we can accept that although law is of general interest to society, the practitioners of law are those advocates and other lawyers most concerned and informed about its daily practice, so in information studies, although society at large must contribute to the shared definition and meaning of the field, it is the practitioners who are the prime participants: The users, although interesting, remain secondary figures for this purpose.

A further possible constraint lies hidden in the notion that constructive interpretation is purposive. This, and the constraint (already mentioned) imposed by the history of a practice, imply that the original intention—of the author of the text or practice "provides the *formal* structure for all interpretive claims" (Dworkin, 1986, p. 58). A query arises with respect to current intentions of people participating in a practice. Dworkin firmly rejected this individualist position, and insisted that interpretation is not what other interpreters think. It is about what the practice means, not what the practitioners mean. Thus we have a further rejection (following Taylor's) of the questionnaire approach. We cannot find out what, say, cataloging is merely by approaching some or all catalogers and asking them: Purpose and intention in cataloging must be discerned from interpretation of the practice itself.

Two other points to note from Dworkin are his description of the stages of interpretation and his inventory of the equipment of the interpreter.

The Stages of Interpretation

There are three stages to Dworkinian interpretation. First is a preinterpretive stage in which the rules and standards taken to provide the tentative content of the practice are identified. (Every new librarian, as a trainee, will go through such a stage.) Second is a stage where the interpreter (who must, even as a social scientist seeking some understanding, be a participant) "settles on some general justification for the main elements of the practice identified at the preinterpretive stage. This will consist of an argument why a practice of that general shape is worth pursuing, if it is" (Dworkin, 1986, p. 66). The third stage, the postinterpretive stage, is where the practice is altered to meet the requirements of the justification. This stage closely matches Taylor's account of the validation process for an interpretive hermeneutic science. Dworkin's account also provides an instrument to help understand how social practices change following changes in the understanding of meaning attributed to them.

The interpreter, however, must be equipped with the necessary beliefs in order to be able to interpret. For Dworkin there are three prime requirements. First are assumptions about what counts as part of the practice in order to generate the data for the initial preinterpretive phase. Second there is a conviction about "how far the justification he proposes at the interpretive stage must fit the standing features of the practice to count as an interpretation of it rather than the invention of something new" (Dworkin, 1986, pp. 67). Finally, more substantive convictions are required about which kinds of justification show the practice in the best light.

Dworkin's interest was to produce a form of interpretation that suits the law. Quite clearly, a wealth of legal argument can be adduced from the final requirement mentioned in the preceding paragraph. It is worth noting that he specifically allowed a degree of independence in these "substantive convictions"—that is, some personal or external contribution can be made in generating a settled or reformed interpretation that may affect the intersubjective view, the shared view, of what the practice amounts to.

Note, too, that although Dworkin's guide to the steps of interpretation is more pragmatic than Taylor's discussion, there are points that demand attention. First, as mentioned, is Dworkin's demand that any interpreting social scientist be a participant. Second is the absence of any discussion of the development of intersubjectivities between radically different communities that do not share the same forms of expression or sets of meaning. Dworkin was writing for the tradition of common law; in the case of information work, there may be a need for more of the "fusion of horizons" (the intersecting of background understandings) that was mentioned in Chapter 2. But how does Dworkin's interpretive attitude actually work in his chosen field?

Interpretation and Law

Dworkin's conclusions about law have already been anticipated. We also need to know both why he considered law needs an interpretive approach and how that approach can be realized.

Law is a practice. It is a community practice, and although we normally think of how the law might apply to us as plaintiffs or defendants, overall its practice is dependent on social consent. That consent suggests that quite apart from internal interpretations of law between its more obvious practitioners, there has to be a more general social interpretation of what law is for and how it should operate, with which internal interpretations are not incompatible. There is, therefore, a level of interpretation that harmonizes the external views and the internal view of law. This, of course, has its parallel in external views of the purpose of libraries that must be matched by internal views or interpretations of librarians or information managers, whatever extra interpretation they may have of the more detailed or technical aspects of information studies. In law, as Dworkin showed, there is a wealth of internal technical argument about the interpretation of law, which has as its object the determination of what kind of theoretical arguments about the way law should be applied are most conscionably acceptable.

In *Law's Empire*, Dworkin (1986) built his initial case for an interpretive approach by showing that current interpretations of law, by other theories, do not explain various paradoxes about legal practice, most significantly the failure of judges to agree. His account of interpretation shows that the purpose of law, which will embed the intentions of the original legislator, is a prime constraint on the range of interpretations available. His account of the three stages of interpretation also shows that practice will inform any theory of a practice and that theory may in turn alter the practice. Similarly, the history of the practice (the precedents) in law will condition the interpretation of statutes by judges when faced with a particular case. Dworkin argued that even with clearly agreed law there can be problems about the interpretation when faced with particular cases. He cited four cases in which the judges—on several counts—were unable to agree on several important points. First, he pointed out that there seemed to be no disagreement in any of the cases about what the text of the law was. There were no problems about the literal meaning of the law. Second, the disagreements could be said to be about what the law should be, or which precedents applied, or even what the law was intended to mean (having accepted the literal meaning of the texts). It was clear to Dworkin, too, that the disagreements were not about borderline cases, where confusion about which criteria to apply might arise, nor were they cases where there was no law. Dworkin (1986) claimed that the disagreements were pivotal, that they were fundamental disagreements about what law is. He proceeded from this to the conclusion that the positivist argument, that there are common rules lawyers use when deciding cases, is wrong. This claim also invalidates all other claims about semantic theories of law, and leaves Dworkin with the position that there must be some other explanation that satisfies the requirement that the theory of law should describe the actual practice of law, including disagreements where they arise. As lawyers do share factual criteria about law—for otherwise without this sharing there could be no debate comprehensible to all parties—then there must be such an explanation.

It is worth noting here that there are some useful parallels between law and information studies. Both are cumulative in their knowledge. As statutes and cases gather through time to constitute a practice of some branch of law, so libraries gather books through time that are held to constitute some branch of knowledge, and as there are discarded statutes and overlooked cases, there are superseded and overlooked books, too. First, in the sense of the instruments of the library and information field, the rules for indexing or cataloging, and so on, there are discarded rules that have been bypassed as understanding within the field improves. Second, and more significantly, librarians, information scientists, or information managers do organize a view of a field when they classify its documents, so when they look for a language or classification that adequately encompasses and organizes a field they impose an interpretation on it—giving the reader a particular view of knowledge, just as the lawyer might have a particular view of law.

Further Techniques

Dworkin's construction of interpretation offers one extra device and one pragmatic tool. The device is to distinguish between concepts and conceptions. The concept (of law, or whatever) is like the trunk of the tree: Using the example of courtesy, Dworkin (1986) said that a particular community may have a concept that respect is part of the very meaning of courtesy. Anyone who denies this is held to be outside the community. From this initial concept spring different conceptions as to what respect really requires. Therefore, in law we might have a concept that gives rise to different conceptions at a different level of abstraction. So, judges may disagree in conception although they agree on the basic concept. Similarly, in information studies, there may be a basic concept that manifests itself in formal expression as a number of competing conceptions, adopted with varying enthusiasm at different times by practitioners who may disagree vehemently among themselves about which conception is the right one, but who share a common tie to the basic concept.

The tool Dworkin provided is the working description of interpretation in application. It may be possible to devise several interpretations of a particular legal problem (Dworkin used the example of compensation for emotional injury), and then see how these various interpretations best fit the known facts of a particular case. "The interpretation . . . must . . . flow throughout the text; it must have general explanatory power, and it is flawed if it leaves unexplained some major structural aspect of the text" (Dworkin, 1986, p. 230). If no interpretation can be found that fits the bulk of the text, then one that captures most or even just part of the text may be adopted. Where several interpretations fit the text then the interpreter must decide between them, on the grounds of which makes the text the best it could possibly be. There are parallels here to Taylor's requirement for coherence and to his fundamental point about interpretation, which accepts the possibility of a plurality of meanings, with the prospect of one offering a better understanding of the text than another, although all remain equally valid. It is in this "equal validity" that there are grounds for judges to disagree, especially if they apply different conceptions of one concept.

Dworkin provided us with one further tool. In building his picture of interpretation, he described a chain novel, with each chapter written by a different author, and each author must read and interpret what has been written before and in the light of that build his own contribution. Dworkin (1986) suggested that judges, when interpreting statute law and the legislative history of each statute, will interpret the text in a similar way—the law is a sequence of chapters by different authors. Again, there are parallels in information studies, both universally and within any one organization, where the practices from the past that still bear on the present must be interpreted in a certain light in order to be shown as forming an integral whole with current practice.

Dworkin's aim was not to provide an interpretive account of law as an academic discipline (although that is in part a by-product of his work), but to provide a guide to the practice of law and the behavior of judges when adjudicating cases. Much of the matter he supplied is technical to law and is not of concern here, but the tools of practical interpretation he showed in application are relevant to other disciplines. He summarized his overall case, like Taylor, to a broader community than the legal one, hardening the argument given earlier that interpretation within a practice must be consistent with what the larger community would also consider an acceptable interpretation: "Judges who accept the interpretive ideal . . . decide hard cases by trying to find, in some coherent set of principles about people's right and duties, the best constructive interpretation of the political structure and legal doctrine of their community" (Dworkin, 1986, p. 255).

How can these two examples of politics and law help in the consideration of the situation of information studies? The approaches of Taylor and Dworkin provide both philosophical background and some tools of practical interpretation. There are still some problems that can be worked further in information studies, particularly the problem of how much an interpreter must participate in a practice in order to be able to offer a satisfactory interpretation. It may be necessary to develop further tools for the application, and it may also be necessary to speculate on the disciplinary context of information studies. As a profession, librarians and information managers have happily imported foreign disciplines that at various times have forged dominant models of the field, and have simultaneously severely skewed the professional educational curriculum and that open up questions about the nature of the discipline of information studies. The range of names, from librarianship through library and information studies to information science and now information management, shows this clearly. Management and computer science are two obvious external influences that have had this effect. Before moving to consider the field of information studies, I briefly consider one other discipline that seems a candidate for interpretive treatment to see if similar problems occur.

Interpretation and Historical Data

History is in every sense an interpretation, given the basic analysis of Taylor. Historians, especially in the English-speaking world, have sometimes sought to operate within a positivist tradition of reconstructing a narrative of the past based on some objective facts, be they demographic trends, indices of production, the results of battles and elections, or the archived memoranda and papers of government departments. From these objective facts, explanations, if not predictions, are constructed about short-term and long-term movements, including some very long movements like the Industrial Revolution.

History is important to this inquiry because, as Taylor indicated, all social sciences are historical in character—they build on the accumulated record of human societies. Even when so-called objective facts or brute data are being used, they are the basis of historical reconstructions. In consequence, history is important to the study of information work, for two reasons. First, as a social science, the discipline of information studies uses historical data about the work practices being studied. Some aspects of the work of a classifier, for example, are considered against an assessment of existing collections: User studies, however contemporary, are using data that, strictly speaking, are "historical"—data about previous human actions—for the prediction of "universal" behavior patterns or the trend in user behavior. Second, some aspects of information studies and associated disciplines are themselves historical—most notably recent trends in the study of the history of the book, but also obviously all aspects of the history of libraries, the book trade, publishing, reading, and literacy.

There are good reasons, therefore, for a resource that will allow a historical approach that is also interpretive. Unlike the position of politics or law, this is not available "off the shelf," but the positivist traditions in historical research can be put aside, and very much for the same reasons, as they have been overthrown in the interpretive account of the social sciences in general. Quite separate from the need to demonstrate this with respect to component parts of information work, it is also important that there is a resource that allows access to an understanding of the more recent phenomenon called the Information Age. We have all been made more immediately aware of this development with the promise of information superhighways, and the information field is held to be both a prime beneficiary of this trend and simultaneously a powerless agent in the face of insuperable social forces. There is a need, therefore, for some form of explanation, more particularly an understanding, of the Information Age that satisfactorily accounts for it as the current context of meaning for the information field.

If such an account is available it will show in terms comprehensible to the interpretive approach that the meaning of the Information Age is not to be found in the positivist conception of historical facts. These facts are really authoritarian statements on the part of the historian about what is and what is not significant in the reconstructed narrative of the past (Skinner, 1985). These allegedly objective facts actually presuppose a meaning. Just as with the brute data of social inquiry, an interpretation is already supplied, in a crude form, and society is seen in terms of the brute data. As a context of meaning for information work, we are more interested in an account of the Information Age—which must also be based on historical data—that takes account of the common and shared intersubjective meanings that are experienced as the background to their current professional lives by all the participants. It is not just the historical reality of the Information Age that is critical, it is the intelligibility of that idea to participants in information work. To achieve that, there is a need to examine structures rather than facts.

There is in the work of Pocock (1985) an approach to history as a discipline that emphasizes the importance of language, actions, doing, and interpretation of texts through time, which allows a reconstruction and interpretation of the past by relating the effect of the interaction of the two contexts of experience and of language. Although the notion of an interpreter constructing "texts" or "text analogues" of a particular practice or discipline has already been considered, language itself has not been considered directly, except to distinguish hermeneutic positions from those of semiology or linguistics. It is almost inevitable that language or discourse be considered, as it is through language that all meanings are mediated, all intersubjectivities established, and through the development of particular patterns of discourse that conceptions of a field arise. As most conceptions of the field of information studies will be constructed from the historical record—albeit of the fairly immediate past—it is obvious that Pocock's ideas can be borrowed to augment the armory of the interpreter.

For Pocock, any historical actor will work within a context of language that conditions and limits the number and kind of things he or she could say, and all that actor's individual "speech acts" will be uttered within that context or *langue*:

> The author inhabits a historically given world that is apprehensible only in the ways rendered available by a number of historically given languages; the modes of speech available to him give him the intentions he can have, by giving him the means he can have of performing them.
>
> The more complex, even the more contradictory, the language context in which he is situated, the richer and more ambivalent become the speech acts he is capable of performing, and the greater becomes the likelihood that these acts will perform upon the context itself and induce modification and change within it. (Pocock, 1985, p. 5)

These statements provide possible explanations of the limitations of particular conceptions, whose exponents are imprisoned within their own time, and explanation of the increasing speed with which alternative conceptions now seem to be developed, as complexity and ambivalence increase the chance of change.

The use of discourse for the construction of conceptions is considered again in Part III; for the moment it should be noted that historical explanations are not inevitably based on brute data or historical facts and that interpretations must relate individual actions and statements to their contexts if meaning is to be recovered.

SUMMARY

Interpretation is not merely a method, it is an approach that conditions the way we look at phenomena, and conditions, too, what we might look for, what problems we perceive, and what solutions can be available to us. This means that we cannot just take a bundle of techniques and apply them to any situation or data and turn up solutions when still working in a noninterpretive frame of mind.

The interpreter expects the social sciences to offer a better explanation of our own lives than is available through simple common sense. He or she will search for some insight that clarifies practice by offering a good theory that brings practice out in the clear.

Practice is made apparent to us through the contexts of language and experience, and it is through language and participation in a practice that we learn its purposes and its meanings. Through involvement in a practice we learn the language of that practice, and through widening our realm of experience by widening our language we learn to develop a language of perspicuous contrast, which will enable us to understand other related practices and contexts and also to develop a more insightful and clearer view of our own practice. The language we use in a practice is not merely technical, it is a discourse expressive of the practice, and use of it and acceptance of the meanings of the practice allows and enables us to make judgments about the practice and to participate fully in it by contributing to the further construction of it. In doing this, we attach meaning, maybe a changing meaning, to primitive data: We do not have any brute data that have objective, unchanging existence and meaning for all observers.

However, just as individuals move into a practice by initially accepting its values, internal goods, and rewards, and latterly come to understand why those values exist, it remains the case that the interpretation, ultimately, is not what we make of it as individuals, it is what the practice means. This requires that we interpret something shared by the participants, not merely the aggregation of their views: The purpose of the practice must be discerned by examination of the practice itself.

Interpretations allow for a series of stages of interpretation, moving from an initial preinterpretation, where there are certain assumptions about what counts as the practice, to a second stage where there may be convictions about what fits as part of the practice and what must count as a new practice, to a third stage where we might know what kinds of justification show the practice in the best light.

Because there may be alternative expressions of the meaning of a practice, we can use a few useful devices to draw out an interpretation. The process of interpretation through time can be seen rather like the construction of a chain novel: Alternative expressions of meaning can be seen as being competing conceptions of what a practice might be; and we can expect that a good interpretation will "flow through the text" of the practice, will be an obviously acceptable and good explanation of what the practice requires, and will not leave unexplained any major part of the practice. Newcomers to the practice should find the interpretation available to them sufficient to make the practice convincing. Eventually, then, an interpretation will give a better account, a better understanding of the purpose of a practice, and a better theory about what it is that we do.

This outline of the interpretive approach, and illustration of its application in other social sciences, is followed in the next chapter by an examination of the second part of the argument: the claim that the so-called Information Age is the current context of meaning for information studies.

4
The Context of Meaning and the Concept of the Information Culture

This chapter completes the examination of the basic building blocks for constructing an interpretive analysis of the field of information studies. The fundamental claims made for the interpretive approach, and its development and application in two social science disciplines, have been considered: The benefits that might be expected to flow from its successful application in information studies are examined later. Before moving to the next part of my project, which is to provide the grounding for an interpretive analysis of the field that should show that it can be expressed in the language of interpretation,[1] there is a need to establish a context of meaning for the field and for some explanation of how that context must function in relation to the interpretation. The remainder of the chapter examines the claims of the idea of the information culture to be used as the current context of meaning. This is then used as a background for Part III.

THE CONTEXT OF MEANING

The interpretive position claims that a picture of social practice and social reality is constructed by people coming to share the meanings of things in their lives, and talks of a discipline when a coherent set of objects, about which expressions of meaning may be forthcoming in various ways, has meaning for a group of interpreting subjects. The reality will change as the interpretation changes to improve practice, to offer a more comprehensive, more up-to-date, or more felicitous expression of those objects. Clearly, the interpretations are embedded in the past. They are historically dependent, only if because our interpretation of life is part of our self-identity: We interpret things in the light of who we

---

[1] The reconstruction of the field from basic data, building an interpretive discourse for the guidance of current practitioners is another task outside the scope of this book.

are, what we have become, what our experience has hitherto been, and how people like us are making the interpretation. This is all background to current interpretations, and the actual process of daily interpretation and reinterpretation takes place against a background, or a number of different interrelated and mutually embedded backgrounds. In practice, we alter our self-identity to conform to some socially arbitrated norms,[2] and the normative behavior that ensues is similarly subject to changes in the background. If, within the context of normal work, home life, the yearly cycle of play and performance, our environment changes in some way, then our interpretations will also change. If individually we win or inherit a vast sum of money or collectively we are suddenly part of a society devastated by war or disease, or professionally we are reduced by adverse government decisions on funding, then our view of our individual or collective environment will change: There will have been a change in the context of meaning for our lives.

Even without such cataclysmic changes of circumstance, there is a context of meaning, a backdrop for all our professional endeavors, which will determine our objectives and reveal to us the means available for their realization. It can be said of all actors or agents, as Pocock (1985) said of every author, that their world is made apparent to them through language, which also gives them the means of forming and performing their intentions, and that the picture is complicated, and change is made possible, by the interaction of context and foreground action. It is not as if everyone is imprisoned within an inescapable frame of time, unchanging and proscribing the chance of transformation: The diversity of the context makes possible a widening range of foreground acts, and in turn that may stimulate further gyrations within the context. Pocock (1985) said of any actor in any situation that change will more probably ensue from immersion in a richer, more complex, and more contradictory language context, which will broaden the range of things he or she can think and do.

Thus, awakening from a past that was not static but relatively slow moving, information studies is in the position of a discipline with many options available to it. This does not mean that the environment is revolutionary, but that because of some stirring up, the background or context within which its practitioners operate and the meaning of the things commonly done can be seen in a variety of ways. We have a number of different expressions about the same thing, our working environment.

From this, several points follow. First, the language we use, what we may call our discourse, which will include the speech acts that determine which meanings we share and with whom, and the speech contexts with-

---

[2] See the later remarks on practice in Chapter 7 for an expansion of this point.

in which these acts are performed, is crucial for our construction of interpretations. Second, the arrival or the sudden awareness of the arrival, of a new context, or at least a new way of describing it, has meant not just a lumbering shift from one mode of professional existence to another, but an opening up, an opportunity to create interpretations that does not presume limitations on our understanding of what we are or the way we express it, but that allows or encourages numerous expressions of what the field is.

After a long period with a relatively stable set of available interpretations, there are grounds to argue that in the last 20 years or so a number of competing expressions of what information studies is can be identified. In Part III some of these will be examined: In this chapter it is claimed that it is the information culture, variously described and interpreted, that has acted as the context of meaning and has allowed this flowering, or this confusion of interpretation, and that seen clearly as a single context, allows a participant in the field to see all these expressions as legitimate current conceptions of the original concept of the field. These conceptions arise, and continue to arise, because this is a practice in practical situations, and what Pocock (1985) claimed for political speech is also true for practitioners in this field:

> Political speech is of course practical and informed by present necessities, but it is none the less constantly engaged in a struggle to discover what the present necessities of practice are, and the most powerful minds using it are exploring the tension between established linguistic usages and the need to use words in new ways. (p. 13)

Using words in new ways allows participants to write, in Dworkin's metaphor of interpretation, the next chapter of the book, which is the history of any practice, but he also required that they maintain integrity with the original practice and interpretation. I next develop a view of the information culture that allows that.

AN INFORMATION CULTURE

There are immediate problems of methodology to confront in approaching the subject of information culture and its relationship to information studies and to an interpretive approach. Can a satisfactory account be developed from the existing literature, which is not founded on an interpretive approach, or is there a need to develop an interpretive account of the Information Age before proceeding further? Such an enterprise would double the size of this work, and there are good technical reasons why it is not necessary. The view of the Information Age that the information studies world has developed has come from the existing literature, and if we are to develop any view of it that is intersubjective, then the same basic information must be used.

The second methodological problem is that the term *information culture* is itself an interpretation or a label for some other phenomena, some definable set of objects. I use the term information culture as a label to describe various reactions to the phenomenon of the Information Age that whether friendly or hostile, recognize that *something* is happening to Western society, centered around information, even though there may be disagreement about the desirability and the real nature of these changes. Initially there is a need to come to terms with the phenomenon itself, so we can speak of the more generally used term *Information Age*. There is difficulty in deciding what these objects that constitute the Information Age are, as the label is used most frequently to describe judgments about trends rather than any body of indisputable objective knowledge. If the label is an interpretation in itself, then what is being interpreted, and for whom, must be identified. As this is a universal phenomenon affecting not just librarians and information managers, there are obviously many groups of potential subjects. Another complication is that many of the expressions of what the Information Age means are actually predictions rather than explanations or justifications. As predictions, they in turn become part of the primitive data on which our interpretation is built. Finally, the set of objects about which we must make sense or coherence is itself a matter of dispute and conjecture. Even terms like *information technology* are used in parallel senses to refer to both computers and practices, to predictions and demonstrations, to development and (more rarely) diffusion.

INFORMATION STUDIES AND THE INFORMATION SOCIETY

The literature of the professional press is effusive, and library reports somewhat silent, on the subject of the information society or the Information Age. Within the research reports of the discipline also, there is evidence of only subdued interest in the topic. This suggests that the character of the information society as seen from within the profession is essentially one of a background influence. In this position it can obviously serve as a context of meaning, but for this point to be established we need to seek sanction from other parts of the literature.

What could be adduced in support of the argument? Typically we could expect to find analysis of the basic information society case, discussion of the role of the information and library profession within the overall information sector, examinations of the impact on the profession of the emergence or consciousness of the information society, and some critique of how the information community should respond to new working and living conditions. There could also be discussions of the impact of information technology.

There are examples of all of the literature types mentioned here, but perhaps rather less frequently than might be expected. Two simple explanations for this could be, first, that although the profession was keen to adapt to information technology and the altered professional techniques that this implied, it was rather less concerned with or even aware of the wider social implications of that technology, and second, that the idea of the information society was held to be relevant to only a segment of the whole profession. A third related possibility is that the idea of the information society was perceived purely in terms of technology, and no wider implications were seen. Fourth, it may be that professional attention was diverted by the specter of information theory, which entranced a small part of the profession, or at least its research component, from the 1940s onward.[3] The desire to apply information theory as developed by Shannon and Weaver (1963) to the development of library and information theory has been long lived and is still not dead: In consequence, the theoretical drive of the subject has not been fully free to consider other less direct ways for that theory to have its full impact, through economic events rather than theoretical breakthroughs.

All these must be considered when deciding what precise context of meaning the idea of the information society gave to the information community, and how far this changed over the years. A few key works can quickly be identified.[4] The evidence of the literature suggests that the discipline and the profession have been overly occupied with technique, with the regulated practice that has brought professional recognition, and have been less critically aware of the discipline's (and the subject's) relation to knowledge, the maintenance and transmission of which has been the core reason for the existence of the profession. Indeed it is ironic if the whole profession finds itself conforming to all of the worst fears enumerated by the position associated in the following pages with Ellul, whereas its comments endorse only the portrait of the age pro-

---

[3] For comment on the disadvantages of this see Suppe (1985).

[4] The works of Toffler have probably had the largest impact worldwide and across many spheres of activity. See especially Toffler (1973, 1981). Among the more strictly professional literature see, for example, Cawkell (1986, 1987), Cronin (1983, 1986), King (1984), Martin (1988), and Williams (1985).

duced by Machlup, Porat, and Bell. The existence of this corpus of literature is sufficient without further examination for the present purpose; the subject of the information culture is obviously important for the profession. The next section considers how that importance manifests itself within the interpretive approach.

THE INFORMATION AGE

> How do we know the information society has arrived? We have but to listen to the commentators and leaders and to perceive the signs all around us. (Landau, 1986, p. 37)

The Information Age refers to a period when society is critically dependent on information. That age, our own, is dominated by information and our society is seen therefore as an information society. There are several separate accounts of the development of the information society. Not all use this term to describe the economic, social, and intellectual processes that are at the center of their arguments. I have chosen to use the terms *information society* or *Information Age* to stand for all these other labels such as postindustrial society, knowledge economy, or technological society. Various central arguments are hidden by these titles. The most important of the arguments to be considered are:

1. That the creation of wealth is now based more on the generation of knowledge or information than on the processing of materials or the provision of services.
2. That the proportion of the working population engaged in information-related occupations is now greater than that of any other group.
3. That we are now more dependent on an intellectual technology and an intellectual class for both the control (and exploitation) of our environment and also of our political system.
4. That we are in the grip of a technological way of thinking that infuses all our ways of thinking in all areas of life and that by its success drives out other ways of thinking and other values, to the detriment of society generally.
5. That there is much more information than ever before and it is therefore important as a necessary resource and as a management problem.

Two general points arise from these claims. First, it is difficult to reconcile them all, and some directly contradict others. The significance of some is not always apparent or proven. The second point is that the rather simplistic shorthand that I claim has achieved the status of common currency in the library and information world and that might be summarized as "information is centrally important to modern life and librarians provide information, therefore libraries, librarians, and information managers and their discipline and profession, are centrally important to modern life." This really cannot be inferred from any of the constructions of the information society that are currently available.

It should be noted that the stances listed are all historical, in the sense that they are based on existing social data and known trends. Some are predictive as well as descriptive. There is another group of studies that concentrates on selective examples of current technological development to produce predictions about social and economic life that are less measured than the other studies. These commonly concentrate on two predictions:

1. Information technology is transforming economic life and we must transform ourselves if we are to survive economically.
2. Information technology is transforming the character of individual and social life and we must adapt to radically fundamental changes in society before they overwhelm us. Some of these changes affect areas such as the character of the family, the structure of political or community life, and the imminent demise of the professions, as well as topics closer to the daily concern of the information professions such as the future of the book and the strategies of individuals coping with problems of information overload.

How can a picture of the information society be constructed from such a confusing background? The conclusion is complicated because despite the fairly wide diffusion of information technology, it is clear that many people, even among those using computers, are resistant to the change or dismissive of claims about the existence, imminent or immanent, of such an information society.

We must also ask how such an information society makes itself apparent to librarians and information managers. General trends in society, which are relatively indirect in their impact on information work, and which will not always be attributed directly to any such concept as the information society, are easily identified. Changes in printing, bookselling, and publishing, for example, may be attributed to general economic conditions, including those stemming from government policies, rather than any other factor. The growth in the size of financial markets and the volume and character of international financial dealing, or changes in the technology of news reporting, or even changes in the profile of the computer industry, may be attributed more to the ongoing flow of technical change rather than being part of some overall shift in the character of society.

It is probably in the introduction of computers in handling traditional information business that the information society has had the most direct impact on the library and information world, yet again it must be asked whether the direct connection is made or whether the change is associated more with some quite unexceptional economic and technical progress. This brings up another set of questions about the information society.

First, we can ask whether or not this is the fundamental shift in the character of society, or whether the current changes that have been given the information society label are merely part of a longer process, still in progress, that will effect a rather different change in the long term. The proponents of the information society present only the former view, and offer only increasing intensity and diffusion of the current trends as future changes. Whether the actual position is different is irrelevant: The critical question for this work is what is perceived as being the case, the fundamental shift or the ongoing process? The latter is far less likely to win committed support than the former, certainly from those whose view about the nature of their practice is not settled. This suggests that for its proponents, the information society is a cultural project, a thing to be realized and advocated and pursued with millenarian enthusiasm. Lyon (1988) warned about the dangers of such a view, pointing out that technological potential should not be seen as social destiny, even though he conceded that the technological convergence at the heart of such views is socially as well as technologically significant.[5]

What would the assumptions and objectives of such a project be? For those of this persuasion the information society is clearly the context of meaning, the only possible context, and it will determine the language they use, the decisions they make, and the interpretations they can form. The ambitions they have and the realms of discourse they inhabit and comprehend, will be determined largely by this project, and their choice of argument or data (economic, social, political) will be dictated by this project. If they are successful in setting the terms of discourse, and this currently seems to be the position, they will also set the context of meaning for all of us. This will include those who, either because its prospects offer them nothing or because they reject the analysis as insincere or too shallow an assessment of the human (including professional) condition, reject the idea of the information society. The context of meaning would, therefore, determine how we could see the librarian or informa-

---

[5] "In so far as the information society idea depends upon versions of technological determinism it should be resisted" (Lyon, 1988, p. 156).

tion manager. Just as the separation of time and the changed character of social and economic life means that the role of the librarian is not seen in the same way it was in medieval or early modern Europe, so now the role of the information manager may be shaped by our understanding of the times we are in. Self-evidently, the arrival of the term *information manager* as distinct from *librarian* indicates that the librarian was seen as inappropriate for the new role, and the marriage in the joint term *library and information work* reflects a later, reinterpreted way of seeing, as the understanding of the role of librarian was readjusted. As our understanding of our context of meaning itself is reinterpreted, so subsequent interpretations or expressions or conceptions of the role of the individual professional or of the whole discipline also change.

Second, if the changes currently afoot are seen primarily as changes in technology with some consequent organizational implications, is it possible to talk about any information society at all? In effect, what is critical for librarians and information workers is not the actual objective reality of an information society (assuming one could be portrayed), but the subjective meaning of such a phenomenon. Almost inevitably the language of an interpretive approach forces itself on us. This allows a broadening of the approach taken to describe current economic and technological changes in a way that accommodates more subjective assessments that reflect shared intersubjective meanings. This is itself necessary because the available economic data is inconclusive, or at least highly dubious (Lyon, 1988) and its interpretation is meaningless unless other more general and subjective views are introduced in support of the analysis.

THE INFORMATION ECONOMY

The central problem with the economic data is that it not only reveals nothing, but actually begs more questions than it pretends to answer. All available assessments of the economic dimension of the information components of society depend on extrapolated data. There are no data that, aggregated from whole economies, directly attempt to measure information inputs and outputs. The information component is derived from examination of data compiled for other purposes. Furthermore, opinion suggests there is no point in changing national accounts to give a direct measure of the information sector (Cooper, 1983).

The unavailability of direct figures immediately reveals that the whole economic argument about the information society is based on a question of definition, or, as we might claim, of interpretation. The figures for the information society's economic dimension are derived from National

Income Accounts, and each analyst will have his or her own view about what should be included or excluded. The usual objective is to show that after extrapolation and aggregation, the traditional division of the economy into three sectors—industry, agriculture, and services—is no longer adequate, and that a fourth sector, the information sector, is now required and can be shown to be the largest sector. The point in time at which it becomes the largest sector can be used to mark the date at which an economy becomes an information economy. Clearly this is attractive, but it is really sleight of hand. Undoubtedly there are new products and services that are informational, but for the most part the exercise is merely one of relabeling existing products and services. This could, presumably, be done with a wide range of concepts. (Frequently, e.g., there is a need to show what proportion of an economy stems from government activity, so all state enterprises and services are separated from everything else.) The figures remain figures, and we really require some level of understanding about what lies behind them. Before turning to the views of those who have attempted to provide some rationale to the idea of the information society (Bell, 1976, 1979; Machlup, 1962, 1980, 1982, 1984) we should note some final comments about the attempts of those who, like Porat (1977), attempt to define the information sector by measuring all economic activity.

First, Porat was forced to decide on every occupation whether or not it was in the information sector. The consequence can be strange: Typists, for example, are information workers, because they transform information from one format to another, so too are telephonists and advertising agents. Second, the information sector becomes enlarged, to a point where library and information service activity is reduced to an insignificant size, by the inclusion of not only almost every office worker but also the complete educational, financial, and legal establishments, among others. Two questions arise here: First, is there a confusion between knowledge and information, and does it matter? Second, is the type of information being discussed the same as that which the library and information profession is concerned with? Lawyers, for example, have information they ally with their training and skill that gives them the knowledge of how to apply the information. Architects, too, can be said to take ideas and by using information and their training transform the ideas into a set of instructions from which engineers and construction workers can build lasting structures. Yet in the analysis of economic activity, there is no distinction between the knowledge component and the information component of the work of a lawyer or architect. Similar comments can be applied to the work of medical workers. Conversely, where there is (as in the financial sector), a lot of information but comparatively less knowledge to apply in taking risks on which companies to invest in, the economic assessment remains the same but it obscures an important difference between activities that are knowledge-based professions and those that merely use information.

The second point about the character of the information being used is important. Librarians deal with recorded knowledge and supply it to other people: The information they supply is metainformation—information about information or knowledge. They are not originators or creators of information; they do not even supply information with the authority of a doctor or a lawyer imparting professional information in their own field. The parallel would suggest that librarians might speak with authority about classification schemes or cataloging codes, but not about real information that is usually sought with some purpose. A librarian might provide texts of the statutes and case law of trespass, but it is unlikely that he or she would offer an opinion on what the law of trespass was. A librarian cannot be pressed on a point of information: He or she must immediately seek refuge behind the sources. Of course, many librarians do supply information, but it is largely noncontentious or noncritical information. Yet librarians remain convinced that they are in, and indeed central to, the information society. Taking the two points together, we might ask whether we really want to talk about knowledge rather than information. However, this becomes difficult for the library and information profession because what it provides about knowledge is not knowledge itself, but metainformation about it. There is obviously a confusion here about the precise locus of the library and information profession within the spectrum of information occupations.

Two other points remain to be made about Porat's analysis of the information economy. First, it is extremely difficult to assess the real economic worth of services that are consumed within companies. This problem of assessing "real" economic charges will also occur with government offices and their libraries. Machlup (1962) previously found difficulty assessing the economic value of housewives' activity in the home and also of finding a suitable figure for education received in the home. In any analysis of the economy, there are obviously large areas that are almost immeasurable, which must render any final figure for the size of the information sector very suspect.

Finally, Porat had to consider not only information services, but also information products. Here again in any division of manufacturing into information and noninformation products there is a lot of relabeling—the construction of computers, typewriters, telephones, radios, hi-fi equipment, cassette tapes, cash registers, temperature gauges, and burglar alarm systems all becomes part of the information sector. There is, I believe, a serious gap between what in the mind of the librarian or information manager counts as part of the information sector and the manufacture of burglar alarms.

For the librarian or information worker, the economic assessment (by economic activity) of the information society remains inadequate or confusing, and cannot reasonably be used to provide a context of meaning for interpretation of professional activity. Can a better tool be found in the work of those who describe the concepts that underlie the work of accounting for the information society?

In the English-speaking world, the whole debate about the existence of an information society was initiated by the work of Machlup in 1962. This work was substantially revised and enlarged in 1980. Machlup started the general debate about the role of information activities in the economy but did not provide the kind of framework of explanation that could actually demonstrate rather than merely aggregate the compelling and wealth-generating power of knowledge applied to social purposes. There is such an explanation in the work of Bell.

BELL AND THE AXIAL PRINCIPLE

Bell's *The Coming of Post-Industrial Society* first appeared in 1973, and his central argument has remained the same, albeit with slight modifications. Along with Machlup, he remains one of the major figures in the information society argument.

Bell (1979) connected social changes to technological developments, and showed how possession of technical knowledge becomes politically important. He identified long-term trends in U.S. society characterized by a shift from a goods-producing to a service-delivering society, the centrality of the codification of theoretical knowledge, and the creation of a new intellectual technology as a key tool of systems analysis and decision theory.

Bell described the slow historical shift from producing goods, but also tied the increase in the proportion of the labor force engaged in delivering services to the change in the character of services provided, from those that were auxiliary to the production of goods to those providing human (teaching, health, and social services) and professional services. Professional services he described as those concerned with "systems analysis and design and the programming and processing of information" (Bell, 1979, p. 164).

It is probably, however, not this shift to information-handling services that is most attractive to the library and information profession, but the cause of that shift—the growing importance of theoretical knowledge, which Bell (1979) saw as the axial principle of postindustrial society.

> The axial principle of the post-industrial society, however, is the centrality of theoretical knowledge and its new role, when codified, as the director of social change. Every society has functioned on the basis of knowledge, but only in the last half century have we seen a fusion of science and engineering that has begun to transform the character of technology itself. (p. 164)

Bell (1979) described the transition of science from the lone 19th-century pioneers to modern research teams where science is closely related to technology, with startling consequences:

> While modern science, like almost all human activities, has moved toward a greater degree of specialization in its pursuit of more detailed knowledge, the more important and crucial outcome of its association with technology is the integration of diverse fields or observations into single conceptual and theoretical frameworks offering much greater explanatory power. (p. 165)

Furthermore, the consequence of this is the production of a new intellectual technology. He saw:

> [T]he methodological promise of the second half of the twentieth century is the management of organized complexity: the complexity of theories with a large number of variables and the complexity of large organizations and systems which involve the co-ordination of hundreds of thousands and even millions of persons. (Bell, 1979, p. 166)

Since 1940 new fields, methods, and techniques have emerged, which "seek to substitute an algorithm (i.e., decision rules) for intuitive judgment. As this formalized intellectual technology is becoming predominant in the management of organizations and enterprises, to the extent that it is as central a feature of postindustrial society as machine technology is in industrial society" (p. 167).

In this new postindustrial society, knowledge and information become the crucial variables and knowledge becomes the source of added value (or wealth). Bell (1979) saw information as data processing of records, data processing for scheduling, and databases. Knowledge he saw as "an organized set of statements of fact or ideas, presenting a reasoned judgment or an experimental result, which is transmitted to others through some communication medium in some systematic form . . . Knowledge consists of new judgments (textbook, teaching, and library and archive materials)" (p. 167).

Bell's portrayal of postindustrial society is very attractive to the librarian or information worker. He identified a different division of the economy than Machlup and Porat, but similarly identified an information sector. He also accepted Porat's measurement of the information sector. Bell's attraction is transparent. His analysis meets all the demands that an information-conscious profession could propose. Libraries are explicitly mentioned as central resources for the storage of knowledge. Information and knowledge are cited as central variables for the new society, and the generation and use of theoretical knowledge is not only characteristic of but critically central to the new age. Bell mentioned the importance of technology in all this, but his emphasis shifts slightly so that the nontechnologist is given a more critical role. First, it is not technology per se but the merging of technologies that is important, and second, the new intellectual technology is paramount, where rule-governed procedures take primacy over intuitive judgments. The continued attempts of the information professions to generate a successful language of information retrieval—through classification schemes and indexing languages, is a good example of an attempt to produce an intellectual technology, whereby knowledge can be made available by anyone who has had the appropriate professional training in the correct techniques. These techniques may not be as impressive or arcane as stochastic processes, linear programming, or the construction of decision support systems, but they do fit within the general picture. Furthermore, in the current climate of the oversupply of information, where potential readers are swamped by the total output and need help in retrieving relevant subsets of the literature, the professional task recedes from that of developing metainformation (information about the knowledge contained in documents) to the task of handling the metainformation itself in information retrieval systems. The library and information profession can feel very much at home in Bell's postindustrial society.

A criticism leveled at Machlup and Porat was that they offered neither explanatory nor predictive tools. Bell gave an explanatory analysis and offered not a predictive tool, but a predictive dilemma, which can be used to heighten the sense of responsibility of the information profession. Bell (1979) claimed that "the expansion of the information economy will largely depend on two developments. One is automation—in industry and in the white collar occupations. The second is the growth of information and its retrieval—data bases, scientific information networks, and the explosion of international communications" (p. 184). Put more dramatically, the information economy idea, which offers such an attractive analysis for the librarian or information manager, will be jeopardized unless information professionals act to secure the information required.

Bell (1979) further cited the much discussed and measured explosion in the quantity of published information as evidence of the need for improved information retrieval. Citing the work of de Solla Price and others on the growth of literatures, he claimed as obvious that only computerized information retrieval can deal with the increased output, coupled with the development of large-scale information networks and the automation of data banks and the generation of a national information policy.

Plainly, all this can act as a very comfortable context of meaning for any interpretation of information studies and its theory and practice. If Bell's account is credible it could easily serve as a working context and ideology.

Yet Bell's analysis is open to objection. It is a credible analysis only to people who believe in the idea of an information society, who are comfortable with change, especially along the lines he indicated, for whom the information society is a comfortable cultural project, and who can identify with the professional and technical classes, who are the major beneficiaries in Bell's account. It could be claimed that some in the information profession are almost willing it into being one of these professions.

There are however many practicing professionals for whom Bell's account is shallow and sectarian. Plainly, the future painted by Bell is attractive mainly to those who can benefit from it, most obviously those who have or think they can get the information-handling skills, and who have the task of handling critical scientific and technological information, which are central to the Bell hypothesis. Bell did not discuss, except by analogy, the position of the losers in the new age. He cited old-fashioned calligraphers who were "relegated to the artisan scrap heap" (Bell, 1979, p. 187) by the invention of printing: The implication is that some occupations may experience similar relegation today. Some nonnumerate librarians may well consider themselves in that category, and even those who do not stand to lose personally may feel uneasy with a philosophy of the field that seems to cater only to winners. The claim of an older spirit of library science to provide library services to all may imply that we reject some of the triumphalism in the available text of the information society. For some that older tradition must be dead; that is, their conception of the field has changed, and with it their conception of professional practice. We have to consider whether the field of objects for which we seek coherent expression has changed, or the subjects who make the expression have changed in their self-identity, and whether this is a consequence of a changed context of meaning.

There has been little in the professional literature until recently that explicitly rejects the idea of the information society or claims that the economic analyses are wrong. The objections raised are concerned more with the quality of life in the new age, and the quality of the working environment for those working with the new machines (see Blake, 1978). Those feeling this way are well supported by other critical literature that is concerned with more than economic success, and that examines ethical and psychological issues associated with the current trends.

THE CRITICAL ALTERNATIVE

> Ours is a world about which we pretend to have more and more information but which to us seems increasingly devoid of meaning. I will argue, as would Ivan Illich, that this is due to the inevitable and ironical counter-productive effect of the way in which we produce, process, and consume information. (Dupuy, 1978, p. 4)

The criticisms of the information society normally turn on two major objections. One is the objection that the analysis of economic conditions is incorrect and the outcome will be rather different from that proposed by proponents of the information society idea. The other objection is that the whole argument is but another name for a trend already discerned and subject of a far more rigorous analysis that goes beyond economic conditions to reveal the impact on man and society of current developments.

No one, it should be noted, denies the existence of the new type of society: What is at stake is our understanding of its true dimensions and our conclusions about its impact. Those following Bell, Machlup, Porat, and the host of authors who have developed their ideas, tend to accept that the information society is a "good thing." Those writing within the alternative tradition are far less certain about the outcome. Indeed Ellul (1965, 1980) argued that the circumstances that produce the new information society are themselves a development of the older industrial society[6] and impose threats to the nature of moral existence because of the constraints they impose on our behavior and the limitations they force on our patterns of thought. There is, in fact, an implicit suggestion

---

[6] This theme is developed in another way by Beniger (1986, 1988), who draws very different conclusions from those of Ellul.

in the work of Ellul that in some way the information society, far from being beneficial, is really something dangerous.

Few readers in the English-speaking world have until recently been aware of this anti-information society tradition. Yet it should be considered as much a part of the idea as the more celebrated materials. This stance may seem unjustified, as it was claimed earlier that the idea of a context of meaning for the library and information profession demanded an idea of the information society that was a shared meaning or experience. What Ellul and others have expressed is to be found in common reactions to the information society idea, albeit not so coherently expressed.

One strand of opposition to current developments emphasizes the impact on the quality of life that current developments in capitalist society are having. Dupuy (1978) saw what he called the informational society as a phase in the history of capitalism's attempts to cope with its contradictions, and he saw its effects as intensifying rather than relieving the problems of advanced capitalism. "Rather than delivering us from material constraints, the informational society intensifies the struggle for survival and strengthens the radical monopoly of economic activity over the social and political dimensions of our life" (p. 4). Dupuy complained that common meanings and, we can interpolate, shared meanings, can only be constructed by people making things together. "Without a common world created by *making* things together, no encounter, no human history, no action would be possible . . . Hence men cannot communicate unless they have a common world which unites them" (p. 5).

Capitalism depends on a degree of specialization that in Dupuy's view increases the alienation felt by individuals in society. He accepted the Marxist point that labor that is not for consumption by its owner becomes a commodity, and he polarized possibilities in our society as either autonomous or heteronomous. The effects of this polarization he described as a set of opposites, where the autonomous mode of production or experience is held up as good and the heteronomous (dependence on others) as less good.

> We can learn, for instance, by becoming acquainted with the things of life inside a meaningful environment, or we can learn within the walls of a professional institution. . . . We can render a service to someone asking for help, or we can refer him to people who provide those services. In contrast to the heteronomous mode, what is produced by the autonomous mode cannot in general be measured, estimated, compared with, or added to other values. The *use values* produced autonomously thereby escape the control of economists or national accountants. (Dupuy, 1978, pp. 7–8)

Machlup found something similar when he was attempting to measure the economic value of education in the home.

Dupuy is not a Luddite, and moved away from the crude polarization to state a more balanced hypothesis. The autonomous capacity to produce use values may be significantly invigorated by the heteronomous mode of production.

> The professional therapist, antibiotics, or the predetermined curriculum may, to a certain extent, improve what people could do on their own or through mutual aid. . . . Yet my hypothesis is that beyond certain critical thresholds, the heteronomous production of values generates such a thorough rearrangement of the physical, institutional, and symbolic environment that the autonomous capacity to produce use values is paralyzed. The paradoxical effect of such a restructuring is that the more pervasive the means brought into play by the great heteronomous service producing institutions, the more they become an obstacle to achieving the ends they are supposed to serve. . . . The service economy has gone far beyond these critical thresholds. Relations with other people, the world, or oneself, which we call education, habitation, or health, but confuse with the educational system, urbanization, or the medical establishment, become things or substances or commodities whose degradation our social engineers, in spite of their endeavours, seem quite unable to prevent. (Dupuy, 1978, p. 8)

Dupuy's (1978) aphorism for the informational or postindustrial society is "more and more information, less and less meaning" (p. 16). He used the term *meaning* in a slightly different way than Taylor, using it as a touchstone for the quality of life rather than as a technical term, but his assault on informational society nevertheless is important for the library and information profession on two main counts.

First, the focus of his remarks is the quality of life of any individual living in a community. The alienating depersonalized experience of modern society is of no interest unless it serves human ends. His complaint is that the balance is currently tipped too far away from consideration of autonomous human beings. For many information workers who do not or cannot draw personal and professional satisfaction from being a successful and important part of the new information society, the idea of serving all the information needs of all members of a community remains a true end of professional life, and for them Dupuy's appeal will be very attractive. At the same time, Dupuy's assault was directed at the very set of professionalized services among which the library and information profession is to be found. Thus the professional librarian who

THE CONTEXT OF MEANING   73

finds in Dupuy's account a compelling argument to reject or resist ideas of professional direction and development conditioned by the pull of the information society will also find in the same argument a stern reprimand for the kind of profession that information studies has made for itself. The librarian who accepts this view of the information society is presented with a professional dilemma. If he or she uses this idea of current society as a context of meaning he or she may well simultaneously have to seek a different concept of professional life.

We can add a further complication to the argument by considering some implications of the work of Ellul. His attack on the Machlup–Bell position is twofold; first, that he foresaw the whole debate much earlier, second, this so-called new information society is properly seen in other terms and is a logical development of trends within industrial society, not a new stage of evolution. Ellul, too, is concerned with the humanistic perspective and the quality of life.

Ellul (1980) found the definitions of our current society provided by Bell and others as limited rather than inaccurate. He claimed that other observers have examined only one element of our society, and that a deeper and more decisive level of analysis would reveal that it is the technological system that underlies and defines modern society. Ellul's first essay on this subject, published in 1955 and called (in English translation) the *Technological Society* (1965) was followed by *The Technological System* (1980). In the latter work, Ellul claimed that technology is the determining factor in society, but it is not the only factor. However, within society there is also a technological system, living in and off the society and grafted onto it.

> We can . . . say that the technological society is one in which a technological system has been installed. But it is not itself that system and there is tension between the two of them . . . the technological system causes disorders, irrationalities, incoherences in the society and challenges the sociological environment. (Ellul, 1980, p. 18)

Ellul's concern was with the maintenance or recovery of freedom. His pessimism, which is to be contrasted with the optimism of Bell and others, is that freedom is threatened by this technological system in our technological society by these technological forces that are too powerful for simple human beings. "This technological environment forces us to consider everything a technological problem and, at the same time, to lock ourselves up in, enclose ourselves in, an environment that has become a system" (p. 48).

Ellul saw this technological system as embracing all aspects of man's environment and constraining his freedom to be an autonomous agent, not because technology imposes some barrier to his attaining whatever freedom he chooses, but because technology limits his capacity to choose by defining what choices or freedom he might want.

> Man can choose. But his choices will always bear upon secondary elements and never on the overall phenomenon. His judgements will always be ultimately *defined* by the technological criteria. . . . Man can choose, but in a system of options established by the technological process. He can direct, but in terms of the technological given. He can never get out of it at any time, and the intellectual systems he constructs are ultimately expressions or justifications of technology. (p. 325)

Ellul saw man as born into consciousness of a technological environment, educated to prepare him for technological functions (and not educated for anything else), and conditioned by agents of adjustment that adapt man to technology. "The entire mental panorama in which man is situated is produced by technicians and shapes man to a technological universe, the only one reflected towards him by anything represented to him" (p. 313). Further, he claimed, technology creates needs or desires that really only exist in order to utilize technological capacity, and that man has no intellectual, moral, or spiritual reference point for judging and criticizing technology.

Ellul, therefore, was worried about technology, and also about technologies. We can find further definition of these terms (the latter usually rendered as *technique*) in his earlier work, *The Technological Society*. For librarians and information professionals who dislike or disbelieve what they are told about information technology and the character of the new information society, Ellul's objectives, and his desire for a humanistic perspective, seem desirable. However, there is an irony in the application of his approach, because all professions based on the reduction of knowledge to some technique (rather like Bell's intellectual technology) are criticized for being part of the overall process. So, as the librarian's claim to professionalism is so closely based on the development and standardized application of techniques, even those now old-fashioned techniques that are not computer based, there is a difficulty for those librarians who readily criticize technique.

How wide does Ellul (1980) cast his net of technique? His view of the technological system and its processes is clear:

> There is production not only of industrial goods, but also of symbols, individuals (by education), spare time activities, ideologies,

service signs, information. What is known as circulation (including that of human beings or information) always originates in production and winds up in consumption. However, this complex system is made possible only by improving an organization that leads to a more and more complete overlapping of production and consumption. Advancing constantly and necessarily, technology makes the technological system the agent of an inevitable affluent society. But, conversely, with everything thus being produced and consumed, the system presupposes a more and more thorough integration of each element, including man, as an object. Man can no longer be a subject. For the system implies that, at least in regard to itself, man must always be treated as an object. (p. 11)

The interpretive stance demands that there is a subject or group of subjects, and Ellul's position might seem to deny this possibility. We may also encounter work in the area of user studies that, for librarians at least, does attempt to objectify the reader or library user. My intention is to recover the definition of the subject by developing the shared meanings of subjects, and to reject the reduction of human beings to objects implied by Ellul. The way this works out is seen in the examination of the individual conceptions of the field in Part III. For the present purposes of constructing a possible context of meaning from the idea of the information society, it is legitimate to retain Ellul's rejection of man as subject, and to continue his construction by considering his initial views on technique. These are expressed less concisely by Ellul himself than by Merton (1965) in his introduction to the English translation of *The Technological Society*:

Ours is a progressively technical civilization: by this Ellul means that the ever-expanding and irreversible rule of technique is extended to all domains of life. It is a civilization committed to the quest for continually improved means to carelessly examined ends. Indeed, technique transforms ends into means. What was once prized in its own right now becomes worthwhile only if it helps achieve something else. And, conversely, technique turns means into ends. "Know-how" takes on an ultimate value. (p. x)

Merton also explained to us the idea of technique, rendered by Ellul (1965) as "the totality of methods rationally arrived at and having absolute efficiency (for a given stage of development) in every field of human activity" (p. 1). Merton (1965) said that "By technique . . . he means far more than machine technology. Technique refers to any complex of standardized means for attaining a predetermined result" (p. x).

All that has been said so far could be seen as suggesting that technique is a passive phenomenon, a new way of regarding things as they are. Such a view would be false. Ellul made his idea more powerful by making it dynamic, and by giving it a primacy in respect to science, which inverts the normal relationship we assume between science and technology.

Ellul maintained that, historically, technique precedes science, but only begins to extend and develop with the appearance of science. Since then, although science provided the solutions to the problems that technique posed, we now experience a situation where it is difficult to distinguish between science and technique, partly because science itself has become a technique. Scientists work in teams, forgoing some of their personal freedoms and research ambitions in order to get access to the large resources modern research requires, and so the new class of professionals and engineers (cf. Bell) is really a class of technicians. We now always associate scientific advance with some technical outcome, and the rapidity of change reflects the close feeder relationship between technique and science.

Ellul extended the dynamic character of technique by claiming that techniques are always put to immediate use. Several other claims advanced by Ellul fill in the picture relevant to the idea of the information society. First, because of the primacy of technical operations, we are in a world characterized by the technical phenomenon. Second, our society has moved beyond the application of technique to mere machines: Technique has invaded the realms of social, economic, and administrative life. Thus, the use of reason in technical judgments both upsets older pragmatic traditions and creates new operational methods and tools. However, because reason simultaneously considers the fixed end of technique, which is efficiency, all means are reduced to one, the most efficient. Only the fittest (literally) technique will survive. Finally, consciousness intervenes in the interest of technique, showing to everyone the advantages of technique and leading to the application of techniques and new methods in fields traditionally left to chance, pragmatism, and instinct (Ellul, 1965).

Ellul (1965), in his foreword, concluded that in the modern world, "The most dangerous form of determinism is the technological phenomenon. It is not a question of getting rid of it, but, by an act of freedom, of transcending it" (p. xxxi). Ellul's own purposes are not of concern here, but fertile use can be made of his analysis. He provided no facts, statistics, graphs, or any of the other impediments of empirical research, but still produced a powerful tool that can round off the picture of the information society and allow the construction of a more complete context of meaning for the information professions than would be available using U.S. sources alone.

INFORMATION TECHNOLOGY

Before building that picture there should first be some consideration of information technology. This is not to consider the role of the construction of information machines within the information sector, nor to consider the response of librarians or information managers to the introduction of information technology in the workplace. The discussion must be placed within a more immediate frame of time, so that the relative newness of the technology is apparent: The concern is with the way a revolution in technology has finally been disseminated to the bulk of practitioners and how the abstract analysis of an information society has become transformed into the pressing reality of a computer-based professional existence.

The concern is with the merging technologies, which for Bell are a critical feature of the postindustrial society. The two crude machine technologies being merged are computers and telecommunications. Alongside this merger there are also changes in scale and in marketing, with attendant economic and social consequences, and there must be an account also of the changes in possibilities for information storage and information handling software that all the aforementioned changes imply.

It remains the case that most practitioners do not work with computers in any immediate sense, although most will most probably work intermittently with a terminal attached to a local miniframe or mainframe, or with a network workstation, which runs some system package dealing with one or several housekeeping routines. Some librarians will use terminals for the online interrogation of databases held in remote hosts and may use one or another of the telecommunication networks to do so. Very few librarians or information managers will use their own minicomputer or microcomputer for anything other than institutionally bought or developed packages or programs, and the number who actually program will be infinitesimally small. Against this we must place the atmosphere within the subject and the profession that now accepts the dominant position of computer systems and services. The work of librarians and information workers may not have been completely computerized, but their ideology has been. The computerization of the basic housekeeping routines and of the major catalog services has been of critical importance in developing this situation.

The use of computers has been under discussion in the library and information profession for 40 years. Courses in computer use and simple programming have been available in library schools since about 1955, but the dissemination of computer use has been more recent. Only since the mid-1970s has there been widespread use of online information services, and although computer-generated hard copy or microfiche has been available longer, the online use of cataloging and classification data has been similarly recent. It should be clear, however, that librarians are not programmers: The library and information professional is very much a consumer rather than a producer of information technology, and normally an end user rather than a developer of software.

A most significant development is even more recent than those mentioned so far. The microcomputer revolution, which has put computer power into so many homes and offices, has actually revolutionized the information business by putting information power in the hands of ordinary office workers and people at home. The political promises of home and office connection to the information superhighway will secure that change. A relatively small investment can buy adequate computer power and access to telecommunications to allow anyone to set up as an information service: This development outside the library or information center has had a major impact in widening the library profession's horizons about what is possible and has also introduced a new threat in the form of possible increased demand from a potential clientele who might easily go elsewhere. The literature of the information society for the librarian includes warnings about the dire consequences of failing to be suitably technologized. These warnings have acquired a new intensity in the last few years. For the library and information profession, the idea of the information society as a context of meaning has found a new urgency, most potently in these recent years since the widespread diffusion of microcomputers and their increasingly sophisticated software. It is against these developments that we must construct the final analysis and picture of the information society.

THE INFORMATION CULTURE: ANALYSIS AND CONCLUSION

To reiterate an earlier point, at issue is the idea of the information society: The empirical evidence is open to several interpretations, and the theoretical environments that have been constructed are ambiguous and conflicting. There is a need for an interpretive tool that can develop a coherent view of the context of meaning for the library and information discipline and profession. A definition or representation of the information society is required that can both win the consent, through conviction, of those practicing in the profession and win the support of the discipline as a satisfactory and adequate framework for analysis. To sustain the earlier argument that theory and practice are mutually feeding one another, and that it is from practice that theory must emerge, there must be something that relates the information society to the practice of library science and information work.

The picture that has emerged is confused and contradictory. There are some empirical observations that need theoretical support. There are also two sets of conflicting theoretical and explanatory arguments (which we can label as the Bell and Ellul positions), which not only are mutually exclusive but are also polarized in attitude and conclusion, and are not clearly related in language.

The situation is, however, not so desperate. It is possible, I believe, to recompose the core of the Bell and the Ellul arguments to develop a composite argument that offers alternatives to the reader, and that then can serve as a broader context for interpretation. This demands understanding about certain correspondences between Bell on the one hand and Ellul on the other, and understanding about which meanings can be construed as common and shared.

The first task is to draw the connection, already hinted at, between the idea of knowledge as used by Bell and the term technique used by Ellul. What for Bell was the new intellectual technology is quite clearly subsumed by Ellul into the general category of technique. What is different is that Bell allowed the development of new knowledge in any way (although the impact of his construction is that the new knowledge will be more of the same: knowledge of the sort that produced the information society). Ellul, on the other hand, with his concept of the survival only of the "fittest" technique obviously constrained the character of new knowledge—which can only be in the service of the further spread of technique.

The different attitudes toward knowledge-technique do impose a barrier to the development of a common or shared meaning for the composite term. For Ellul, technique is what we may find irresistible but must transcend. For Bell it is the tool that allows further progress, and may be seen in itself as a source of wealth and power. This argument can be taken one step further back to consider the people who use the knowledge. Here Bell and Ellul were closer: Bell's intellectual technology is algorithmic, which is very close to Ellul's description of technique, and in both interpretations the knowledge creators and handlers can be seen as a technical class. The difference is that in one case the technical class is viewed as the new power group in society and in the other it is, although powerful, seen as a class diminished and diminishing society through having merely technical competence.

With these seemingly incompatible accounts there is the "language of perspicuous contrast" that Taylor (1983) called a major tool in the development of an interpretation.

It is through this language of contrast that a clearer understanding of aspects of anyone's position becomes available, and thus allows them to move on to a better interpretation and practice. Seen in this way the close correspondence between knowledge on the one hand and technique on the other assists in the development of interpretation. The conflict between Bell and Ellul comes to be seen and used as an aid in the construction of a more advanced conception of the context of meaning for the information and library field.

This morass can be untangled to present a table of views that encompass the different positions (see Table 4.1). From an expanded version of Table 4.1, it would be possible to develop crude guidelines to the position of the various conceptions of the subject in Part III. Thus, there are grounds for regarding the information society as a context of meaning, even though the views about it are so disparate and opposed. It is because there are arguments available to us about the nature of the information society that it is possible to say that it must form part of, and inform, the discourse of all active in the information or library profession and discipline. Enthusiasts for and opponents of the information society argument have available alternative expressions of what that kind of society means that can be applied to support the contrasting positions they take: The idea of the context remains, even if its impact is the subject of differing interpretations.

To the immediate objection that, if there is no agreement about the meaning, then there are no common or shared meanings, it can be answered that the strength of agreement about meanings is to be seen as a continuum from strong to weak, and as the meaning shared is stronger, so the conceptions of the profession are more likely to coincide: Where they are weaker, professional cohesion is correspondingly reduced.

TABLE 4.1

Attributes	Bell's View	Ellul's View
Machinery	Favor	Reject
Professionalism	Favor	Reject
Individuality	Reject	Favor
Knowledge / technique	Source of material wealth	Cause of spiritual poverty
Horizons	Expanding	Narrowing

The need to produce some embedding of this idea from practice still remains. What can be stated now is that practice usually has some end: Most typically immediate ends in serving a particular client and longer term ends that are embodied in the structure comprised of continuing daily decisions and that collectively reflect the convictions of the practitioner about the nature of the practice. The latter can be said to reflect the practitioner's view about the working environment, and as such can be related to one of the conceptions of the information society. Indeed it is quite possible that the views of any one practitioner may move from one to the other of the two representations of the information society already described at different stages in the development of a career.

It is clear that the requirements of a hermeneutic science for the information society are met: There is a group of subjects for whom the meaning must exist, there is a field of objects about which we can make some coherent sense, and there are alternative expressions about those objects. It is the strength of the interpretive position that two competing views can be admitted, especially in such a case where the objects being described are substantially the same (except in their language) and over which there is so little disagreement except about their interpretation.

The second task is to resolve the inconsistency in coverage between Bell and Ellul. The latter was explicitly concerned with all of society. Bell was more particular, and confined his analysis to that part of society concerned with the economy. He did not, as he might if he had used Ellul's broader scope, explain the impact on other aspects—the polity and the spiritual aspects of life. This discrepancy does not pose any problems, because within the library and information profession few conceptions would be centrally concerned with the polity (the political structure of society), and their situation in our analysis would anyway not be different. An example would be any conception that placed ideas of service to society higher than any view of the techniques used to achieve that end, such as a conception of library science or information management as service that ignored mere technical skills and valued compassion and concern more: The limitation of Bell's position is not in that respect a restriction.

With this context of meaning established, the next task is to review the different ways in which information studies has developed understandings of itself and how commentators and practitioners generate different views of the field.

Part II
Preparations and Objections

In this part of the book, I consider the legitimacy of the interpretive approach for information studies as a preparation for considering various conceptions of the field in Part III.

In Chapter 5, I argue that there are good grounds for proceeding with an attempt to build an interpretive model of the field. Chapter 6 considers various objections to the claims advanced about the interpretive approach: first, the objection that there can only be two possible interpretations of the field, and second, the objection that the only possible conceptions or models of the field must be those associated with the unique techniques of the field—cataloging, classification, indexing, and so on.

The final chapter in this part, Chapter 7, considers the relationship that develops between any practitioner and his or her field, and this picture is used as a preface to the consideration of three models or conceptions of the field in Part III.

5

Interpretation in Library and Information Studies

In this chapter, questions about the relationship between the interpretive approach and the library and information field are answered, in particular the question of whether the approach is suitable at all. Can it be said that this field is one that meets the requirements as put forward by Taylor for an interpretation? Other questions that follow from this include the conditions to be satisfied, the apparently difficult case of information science, other conditions that must be met, the means of applying an interpretive approach, and the grounds for that approach in the field.

IS THE INTERPRETIVE APPROACH SUITABLE?

Information studies lacks a firm theoretical base, and claims advanced about the theoretical base of even information science are debatable. The literature of the philosophy of the field reveals many schema and few convincing statements: Despite the widely held view that a firm epistemological base is needed, or even exists just waiting to be discovered, no one has successfully described what it is. Brookes (1980b) was convinced that the field had this foundation theory almost within reach: He claimed that "we have access to the data needed to establish the missing general theory. The missing theory is very important indeed" (p. 23).

In the early 1980s, Brookes attempted in several publications to establish such a theory, but failed, or failed to capture the support of the discipline for his views. This failure makes the task more difficult: Whereas the enemy of the interpretive approach in the social sciences is clearly defined—the logical positivist with his objective facts—we do not have so easy a target. The task is complicated further because of the methodological diversity within the broad field of library and information work, which requires first that it be shown that the field really is among the social sciences. Whatever may be said for the bulk of practice in the broad field, there are pertinent claims from experimental information retrieval to consider that subfield at least to be an empirical science, whereas the group of subfields that can be loosely labeled historical may be consider themselves as part of the humanities. Such claims challenge the idea that all our practices can fairly be included within those areas that can be subject to an interpretive approach.

The response is threefold: first, to show that the field is shown in its best light as a social science; second to show what conditions must be met in order to offer an interpretive account; third, to show how the interpretive approach can be applied to the discipline as a whole.

CONDITIONS REQUIRED

The first condition that must be satisfied is that the field be regarded as a social science. This can be broadened to the statement that it not be a natural science. Brookes (1980b) gave some assistance when he recognized that "the problems which confront us most urgently now belong to the *social* rather than to the *natural sciences*" (p. 27).

The humanities, like the social sciences, which have already been examined, are, according to Gadamer, suitable areas for hermeneutics (Outhwaite, 1985). Therefore, if there is a conviction that information work is properly studied as a human or as a social science the first condition is satisfied. Gadamer (1976) claimed that "the modern social sciences stand in a particularly strained relationship to their object, ... this relationship that especially requires hermeneutical reflection" (p. 40), and proposed a hemeneutics that is not "a methodology for the human sciences, but an attempt to understand what the human sciences truly are, beyond their methodological self-consciousness, and what connects them with our totality of experience of the world" (Gadamer, 1975, p. xiii). The basic distinction he drew is between the sciences that meticulously research a given area of reality, and those that "are more a matter of re-interpreting a partially known reality in terms of current concerns" (Outhwaite, 1985, p. 32). I claim that this covers most aspects of information work. In respect to historical studies in the field that might be held to be between the humanities and social sciences we can be similarly confident. Gadamer's description of the hermeneutic approach also enables us to include the interpretation of special literatures whose aesthetic rather than utilitarian virtues are dominant—for example, children's literature, rather than dictionaries and directories.

There remain two other areas of professional activity that might be considered outside the social sciences. First, information science, which is discussed in the next section, and second those productions like catalog codes and classification schemes that might be held to be about (respectively) real objects and schemes of human knowledge. Cataloging is of course not about real objects: We do not give primacy in cataloging to the physical attributes of books but to their logical content (we describe a book not as a block of wood that has been processed, or as a sheaf of paper with markings, but as something with meaning—the words William, Shakespeare, and Hamlet are interpreted by us, according to where they appear in the book). Classification schemes can only make sense when they too successfully convey some view of knowledge as a whole, or one small part in relation to other parts, in a way that claims to be a common meaning for all users. I realize that this proposition is entirely contrary to the claim of E. C. Richardson and in part to Sayers. However, the latter qualifies the former's view that "there is an order of things ordained by Nature and that the classifier's relation to it is one of inquiry and discovery" (Sayers, 1955, p. viii). Sayers accepted Bliss' substitution of an arrangement "in accordance with the educational and scientific consensus"—in other words, with intersubjective meaning. Sayers (1955) accepted that "the librarian will succeed in so far as his arrangement of books on these sciences and arts corresponds to the arrangement of their material made by the workers in them" (p. viii).

The Question of Information Science

The remaining area to consider is that which often claims to be an empirical science and has certainly attracted most successful attention from people with natural or mathematical science backgrounds—information science, or, more specifically, experimental information retrieval. Several authors have tried to produce explanations or theoretical bases for information science that are explicitly mathematical or relate the field directly to the mathematical theory of communication published by Shannon.[1] It is also true that experimental work in this area has been extremely successful in using computers to work with algorithms developed to solve problems of retrieval, given the imprecise nature of the raw material they have to work with. This raw material is the raw material of indirect discourse between authors and inquirers. To treat a subject inquiry as brute data is to make the same error that Taylor rejected in social surveys. Currently, the major critical area for future development of information retrieval systems is the problem of meaning, particularly contextual meaning, and other advances in automatic

---

[1] See, for example, Heilprin (1985).

cataloging (or knowledge representation) are awaiting a satisfactory automatic parsing system. Resolution of these problems is complex and researchers are turning toward hermeneutic solutions.[2] In its basic data and techniques, information retrieval can be seen as coming firmly within the range of the social sciences addressed by Gadamer, Taylor, and other hermeneutic philosophers. The position is not as clear cut as this, but it is possible to talk of an information retrieval world in this way.

OTHER CONDITIONS

The remaining conditions that must be satisfied are those identified by Taylor (1978) and discussed in Chapter 3. That is, to recapitulate, there must be a field of objects about whose coherence and sense we can speak, there must be a distinction between the meaning (the coherence or sense) and its embodiment in a particular expression, and there must be a human subject or subjects for whom the meaning exists. Further, the meaning that must exist must not only be for a subject but must be of something—that is, we should be able to distinguish an event or action from its meaning. To take a most obvious example, the act of filing cards can be described quite separately from a description of its meaning. Finally, that meaning can only exist in a field, in relation to the meaning of other things. All the elements of any enterprise have meaning only in relation to one another's meanings. Consequently any change in an element that also changes its meaning (changes without changes in meaning are possible) may affect the meanings of other elements, too. To take a simple example, classification schemes do not explain what a particular subject is, only what it is not—history is not chemistry or theology; we learn about what constitutes a subject from the available alternatives. Similarly, a change in the social sciences schedules that changes the usage of the politics classification may have repercussions in meaning for the history schedule, or at least for its application.

Are these conditions found in the information field? There are considerable problems to overcome, and part of the answer must be deferred to later parts of this work. There are many competing models or conceptions of information work available, and it is clear that although they are competing models, they are not all different expressions of the same thing or things: Information science is not another way of talking about historical bibliography. Similarly, if these models compete it must be that the subjects for whom they have meaning may not accept all of them, so there may be difficulty in speaking of a field with a coherent

---

[2] See Rommetveit (1986), and Winograd and Flores (1986), especially Chapters 3 and 5.

sense about which we can speak sensibly. Indeed, the very plurality of linguistic usage suggests uncertainty about the nature of the field. Buckland (1988) restricting his scope to library theory, listed seven different types of activities associated with libraries, and concluded that they are quite diverse and that the relationships between them are not clear. He emphasized that although specialists understand their own area, it is tolerance and *understanding* (his emphasis) of other areas that is important for effective achievement.

It is legitimate, however, not to be concerned about descriptions of the field. To use these is to fall into the trap of using linguistic labels as brute data. I think it is uncontroversial that all subjects for whom the terms librarianship and information work have meaning will well understand, as a shared meaning, the world of objects and actions and events to which this applies. There will be variations in awareness and sophistication, but the only difficulty I anticipate is over the question of including the nonprofessional users of libraries and information services within the group of subjects. On balance, partly because I consider that as the clients of service they have to share the common meaning of, for example, library or catalog and in turn they partly determine meaning in the wider community for the library, I include them only where they seem to have clear status as participants. This may seem a different approach to Dworkin, who really was not concerned to include in his subjects for law the accused or the plaintiff, but only those interested in the character of decision making in law in a community. This last group could be very wide and include those completely outside any experience of the law. Similarly, the meaning of library will in part be determined by the meanings shared by people who never use library services. There are, therefore, interlocking levels of shared meanings—the wider community, the library-using group, and the smaller group of library employees. Although these groups of subjects will share appropriate intersubjectivities at each level, I think there is no difficulty in determining the objects about which they seek to make sense. To use the language of Dworkin, we can say that there is probably a shared (intersubjective) meaning for the concept of library, but that the various subjects will have their own, possibly widely differing conceptions for that concept.

We should, however, not leave this question without making some broad statement about the world of objects, which we hope makes sense. For current purposes, information studies, as a discipline and profession, can be seen as concerned with the accumulation of knowledge and the organization of it for social use, and with the technical skills that both bring about the best view of that and are employed to resolve remaining problems.

The remaining question to resolve is whether or not there can be expressions about this field of objects that are different from the objects themselves. I think this case has already been answered by discussion noted earlier about the significance of the humble task of filing cards (or its current electronic equivalent). Anyone asked—to reiterate the question posed at the start of this work—"What are you doing?" when filing catalog cards can answer stupidly and unhelpfully that they are putting cards in a drawer, or (more usefully) that they are helping to build the catalog, or making information on latest stock available to all users of the library, or putting the cards in alphabetical order with other catalog entries. For the field as a whole they can offer answers about their purposive strategy that may vary equally. It remains the case, though, that the interpretive claim is that many expressions may be legitimate and a good interpretation will produce an expression that is better. Thus every new interpretation will generate a text, or text analogue, for the field that gives a better fit to the whole field than previous expressions. This question comes under closer scrutiny later.

MEANS OF APPLICATION

How can an interpretive account of information studies be constructed? I propose to follow the example of Taylor and Dworkin, avoid a top-down description of the discipline, and concentrate on building up the picture from the practices that make up the discipline. However, there are two immediate problems. The first is that the analogy that was made with law suggested that the bulk of lawyers are not concerned directly with the process of making judicial decisions or even in most cases anticipating on what grounds they will be made. The work of the average lawyer, like that of the average librarian, is humdrum and far removed from the heady excitement of judicial decision. Is the right course of inquiry, if the analogy between the professions is good, to ignore the practice of librarians in libraries and concentrate instead on the areas of decision making that are analogous to judicial decisions? The second problem to be faced is that there is not just one practice but two distinct types of practice. On the one hand there is the practice, or group of practices, that constitute library and information work, and on the other there is the practice of theorizing and explaining practice, or about practice, and researching for improved practice—an area that for convenience I call the discipline, as distinct from the profession, of the library and information field. Which practice should be the focus of inquiry? The analogy of politics concentrates on the disciplines of studying political behavior rather than the practice of politics, and similarly with law: There is a concentration on the sense of what the discipline of law amounts to, as opposed to the behavioral minutiae of form filing, getting adequate numbers of witnesses, or exchanging contracts.

A solution to both problems can be found in consideration of the educational function, which in law and in information studies is slanted more toward vocational than purely speculative academic work. If the point of an interpretive science is to develop the theory from practice, which will in turn improve on practice, moving understanding forward from a state of prejudice to one of increased clarity, then merely teaching even the best practice is to fail in the duty to the student and the profession. It is in the educational function that students are confronted with the interpretation of current theory on judicial decision making—law schools teach jurisprudence alongside company law, but lawyer's offices contain departments only of the latter. This analogy I believe can be shown to hold good—or rather ought to hold good—in the library school or departments of information management. The practice we are discussing is not a real practice, it is a belief about practice as informed by the interpretations that are initially imposed on practice by professional education, and are embellished by experience. By experience I do not mean the experience of performing work tasks; I mean rather the continual updating by reflection of all those points that any novitiate connects with a practice and that are constitutive of its character—including research, theory, and daily experience. To work over the practice to develop some intersubjective meaning actually requires that the interpretation be informed by something. The claim of an interpretive approach to be able to construct improved meanings must be dependent on a source of improvement. This could of course be some distilled inner thought and reflection, but even that is unlikely to be fruitful without the injection of some external stimuli, most commonly external knowledge about practices in other disciplines or places. Such external stimulus would be the expanded context of language or experience Pocock (1985) mentioned. If information studies as a discipline is to maintain itself as a social science then it must be open to general movements in thinking about, and within, the social sciences. As was the case with politics in Taylor's construction, the discipline must, epistemologically, keep very close contact with the parent disciplinary group.

The practice to be used for the basic primitive data is, then, not the practice in this library or that information service but some constructed practice that is the closest it is possible to get to a clear set of shared meanings. The requirement of an interpretive approach is that we work from some text or text analogue and move toward a further text—the interpretive account. There are obviously texts available, which through wide exposure or popularity, can be said to be in some way representative of parts of the overall practice. However, there is another difficulty here, which is that such views may be only the interpretations of particular individual members of the community, whereas what is needed is some set of shared meanings. So, common observations about common practice and common statements about the nature of the practice that the texts describe should be added. Effectively what I claim is that no one available published text offers a best interpretation of the practice, and the interpretation must be constructed from a number of sources. Because published texts are historical, if only in the sense of being available some considerable time after they are formed as interpretations in the author's mind, and because other forms of discourse are more current, the textual record can be embellished with whatever else is available that shows sufficient commonality of meaning with the set of shared meanings. In the case of information science, for example, there are several basic texts that may be considered as competing expressions of more or less the same thing. Different universities may choose different texts and practicing information scientists are likely to use some recollection of the text preferred at the university they attended plus considerably more information gleaned from discussions at conferences and with local colleagues, from the professional and commercial press, and from other external sources. The different versions that two people from different information units will have will again be competing expressions: Dialogue may generate a new interpretation conveying more meaning, which will improve the practice of both practitioners.

What sources of text are available? The situation of law is more clear cut: Apart from the text analogue of behavior, there is the body of statute law, common law, judicial decision, commentary, and academic review. Although parallels for these cannot be identified so precisely in information work and its literature, the same tasks are being performed. What is more difficult to pin down is the text analogue, or what is constructed from the behavior of practitioners. This is because the behavior of lawyers is more purposive, with more obvious immediate and long-term objectives, than can be the case for librarians or information managers. In few cases can information professionals concentrate on the purely intellectual and logical, as opposed to the physical and administrative, elements of each task in their practice. Because of this difficulty it becomes necessary to treat behavior within the practice, by which I partly mean views of that behavior, rather than the behavior of practitioners, within each conception discussed in Part III.

To aid the process of generating the text, practical tools are needed that allow not only the identification of the shared practice but also the construction of theory from it. This is difficult. There are those tools taken from Taylor and Dworkin (see Chapter 3), but we might also consider some other, complicating issues that arise from the origins of hermeneutics. Hermeneutics has a reputation (undeserved) for being uncritical, stemming in part from its origins in Biblical criticism—where the principal concern is the manifestation and restoration of original intentional meaning. This itself gives rise to two immediate problems; first that there is no obvious check on the limits of understanding—especially, for example, when dealing with corrupted texts or incomplete or distorted communications of any sort—and second that the linguistic medium is "part of more general social processes, which should not be reduced to communication alone" (Outhwaite, 1985, p. 37). There is still the problem of how to construct a text of such a disparate field. My claim is that the concept of the field has in the last half century or so been given different expressions at various times. Most of these are still extant, at least vestigially, although their influence has waxed and waned through time. These expressions can be labeled *conceptions*, following Dworkin's model. So, the field can be spoken of in the guise of historical bibliography, or information management, as different conceptions of the principle or concept.

This work examines three different conceptions of the concept of information studies—historical bibliography, information science, and information management. Each of these conceptions has at one time or another been a significant influence in the field, providing a driving force in forging the profession's image of itself, or in defining changes in the professional curriculum, or in characterizing the profession's central preoccupation at the period of that influence. Several conceptions have run in parallel, and the degree to which they conflict will be brought out in examination of their language and their interpretation. There is a greater concentration on more recent conceptions that are currently competing for attention in the profession, and these are the conceptions that most particularly are developed against and within the context of meaning given, or imposed, by the information culture.

There is no claim that this list of conceptions is exhaustive or that it could not be improved with substitutions. I do claim that as a first exercise in developing an interpretive account of the field the chosen examples will serve to show that objections to the use of interpretation in information studies can be overcome. The field can be depicted in terms of these conceptions, and arguments about the current nature or character of the field can be answered, in part, by reference to currently extant conceptions and their relative strength and vitality.

The idea of these conceptions also begs questions, which in part give an agenda for the discussion of each conception. Must there be a separate text for each conception? Can there be any meaningful answer to the question whether one is a better conception than another? How closely do they relate to one another as well as to the original concept? If different texts are produced for different conceptions are they really texts of different disciplines, different fields of objects with their own coherence and set of subjects? The fields of both historical bibliography and information management, for example, appeal to subjects outside the traditional professional group. If there are to be comparisons between these conceptions there must be an account of how these can be created or constructed by participating subjects. There must also be a demonstration that it is reasonable to talk of the sense or coherence of information studies as a whole rather than of one or more of the competing conceptions. This latter is required to show that there is one field, based on one underlying concept, rather than a succession of fields based on different concepts. The language of perspicuous contrast can be developed, and examples of the fusion of horizons between different conceptions offered, only if each conception embeds some intersubjective set of shared meanings about that conception. Without an expression and interpretation for each conception, there is no base from which to proceed with comparisons. In some cases it may also be desirable to show that the move from one conception to another is the outcome of an interpretive theory, which in a postinterpretive phase has led to an improved, or at least clearer, practice, which in turn has become the preinterpretive practice of the succeeding conception.

This examination must be placed against the background of the current information environment, the Information Age, rendered here as the information culture. The conceptions should express a constructive interpretation of the information culture and the information field, and must have coherence for the group of subjects who constitute that practice. The validation will be found in the best expression of the best interpretation in whatever constitutes the best improvement in practice. The drive to the best practice (reflecting Ellul's determinist technique) will also offer an explanatory framework for that interpretation. This will be discussed further in Chapter 7, which considers the relationship between practitioners and their practice and the theory that is generated from practice.

THE GROUNDS FOR AN INTERPRETIVE ACCOUNT

Are there good grounds for adopting an interpretive account of information studies? I have been careful not to mount a direct assault on positivist schemas of explanation, or to examine the current state of theory in the discipline. The strength of the interpretive account will itself reveal the inadequacy of alternatives.

The principal requirement for a hermeneutic science as identified by

INTERPRETATION IN LIBRARY AND INFORMATION STUDIES 95

Taylor can be met. There is also a means of applying the interpretive approach to the field, and benefits will flow from it. Additionally, as the interpretive approach, as applied by Taylor, is one that ties politics very closely to overall social theory, it is reasonable to expect the information field to benefit similarly from a closer association with more general social theory.

At the beginning of the review of the interpretive approach, I rejected (following Outhwaite) any approach that veered toward *psychologism*—the interpretation of a field through the views of one or many individuals. This approach is anti-interpretive because it does not concentrate on the construction of intersubjective shared meanings, and thus offers little assistance in understanding whole fields of study and really contributes only to individual biography. Multiple biography does not constitute a discipline or a profession.

In connection with the dangers of psychologism, it should be noted with respect to the approach known as symbolic interactionism that similar problems arise. Although an approach refreshingly close to the hermeneutic interpretive tradition, it is also one that can be labeled psychologist, concentrating more on individual reactions and responses to environments and the mind-based construction of the world than on the generation of shared and common meanings that mark the interpretive approach. Symbolic interactionism was favored by Shera in his later work as the best methodology for the field to adopt in attempting to understand itself. Symbolic interactionism is based on a phenomenological approach and is really in part a technique for gathering data: It requires participant observation for data collection and for "taking the view of the other" in analysis. This obviously will work more toward mass biography than the construction of shared meanings. This point is of more critical significance in the library and information field than it might be for other social science professions. When we consult a social worker or lawyer we really do want him or her to see or take our point of view, take our side, and work through the image of law or regulation to help us to our goal. Library and information work is concerned more with the shared interpretation and construction of a solution through sifting the mass of recorded knowledge. Furthermore, the business of running a library or information service is more a shared than an individual exercise. If a legal firm expands, it may take on more staff and even separate them into departments, but each individual lawyer will be seeing individual clients: The library or information agency builds its service in a different way, which requires much more emphasis to be placed on shared meanings—whether it be in interpreting classification schedules, or developing a manageable view of the subject literature of a particular field. The information field demands that the professional practitioner and the user not only share those meanings among themselves, but also develop a sense of shared meaning with the access tools to the literature.

With the confidence that there is a viable enterprise, the next task is to consider what objections can be mounted against it. The next chapter examines and dismisses three separate objections.

6
Objections to the Interpretive Position

In information studies, there is no dominating ideology such as is found in modern natural science. It cannot be claimed that there is one overall perspective of the subject or discipline, and that all work within it conforms to one particular paradigm. It is, correspondingly, difficult to establish an idea of how coherence across the field as a whole can be constituted. The historical record shows traces of the existence of several paradigms of the subject, some coexisting or at least coeval, with no clear succession between them. In terms of each individual conception, this does not pose problems for the interpretive position. The overall interpretive purpose does, however, become more confused if the concept of which the conceptions are held to be embodiments is itself so weak or ambiguous as to be the subject of a low degree of shared meaning among practitioners.

The most public debates have been between the competing claims of information science and library science that reveal an unsatisfactory situation within the overall community.[1] This section examines the traditional division of the field into library science on the one hand and information science on the other and shows that this division is neither necessary nor desirable.

IS THERE ONLY LIBRARY SCIENCE AND INFORMATION SCIENCE?

There may be good grounds for considering library science and information science as examples of the use of perspicuous contrast for the development of understanding, but that is a reading we would have to impose on the texts because it certainly does not stand out as authorial intention. However, the distinction in the conception need not be so problematic. Dworkin showed that several competing interpretations of

---

[1] See, for example, Rayward (1983), and the continuation of that debate in the *Journal of Library History*, *20*(2), 1985.

the legal tradition (in common law societies) may compete, and through time may pass in and out of fashion, and still allow the law as an idea to retain a powerful sense of identity and self-definition. Within the longer tradition of library and information work, it is not unreasonable to expect the same. In doing so, it is necessary to be clear about the way our paradigms of "librarianly" activity are being challenged and overthrown, and how the profession and the discipline regulates, through a powerful sense of what is good practice, the idea of what librarianship or information management is.

There are three preliminary questions to resolve before proceeding further with the general discussion of the field. The first is why the traditional division between librarianship and information science has not been retained in this work, as a basis for dividing the field into separate conceptions. The second, related point is to ask how the more complex division into three (or more) conceptions can be justified. Third, there is the question of how the proof of the interpretive case is to be established in each of the conceptions. This point is in part discussed in Chapter 7, and in part in the chapters devoted to individual conceptions. In this exercise it should be remembered that the treatment I give each conception, including that of the field in general, is not an attempt at an exhaustive appraisal of the field. Each should be considered as a cameo, indicating how a more exhaustive study might proceed.

The literature of the field shows most clearly a division between librarianship and information science. Rayward argued that these traditions are actually converging, and themselves represent not always distinct lineages from other related disciplines—documentation, informatics, and other names have all been used. Rayward's views have not gone unchallenged, and authors like Kochen (1983) have sought to emphasize the distinctiveness of information science, whereas others like Wilson (1983a,) have traced different patterns of development. The main concern of these authors is different from mine, but it is possible to identify both implicit and explicit statements that assist my general case.

It is not clear, even from Rayward (1983) that there is a straightforward division between librarianship and information science. He set as his purpose "to explore some of the relations between librarianship, bibliography, documentation, library science, and information science" (p. 343). All these he considered as "[P]art of a historical process that has led to different ways of envisaging, creating, and investigating the interrelations and relative effectiveness of formalized modes of access to recorded knowledge" (p. 343). Rayward continued: "[N]ot long after librarianship emerged as a profession whose practitioners were chiefly absorbed by the administrative and operational challenges presented by libraries, there arose a countervailing resistance to the conceptual nar-

OBJECTIONS TO THE INTERPRETIVE POSITION 99

rowness that such a professional preoccupation involved" (p. 343). He concluded with respect to the different conceptions of the field that "librarianship, bibliography, documentation, library science, and information science may be considered as incorporating modes of study and investigation that not only express subtle occupational distinctions but also represent attempts at obtaining these new and increasingly general perspectives" (p. 343).

Other authorities take issue with Rayward over some of these claims, and also advance other countervailing arguments that are considered later. Rayward, like others, legitimated the diversification of labels for activity in the field, yet for him the purpose of these labels was different from mine. First, he saw them as representing "subtle occupational distinctions"—a claim that need not be disputed, but that should really be secondary to the intellectual conception of how the congeries of objectives and explanations associated with any one conception can better illuminate the overall purposes of the discipline. It should also be noted that although Rayward's claim about historical process is not only acceptable but also supportive of the general argument about the generation, spread, and decline of conceptions of a field within other interpretive arguments, his claim about what this process has led to is really tangential to any claim advanced in this work. It is not clear to me that the different conceptions of the field are more concerned with "formalized modes of access to recorded knowledge" rather than some more immediate professional reaction to established practice. Rayward's idea of a "countervailing resistance to conceptual narrowness" (in librarianship) is a far more powerful tool, used either in the sense of a succession of countervailing resistances to librarianship, or as a succession of resistances to one another. In either case the idea of the opposition can be accepted without also accepting his claim that each conception in turn represents an attempt at "obtaining . . . new and increasingly general perspectives"—which relate to Rayward's own explanation of what the conceptions were for, rather than an assessment by him of what each meant for its subjects—that is, its practitioners.

Rayward (1983) also claimed that certain developments he identified "[A]re important as indicators that librarianship and information science, the latter arising in part from the documentation movement, have certain formal connections. These connections may well imply that there has been a disciplinary convergence of librarianship toward information science" (pp. 343–344).

Saunders, from a different perspective, supported views about similarities between librarianship and information science. Arguing for a unified professional organization in the United Kingdom, Saunders (1989) noted "the extent to which all these organizations are pursuing essentially similar goals and implementing them by similar means" (p. 40). Elsewhere, Rayward (1983) argued that there is a disciplinary continuum from librarianship to information science that at best is a source of innovation and strength, but at worst, because of the tendency toward an ever more general perspective, blurs traditional distinctions and unsettles professional convictions.

It is necessary to consider how Rayward's convergence and continuum relate to interpretive ideas of self-definition and explanation through the use of a language of perspicuous contrast, and to what extent other labels and conceptions can legitimately be used. The tendency to reduce all perspectives in the field to librarianship and/or information science, which Rayward initially eschews but finally admits through the back door of the continuum, is one that other authorities have more trouble resisting, and the relative use of these terms by, for example, Kochen and Shera can help illustrate the general position in the field. It is against the background of all these comments that we must consider the developments of separate conceptions, and also, more critically for the interpretive case, see to what extent other views offer direct support, or can be shown not to be inimical to such constructions.

How then do other authorities depart from the rather general perspective of Rayward? Three general themes can be discussed. First is the argument that practice has had a supremacy in the discipline that has not been adequately appreciated. Second is the argument that information science is the theoretical force behind the practice of librarianship. Third is the argument that information science has superseded librarianship.

Batty and Bearman (1983) responded critically to Rayward, although accepting his overall case, by drawing more attention to the development of theory of and by practitioners. This is rather different from the development of theory from practice, but still lies within the framework of a field being for a particular subject or group of subjects. Without using the idea of interpretation, Batty and Bearman came close to the idea of theory developed from practice:

> Rayward's suggestion that the formation of a theory of librarianship and library research began with the founding of the Graduate Library School in Chicago seems less cause and effect than a *post hoc ergo propter hoc* argument. There had been many scholars, thinkers, and workers concerned with many aspects of library science between 1840 and 1940, most of whom owed no debt to the Graduate Library School. It is true that Jewett, Cutter, Bliss, Sayers, and Ranganathan addressed individual aspects (although Cutter and Ranganathan came close to addressing the whole field). It is

probably true to say they did not develop a theory of librarianship—but we wonder if one has ever been enunciated. It is true also that much of the work in the late nineteenth century addressed practical aspects of library science—but there are many fields in which research customarily addresses practical aspects of the discipline. . . .

The profession may do itself a disservice if it seeks to emphasize only "respectable" research. Rayward alludes somewhat disparagingly to the empiricism of the nineteenth century—yet, like medicine and law, we are a profession with a job to do. We hope to improve by learning from research, but we can also improve through carefully considered practice. (pp. 368–369)

This approach is very close to one that sees library theory developing from research into practice, but it is not quite the interpretive loop from practice to theory to improved practice, nor does it include research as part of practice, as I do. Batty and Bearman ignored the temptation to substitute labeling for analysis and they concentrated on the practical nature of the professional task; yet they do not develop any language, or illustrate their arguments with reference to any language, that might serve as an interpretive tool for the whole discipline. In fact, their aside about the lack of theory of librarianship might suggest that they can only see the practice tackling the question of theory development—of improving the conceptions and, perhaps, changing the concept—as a piecemeal process.

Batty and Bearman gave grounds for showing that an interpretive approach to the discipline is possible, but they did not identify sufficient characteristics of the process for us to say that there is already an explicit or implicit interpretive study available.[2] Some of their comments, however, do enhance the view that an overall theory of all versions of the field of library and information studies has not been attempted, and this could be interpreted as support for the existence of differing conceptions of the field. To satisfy the conditions of the interpretive stance, however, it should be possible for these to be discussed within a general interpretive framework. As the comments of Batty and Bearman do not make plain whether their idea of the "whole field" is one that embraces

---

[2] The work of George E. Bennett (1988), may seem relevant here, but although Bennett's concern is with the identity of the profession, his purpose is different from mine: He played upon the variations among Rayward, Shera, Kochen, and Wilson as evidence of disciplinary uncertainty and claimed that "library-and-information-science" is a new identity. I claim that interpretation accommodates all of these separate views and that no one single identity needs to be found.

all the conceptions mentioned by Rayward or is merely a description of functions within traditional librarianship, it is impossible to move further on this point solely with the available information.

Batty and Bearman were fundamentally sympathetic to Rayward and to librarianship. This suggests some shared conception of the discipline. Kochen (1983), on the other hand, expressed almost antagonistic views, separating the type of information science concerned with written records or documents from some more general information science, and concluding that the "present state in the development of the five fields under discussion is characterized by strongly divergent orientations to information science" (p. 376).

He earlier commented that "to suggest that the primary focus of information science should be library and information *work* is stifling and unproductively restrictive" (p. 372). Kochen saw the information disciplines in a different light: "What matters is that investigators who identify with the information disciplines formulate researchable problems and make discoveries, and contribute insights that clarify the nature and dynamics of information and knowledge" (p. 371).

Kochen saw information scientists as part of a scientific research community, and was unconcerned about their epistemological roots so long as they worked at the same problems.[3] Initially Kochen's stance must seem a major stumbling block to any interpretive approach, but his objections can be overcome with little difficulty. First, his objections to work as a proper focus for information science is indeed a difficulty, but the interpretive approach is concerned primarily with the idea of a practice, and if research work is seen as part of any practice, then the Kochen difficulty is obviated. There are other problems, however, in connection with Kochen's view of information science, that give it an entirely different set of concerns to those of the five fields listed by Rayward. This standpoint reiterates the "countervailing resistance" of Rayward from a traditional view of librarianship vis à vis a sequence of other disciplines also concerned with written records to another resistance where all these are set against a rather more electronic version of information science. This is a serious objection, but it offers comfort in at least one direction: The conceptions of even information science can vary, and this seems to make a straightforward opposition between librarianship and information science more difficult to maintain. Using other labels for concep-

---

[3] Saunders (1974) got close to this viewpoint when he suggested that "we reserve the term 'information scientist' for those engaged in theoretical work on the science of information" (p. 69). In a more robust way, Saunders countered this remark by almost immediately suggesting that "perhaps the whole search for a scientifically acceptable 'information science' is an artificial exercise and a sign of professional immaturity" (p. 69).

tions of the field can be no less legitimate, and there is no fault in ignoring a more procrustean, simplistic, and adversarial representation.

There are, however, other conceptions of the relationship between librarianship and information science that beg examination, if only because of the personal authority of their authors. Shera's (1983) final views have been mentioned before. They are significant here because they put that relationship in a particular light and, more helpfully, because he also pointed us toward a more practice-based or behavior-based source for library theory.

Shera was reduced to saying "That librarianship is what librarians do and information science is defined by the operations of the information scientist. We could say with, I think, some degree of accuracy that librarianship is a service and information science is an area of inquiry that seeks to measure and improve the efficiency of the librarian" (p. 379). He, however, recanted a view he held earlier, that information science provided the intellectual and theoretical foundations of librarianship. He explained away this earlier conviction by claiming that:

> The major figures in the history of American librarianship were doers rather than thinkers; they were concerned with process rather than purpose. . . . Librarians even went so far as to evolve a new discipline called information science. . . . Information theory, in contrast to the theory of librarianship, is severely limited in its communicative potential. Its objective is to provide the librarian with a system giving functional or operational access to the contents of documents. Information scientists give all of their attention to design, production, implementation and control of the system. . . . Our so called information systems are nothing but data systems.
>
> Librarians have become so concerned with process that they have confused substance with instrumentation. (pp. 383–384)

Shera claimed that the library is based on the social sciences and the humanities, and is not and never has been a scientific enterprise. With his concentration on doing, or practice, he allowed room for the construction of an interpretive account of librarianship. His strictures about information science, however, need some further comment. Obviously, information science for Shera is very different from that of Kochen, and whereas the latter found it the true discipline for the current age and rejected all sciences and "-ships" that were concerned only with printed documents rather than information, Shera found his devil in the scientific and technological character of information science, so much so that in their mutual distancing of the two disciplines it could be asked if there is any room for a relationship between them, if they can actually be seen as different conceptions of the same thing.

There is, I think, a confusion that must be cleared up immediately between separate conceptions of the field as information science or information management, or whatever, where they represent a particular interpretation of the field, and comment about the field as a whole, which may embrace one or more of these conceptions. Any examination of, say, law, will reveal that alternative conceptions of law are known to exist even though several or most of them are not currently in use. Shera (1983) in fact helped us by observing that information science deals with only a part of what the librarian does. He also admitted a relationship, however strained, when he damned scientific technology to a "thinking with processes" role in librarianship. Information science for Shera remains an area of inquiry or research; it is not a service or a practice. Yet, as mentioned earlier, research can be part of practice, and the theory that the interpretive approach sees developing from practice, by self-definition, will include an account of research. Shera's objection to information science was that it is scientific. He brought into the battle an alternative social scientific focus and declared that librarians "must look to symbolic interactionism" for the proper foundation of a theory of librarianship—which Shera (1983) described as a "process by which people relate to their own minds and the minds of others; the process by which individuals take account of their own or others' needs, desires, means and ends, knowledge, and like motivations" (p. 386). Here, it can be said, Shera was merely bringing into play another conception as an improvement on the conceptions he rejected. It should be noted that Kochen and Shera share enough in terms of shared and common meanings for them to be able to disagree, and also that Shera's appeal to symbolic interactionism is a lure of which one should be wary.

Shera left us with an indication of the social science and humanistic bases of librarianship and of the possibility for library theory to be developed from other sources than those currently in use. Finally, although his own strictures are against information science, it is clear that the conceptions available are wider than suggested by a simple opposition between information science and librarianship.

In conclusion, it can be said of library and information studies in general that there is no simple polarity between librarianship (broadly or narrowly concerned) and information science, that the development of other conceptions of the field is legitimate and possibly powerful and productive, and that it is possible, despite the opposing stances taken by various authors, to undertake the development of an interpretive account for the discipline.

How would that interpretive account proceed for the field in general?

To follow Dworkin, one could argue that any development would be just another conception of the field. Reviewing the historical account of Rayward, Wilson, Shera, Kochen, and others, it is apparent that the field is open to alternative interpretations and that the thrust for these within the field has commonly come from practitioners: If the later 20th century has produced a profusion of technicians and instrumentalists rather than grand theorists, then that is a consequence that any new interpretive account may serve to redress through the generation of a new revisionist conceptions.

What is not yet clear is whether the integrity of purpose of the field has been maintained. Shera and others have acclaimed it, and by reasserting the humanistic origins of librarianship are seeking to redress the balance away from technical fascination. Although the grand theorists tended to be practitioners, the alien invaders whose vigorous disciplines brought in new conceptions will not have had any cause to maintain the consistency or integrity of purpose, and the very vigor of intruding epistemologies, methodologies, and techniques may well have undermined that integrity. When individual conceptions are examined in Part III, it will become apparent how clearly the integrity of the field has been maintained, and how closely the interpretive approach can be sustained.

Before moving to these conceptions, one other question needs to be tackled. Are not professional techniques the only things that can claim to be the basis for any conception of the field?

IS THERE ONLY PROFESSIONAL TECHNIQUE?

This section considers and dismisses the view, implicit in some significant literature, that the only areas of activity that can claim to be the basis of any interpretation of the field are core professional techniques such as classification, cataloging, indexing, and so on. The traditional techniques do not in themselves allow the construction of meaning for the field. Also, because the interpretation of the field will determine which techniques are relevant, to give emphasis to the latter, in themselves, as the literature seems to do, could subvert the judgment of practitioners. This work has introduced the ideas of interpretation, conceptions, and a context of meaning, to give an understanding of a practice. None of these is to be confused with any higher purpose (professional or moral) a practitioner might have. For example, the professional goal of Universal Bibliographic Control, which obviously gives an important place to enumerative bibliography, is just a goal or mission. Similarly, the aim of public libraries to afford education to their patrons, and to build a collection accordingly, is just one of several possible higher purposes that might motivate a practitioner. In neither case is there any obvious conception of the field at work: There is no interpretation of the field, although an interpretation, in the form of a particular conception, might inform a practitioner's sense of mission or purpose. There is, however, the risk that the prominent professional techniques employed in these missions or purposes might themselves come to be seen as the relevant conception. This is partly because the professional literature is strongly technical in nature, and rarely explicitly identifies an understanding or conception of what the field is, and partly because the technical competencies of practitioners are seen by lay outsiders as close to the essence of what constitutes professional practice. These competencies are also perhaps what give practitioners the basis for their claim to professional status, being the closest the library and information field has to any arcane or peculiar knowledge. The position is complicated by the fact that execution of many of these techniques is based on following a rule or set of rules.

The following sections show that these technical competencies, even though they impinge on so many of the other conceptions, cannot question the degree of independence of those conceptions, and the latter cannot be seen merely as slants or perceptions of this technical area of practice. This congeries of techniques, which are universally prominent throughout the library and information field, do not constitute a conception of the field in themselves; moreover, they cannot be seen as the only real conception of the field, even of a field of traditional librarianship. The independence of my position from such a claim is supported by showing that it would not matter for my argument even if traditional techniques did constitute the only conception.

Introduction: The Difficulties

It could be argued that these techniques are always taught and understood within a wider context, and that there is no case to discuss. I think the position is more complex and demands further examination. The first problem is that outsiders see and assess a practice by its visible appearances and by their own requirements. That is, a test of a practitioner seems to be how good he or she is at the job. I do not hire a lawyer because he believes that lawyers should help the poor, or because he is concerned with injustice to the wrongly imprisoned (although such things may make him available to me). I hire him to win my case, and I do not care what he thinks about the law. Similarly, I want my doctor to diagnose and treat me correctly: I want a good, clean, quick appendectomy, or whatever, and I will judge the surgeon accordingly. I do not want a particular doctor because he has a certain view of medicine or because he feels he has a special mission in life: I just want the job done well. In other words, technical performance is the consumer's test of the practitioner. Being good at the technical skills describes our assessment of professional performance. If a technically competent surgeon is a good surgeon, then the same must be true for practitioners in the library and information field. It could then be argued that a conception of the field as its technical practices was an acceptable one.

The obvious and simple rejoinder to this is that there is more to successful practice than meets the eye. Doing appendectomies is not like changing oil filters on cars: There is more professional judgment brought to bear, and the surgeon can cope with any unusual case, taking the total state of health of the patient into consideration. The process is the same as for the most complex medical treatment, even though a particular operation may be simple. The use of professional judgment reflects the surgeon's (or lawyer's, or information manager's) sense of what the field is and how it is to be understood, taking account of all contingent factors. In other words, his or her conception of the field and the current context of meaning shapes the practical judgment. This is not the same as any sense of mission or higher purpose.

The second problem about techniques follows closely from this last point. If techniques are always understood as serving something else, why does the literature not reflect this? There would be some good grounds for assuming that any discussion of, or textbook on, techniques would make clear their relationship to some view of the field as a whole, or some higher purpose. A quick sampling of some introductory texts shows that techniques are occasionally related to a mission or higher purpose, but the relationships among the purpose, functions, and techniques are rarely explained in a way that matches a conception of the field, and certainly not in a way that gives meaning to the field. Sometimes what I call conceptions are merely stated baldly as being different types of information profession, without further rationalization. In other works the techniques seem to have primacy, over space if not place, and are sometimes identified as a core of the subject.

Urquhart (1981) developed a set of 18 aphoristic "Principles of Librarianship" that do not collectively obviously constitute a conception, or even match his definition for an individual principle—"A principle of librarianship is a guide for action by librarians" (p. 10). Some of his individual principles are clearly technical; for example, Principle 5 states "Libraries must be able to provide adequate access to the records users may wish to consult." Others are extremely general, like Principle 1 ("libraries are for users"), or Principle 17 ("Libraries can be valuable to society"). Urquhart is not alone. The 1976 IFLA standards for Library Schools listed 12 core areas for library education. The first concerns some higher purpose ("The role of the library in society and as a communication agency") and the remaining 11 cover principles and methods of various technical competencies. Although the broader topic has prime place, it is quite clear that technical competency has more space and is of greater importance. The Library Association (UK) also concentrates attention on techniques. The Working Party on Future Professional Qualifications reported with respect to professional education that "a first course should be based on the core studies of bibliography, management, and information handling" (The Library Association, 1981). The Unesco introduction to the field has a similar concentration. The preface states:

> The task, then, was to provide for all those who, embarking on a career in this field, search in vain for a straightforward textbook that would offer them a clear view of their future mission and its importance.... It is our hope that it will serve as a handbook which will succeed in strengthening the motivation and improving the skill of those beginning or pursuing a career in a library or information unit. (Guinchat & Menou, 1983, p. v)

However, after those brief statements, all the chapters deal with technical competencies. Two chapters at the end deal with education and training, and with the profession. The first emphasizes technical competence in its description of general education programs:

> General training in library and documentation sciences usually covers the following main subjects: (a) human communication and user study; (b) documents and information sources: selection and acquisition; (c) processing: cataloguing, classifying, indexing; (d) secondary documents: exploitation and dissemination retrieval; (e) equipment and technology; and (f) the organization and management of an information unit. (Guinchat & Menou, 1983, p. 326)

The latter gives a profile of an information specialist that identifies general personal qualities (usefulness for others, ability to communicate, adaptability, judgment, curiosity, perseverance, and modesty) that could apply to a wide range of practices.

Historically the field seems to have found technique irresistible, even when its leaders knew better. Even in the Chicago Library School, Wilson seemed to have concluded that the goal of library science should always be to emphasize "technique, organization and administration," although his final paper to the School called for the development of a "theory or philosophy of library science" (Houser & Schrader, 1978, p. 50). More hearteningly, Reynolds and Daniel (1974) did identify something like a connected set of conceptions, although they did not use that vocabulary.

> In the past, many attempts to explain the nature of librarianship have been predicated solely on the basis of library activities. These explanations, in essence, tend to reduce the concept of librarianship to a simple description of an organizational response . . .
>
> The study of library and information services can be approached in as many ways as there are conceptual frameworks capable of acting to organize and explain the phenomena and behaviour associated with libraries . . .
>
> As a consequence . . . a series of information fields have developed which attempt to bring order and precision to activities associated with information and its use. (pp. xv–xvi)

Thus the literature is not clear about technical competencies. Although some authors do identify different occupations, there is no explanation of the relationships between them or how they might arise. Even in works that identify something other than technique, the latter command most attention. Traditional techniques seem to have a very important role in the literature. The task remains to explain why they cannot be identified as a conception.

Practice and Procedures

The crux of the case for dealing with all these difficulties with the traditional practices (as opposed to practice) is that they are just practices; they are the equivalent of legal procedures and do not in any way impinge directly on the way the field is construed by those who think about it or construct its meanings. It is of course true that the daily practice of these procedures may, as the interpretive position allows, inform theory without actually determining the path of development that theory may take, just as theory will in turn inform practice with similarly indeterministic effects. It is also true that the sense of being a librarian or information worker is most obviously transmitted by the experience of doing these practices or procedures, or at least a practitioner can be recognized in someone who seems to know about them, just as a member of the public can recognize a librarian in a library by observing someone who seems to be doing what it is supposed that librarians do. In this crucial case the outsider does not share all the meanings and has no way of doing so: He or she can only make rough guesses about who might be a librarian, just as patients in a hospital will recognize medical staff by their white coats, or lawyers in court can be recognized by their special clothing, or their individual roles identified by their physical position in the court (judge on the bench, etc.). In any of these cases, those making decisions can go through recognized routes and stages toward their decision, following the same procedures, but perhaps arriving at radically different decisions.

This revisits the original problem Dworkin tackled in introducing the idea of interpretation when judges confronted difficult cases where several judges hearing the same evidence and using the same law would arrive at different conclusions. So it is with cataloging and classification and indexing. There is an example in the change in cataloging rules whereby the concept of so-called corporate authorship was dropped, a responsibility statement was introduced into all entries, and the notion of corporate responsibility was used instead of corporate authorship. In this case the procedures for description were changed, and the actual practice changed to reflect a new theory about ways of describing difficult material, which in itself arose because of difficulties experienced in practice. However, the meaning of the object being described did not change and the meaning of the ultimate product, the catalog, did not change either. What has changed is the perception of the role of the catalog or bibliographic record in an age that can transform access to material through the use of advanced technology.

The case is more obvious at a more general level with classification and indexing. The ultimate purpose of classification remains the same, whichever classification scheme is used: The decision of a library to use Bliss rather than Colon, or whatever, is based on that library's own construction of its needs, just as the decision of an individual classifier operating any scheme to follow one or another of the warrants available will reflect local needs, too. The case is the same with indexing: The choice of one indexing language over another is like the choice of one view or interpretation of law over another; in difficult individual cases the choice will be more poignant and may lead to decisions about the way a particular indexing language should develop.

Similarly, as Wilson (1983b) showed, the interpretation of cataloging and the catalog will, or should, change with changing circumstances, and needs periodic review and reconsideration in the light of changing external conditions. The point is that the procedure is not the conception; it is part of the expression or manifestation of the conception. It would therefore be wrong to take any book of procedure and claim that it was a (or the) conception. To cite an example used frequently before, the practice of filing catalog cards in a drawer does not have as its meaning or ultimate purpose conformity to some set of rules about filing, rather observing those rules give effect to some other objective that requires the filing of records in some order.

From this it follows that the sense or idea of practice cannot be limited to the physical actions of people, or even to the rules used to govern or guide those actions. Going back to the earlier example of an interpretive concept given by Dworkin, that of courtesy, it can be said that the act of taking off one's hat to a lady (or to a cat or an armchair, whatever that practice demands) is not the real sense of the conception, it is an act that has symbolic value, showing perhaps unnecessarily that the conception of courtesy is recognized. Similarly, the practice of opening a door for a lady, although having practical value, also has a symbolic value, which is to embody the conception of the practice of courtesy. In the case of information studies the various sets of procedures do not in themselves constitute either the conception or the practice. The art or science of cataloging or classifying requires more than the relevant standard, not only because of the variations permitted by the standard, but because the standard only makes sense if various external values are known and shared. The situation is similar to a game like chess or cricket: Knowing the rules is insufficient; it is necessary to know the game, and to play the game by the unwritten agreement accepted by all initiates. Furthermore, it is clear that catalogers or classifiers or indexers are able (admittedly not always with complete success) to perform these operations without complete knowledge of the rule sets they are allegedly employing.

Users of library catalogs or information services are in a position where, even more so than with the practicing professional who is creating a catalog or index record, professional knowledge of the rules is almost irrelevant. In virtually all cases, users of catalogs, bibliographies, and indexes will be able to use them successfully (maybe not as successfully as they might) without comprehensive knowledge of the rules applied. Where there is difficulty with some product—say with an abstracting service or some complex product like the ISI citation indexes—the problem the user has to overcome relates more to the organizational characteristics of the product, maybe to some overriding idea (as with citation indexes) and possibly with the notation used. Knowing the rules is not important for users. This point is more apparent with the use of online services, where users or intermediaries require a rudimentary knowledge of the relevant query language and perhaps some familiarity with a control vocabulary, but they certainly are able to use the system (maybe with reduced effectiveness) without total comprehension of the cataloging or indexing rules used, nor do they need to know how thesauri are constructed.

Rule Dependence and Conceptions

The point is that these technical areas of information studies are characterized by a high dependence on rules, and confusion could easily arise because of this as to what constitutes the real field. I claim that those conceptions considered in subsequent chapters are given definition by some overarching philosophical stance concerning what the field is really about, but are given effect by the way in which the various sets of rules are brought into play and the way their relationships and relative importance are constructed by that conception. It can also be claimed that the picture of what any conception is cannot be constructed merely by listing its technical instruments or procedures. Not only is technical performance not the conception, it does not even reveal the conception. There are two other important observations about the areas of professional technique.

First, those people who live their lives, or seek to constrain all our professional lives, within the confines of various sets of rules and procedures really do not have a conception of the field at all. Their position is one that attempts to invert the normal relationship between overall view (or conception) and implementing means (the rules). Of course we cannot leave the situation with such a simplistic statement. The people thus described do have what might erroneously be called a conception because it meets many of the requirements of the interpretive approach—there is a set of objects, and a set of subjects for whom those objects have meaning. In this case, the objects are the sets of rules in themselves, and the argument to consider this as an interpretation fails because although there is a group of people who share the meanings, there is no expression of the objects independent of the objects. The very nature of the rule-bound approach is one that cannot allow alternative expressions about the objects that are admitted to be of equal value.

It is when this problem is uncovered that it obviously becomes overwhelmingly difficult to consider these technical competencies as a conception. The difficulty is that of fusing the horizons of two separate groups of people who inhabit the same library and information universe and share many of its meanings; the users (and maybe some practitioners) who see the field as these so-called professional activities on the one hand, and the (bulk of) practitioners on the other who come to see the field as one or another of the various conceptions (not necessarily limited to those discussed in later chapters). This problem of fusion can be overcome in a number of ways, the easiest of which are to say either that the users are not really part of the interpreting group, that they are not really part of the profession, or to say that whereas the users may have views about libraries or books or information-bearing media or information, they do not have any conception of the profession or the field of study. Dworkin's requirement that an interpreter of a social science discipline must be a participant to gain a proper understanding of the practice obviously supports this position.

Rules and Theory

The second problem to consider in relation to all these technical professional skills concerns the nature of the sets of rules and the development of theory. For any set of rules to be acceptable, it must have some external plausibility and internal coherence. For example, a set of cataloging rules must offer means of bibliographic description of most of the types of items that are to be included in the catalog, and there must be no confusion, ambiguity, or conflict between the rules. Good sets of rules, therefore, will conform to some external reference about the former point, in a way that need not necessarily be rational, and will have an internal rationality that is both apparent (so as to be usable) and consistent, thus maintaining the integrity of the rules. As rules become amended in time, they will retain credibility to the extent that these requirements continue to be met. The requirement for some internal rationality and for some external reference to the material being handled leads to the development of a theory (of cataloging, classifying, or filing) that takes the form of a set of axioms that ensure the internal rationality by making reference to the so-called external reality, the material being handled.

There are two difficulties that arise over this. First, the so-called external reality, the actual physical item that must be bibliographically described, attains the status of brute data or empirical fact, when what is really perceived is a bibliographical construction, an interpretation of reality. The notion in the public mind, whether lay or expert, about a particular text is not conditioned by bibliographic description or published artefact. The idea of what constitutes Hamlet (the play by William Shakespeare . . . modern catalog codes could probably catalog cigars or small villages, too) is not given its reality by any particular text or description. (In fact it would be extremely difficult to make any meaningful statement about Hamlet or indeed most works purely on the basis of the most elaborate bibliographic description or subject analysis, which can only be synecdoche or metonymy.) Therefore the stuff on which codes are built is not any body of objective fact. The theory and the code are both interpretations. The second difficulty is that these theories about codes (the axioms that ensure good codes and good use of them), because they are seen as the exclusive property of the library and information profession, tend to become symbols for, and even the reality of, theory for the whole field. Thus, a body of guiding rules that has the attraction of an apparent rationality based on empirical observation can pre-empt any other type of theory building and limit the profession and the discipline to a particularly technical form of theory. An interpretive approach to the whole field need not exclude the construction of well-thought-out codes or the use of logical guidelines in these technical matters, but it would offer the extra attraction of the construction of a social theory at a more general level and one that would promote clearer thinking at levels where currently wild speculation seems to be a major resource, as, for example, in discussions of the information society or information management.

The Only Conception?

There are two technical points to be made about the way we handle the arguments about conceptions. Even if it is admitted that this area of technical competencies is a conception, and maybe the only conception other than information science (an argument I do not concede), there is no problem in consequence for the interpretive position. This arises because there is no requirement within the interpretive position for a number of conceptions to exist. The sequence of conceptions is a construction we get from Dworkin: It is an embellishment of the basic position that requires only that a number of equally acceptable interpretations be possible and that they also be acceptable as simultaneously available alternatives. I claim that the field of information studies requires a context of meaning, which is currently the idea of the information culture. Two sets of expression about the field that reflect different approaches to this context are sufficient. Should these traditional or technical skills be seen as the only conception other than information science, the case for the interpretive position can still be maintained, so long as the two conceptions can be defended as such and maintain the integrity of the original concept.

The Totality of Conceptions

The final claim to consider is another technical point on handling arguments about conceptions. It could be claimed that because these technical areas of professional competence embody the corpus of professional techniques and skills that are unique to information studies, all the other conceptions should be ignored and the concentration should be solely on the various areas of indexing, cataloging, and so on, as the various conceptions of the field. It would then be claimed that this book could have far more concrete material to work with and would be able to deal with the different areas in greater depth.

I have already disposed of some of the arguments about this claim in connection with the idea that skills can be equated with conceptions. The argument that there can be different conceptions of what cataloging or indexing is can be dismissed by repeating the point that technical problems, even though they may illustrate some problem of interpretation, can never in themselves uncover the real difference of opinion or understanding that can divide the profession. Reducing and confining discussion to the technical level obscures the real issues. This can be illustrated by reference to two simple and self-evident examples. The use of bibliographic description by national bibliographers, library catalogers and historical bibliographers differs in purpose. The library catalogers and the national bibliographers have similar but different purposes (they are both describing an idealized item, not a physical entity, but library catalogers must meet real local needs of real users, whereas the bibliographer is cataloging for all possible users). The historical bibliographer on the other hand is describing an actual physical representation, maybe one only, rather than the class of objects that the cataloger seeks to cover. The difference in practice can only make sense against the background of what the two or three different sets of people see as the purpose of their labors—in other words, what conception they have of the field. The discussion about the differences in practice could not be resolved merely by reference to the technical practices and procedures. Similarly, the difference in attitudes toward cataloging, classification, and indexing that exists between librarians and information scientists cannot be explained by reference to the technical procedures (which are uncontroversial).[4] The difference is only explicable in terms of an overall approach to the field—so we need to be able to talk of a conception of the field as information science, or whatever.

Thus technical discussion at this level can resolve nothing, and so discussion in depth of cataloging and so on will not advance understanding. Indeed, it is an implication of this work overall that the profession needs to escape from a technically bound discussion of the field, and that a more general discussion is overdue. The argument that there are several general conceptions is advanced to show the breadth of the field and to reveal the power of the interpretive approach in accommodating a seemingly diverse set of beliefs about its nature.

Some aspects of these technical professional skills are now examined

---

[4] I mean that there is no controversy about what the procedures are. There may well be controversy about what they should be.

in their relationship to the general context of meaning and to the other conceptions. Because we are at this level closest to a consideration of what librarians and information workers actually do, in terms of what they can be seen doing, it is obviously important for the argument to offer evidence to show that these daily practices and procedures that give effect to interpretations take place against the background of something like one or another of the conceptions to be examined.

Relationship of the Conceptions to Technical Skills

This section is concerned not with the practice or its relation to theory (or conception) but with the way the technical skills of the field are related to the conception. As was explained earlier, there is an apparent conflict between the idea of a conception and the existence within it of a procedure based on a universal rule (such as an international standard or an international product like DDC or AACR) that seemingly must enforce universal common practice whatever the conception, and so erode distinctions between conceptions. This conflict does in reality exist and it exhibits a tension that the interpretive position accommodates and recognizes as a force either for change or for continuity.

We cannot be so axiomatic about any practice or conception as to say this is what that conception is, and that any deviation destroys the conception. As has been seen, the interpretive position is in part dependent on such deviations, which will lead to new conceptions or reinterpretations. The existence of the universal rules operates in two contrasting ways. First, in a positive way, they help to ensure some consistency and integrity for the conception, and it could be said that the appearance of some such rule-based skill within a conception would help to identify that conception as a conception of the library and information field. Second, it cannot be said that the absence of, say, any adherence to AACR excludes some conception from consideration. Third, a tension must exist where a conception is borrowed from or exists alongside an independent discipline (such as information management or information science) especially where there may be a distinction between the two. In these cases, the existence of technical skills may either force a parting or, if the conception is strong, a redefinition of the importance of those skills to the profession as a whole. There is a clear parallel in the case of law, where the practice of law may be invariant except insofar as procedures change, and perhaps even significant components of practice may be excised. However, the law will remain the same and the interpretations may vary independently of change or its absence in legal practice. Thus juries may disappear in compensation cases without changing the law or its interpretation in difficult cases, and without it ceasing to be law because there is no jury. Therefore it may be that the conception of information management allows the practice of the discipline even though some component like the construction of catalogs may be severely restricted and the relationship to something like collection building may be completely severed.

The various conceptions can be said, therefore, to coexist with a body of skills or traditional procedures and practices, but are not determined by them. More importantly, the ebb and flow of professional thinking that responds to the realities of daily life and that functions within the structure of a conception of the field will affect both skills and the conception. The body of skills that form the armory of professional practice will be changed as practice shows necessary, and the force of that particular conception will be maintained, eroded, or enhanced as its armory is equal to the tasks of professional life. It follows from that position that a successful practice (of any profession) will find or develop appropriate skills, either forging new ones or adapting old ones to surmount professional problems. Thus we cannot say that library and information work is doing cataloging, indexing, classification, or whatever, because as practicing professionals operate within their current conception of the field they will use, adapt, or abandon these things as their interpretation of their position dictates. To characterize the field by its formal instruments, on the other hand, is to enforce its inability to change.

A Working Example

Taylor (1978), when examining interpretation in politics, did not use examples of how people in the discipline of politics thought that discipline should be viewed: He used as a principal example the case of voting, a fairly standard political problem. However, the position changed when Dworkin's interpretive approach to law was considered. A practice like law or library and information studies requires a slightly different approach to that proper for a purely academic discipline. In these cases it is necessary to find just what is the discipline or what constitutes the practice rather than its procedures or its public displays: Getting a search on title deeds, or filling in forms for legal aid, or conducting a brilliant cross-examination of a witness are all legal activities, but they are not the law, not what we understand when we think of law.

How does the interpretive approach condition practice? What has been argued in previous chapters is that if you see information studies as, say, information science, then that will condition your approach to all practical everyday problems in the field: Some you will ignore, to others you will bring particular purposes and skills, and still more will not be seen as problems by people with another conception of the field. What has been argued in this chapter is that however pervasive they are, sets of rules for particular procedures cannot be regarded as conceptions of the field. However, many rule-bound procedures are central and critical to many conceptions of many fields, including information studies: How does the interpreter deal with the problems arising in, say, indexing? Is the approach taken any different from the way anyone else would view an indexing problem?

Luckily there is some work by Frohmann (1990) that provides a clear illustration of the case. Frohmann's concern was to refute mentalist claims, which seem to be widely held or accepted in the field, that (from Farradane) the indexing process is an attempt to simulate the structure of thought, and that (from Beghtol and van Dijk) the aim of classification theory is the discovery and precise specification of the rules governing intellectual or cognitive processes peculiar to classification. His purpose is not of direct concern here, but it is clear that his claim is one that can be used in support of the interpretive case. Frohmann's (1990) abstract conveys the significance of his work:

> A rule governed derivation of an indexing phrase from the text of a document is, in Wittgenstein's sense, a *practice*, rather than a mental operation explained by reference to internally represented and tacitly known rules.
>
> The conception of rules as practices shifts the theoretical significance of the social role of retrieval practices from the margins to the centre of enquiry into foundations of information retrieval. (p. 81)

It should be said immediately that Frohmann was not attempting to present an interpretive analysis of reasoning, but he was using as a major source Wittgenstein's remarks on following a rule, and it is to Wittgenstein, among others, ultimately, that those theorists advancing nonpositivist views about the social sciences appeal. Frohmann showed that there cannot be an objective approach to indexing that represents the mental operations that we all inexorably go through when indexing. He argued that rules about indexing are not discovered but constructed. In other words, they are a social product and we can talk about building a shared set of rules that express the meanings we share about certain objects, but there are not, and cannot be, hard and fast views about the right way to index.

This illustration of an interpretive approach to a problem (in this illustration I am accepting Frohmann's views about indexing) shows that interpretation looks for the social origin of a practice, and once it has been identified as a social practice disallows any brute data or brute theory: All further discussion about the problem, in this case indexing, is seen as taking place within a community of people who when indexing are imposing a purposive constructive interpretation on the practice, which reflects shared meanings. This allows us to construct our rules and procedures in accordance with our practices, rather than to force awareness of what we are doing into a subsidiary role to what the procedures and rules are scientifically discovered to be. It is when we know what our purpose is that we can know what rules we require, or, as Frohmann (1990) put it: "In order to construct rules we need to know the game we are playing" (p. 99).

Information Culture

The final remarks to be made about the older technical skills in the field relate to the idea of the information culture. In the literature the majority of comments relate to information technology,[5] but Williamson (1984) at least recognized a wider dimension, portraying a familiar litany of changes to lifestyles that will be the consequence of new technology: "Subject access to information is but one aspect of the larger problem of on-line access in general, which, in turn, must be seen in the context of a social environment in which technology is expected to change enormously the life-styles of individuals and groups of people" (pp. 51–52). In this there is clear recognition of a context of meaning for all aspects of the online process, which is close to component parts of the information culture. Williamson's attitude to this is accepting and uncritical, as is the attitude of other commentators whose remarks are restricted to the more direct impact of information technology. At a simple level, the inquiry into the effects of new technology has been directed toward an understanding of all the new ways in which information may be accessed, both in terms of the character of delivery and the impact of remote and almost instantaneous access by large numbers of users who have now no need of any intermediary. At a more reflective level, commentators have noted that the character of information instruments has always been limited or determined by the limits of available technology—and that the choice of card over book catalogs was an earlier example of this. This suggests an awareness that the library and information

---

[5] See, for example, Austin (1986), Davies (1987), Simonton (1980), Williamson (1984), and Wilson (1983b).

profession is not only operating within a new machine context but also that the character of what can be delivered by the profession is also so determined, which is to say that the context of meaning is one that closely matches the idea of an information culture where a technology (in the sense of both Ellul and Bell) gives the context within which the skills and procedures are developed.

The Next Step: What About Practice, Theory, and Conceptions?

There is one more significant task to tackle before examining how interpretation works when models or conceptions of the field are considered. The interpretive position emphasizes the significance of the meanings generated by those who are participants in any practice, and it is important therefore that there is a clear view of what practice can mean to any practitioner, not in the sense of what he or she does, but in the development of a relationship between practice and personal identity. I turn to this task next.

7
Practice and Theories

This chapter considers two questions: first, what the relationship is between a practitioner and his or her practice and second, what the structure of theory is that supports the interpretive case, especially in this field. An answer to the first question will give the basis for an understanding of how any participant joins in the construction of shared meanings—votes with his or her feet, as it were, when constructing interpretations. In the case of the library and information field, there is also a need to understand how it can be viewed by participants who are also simultaneously concerned with the construction of their own identity. An answer to the second question will help to show how all the arguments about interpretation and practice hang together. An addendum will look at the way knowledge claims, especially for professional knowledge, come to be advanced and sustained.

PRACTICE, PRACTICAL REASON, AND TECHNICAL SKILL

Any practice will comprise a number of practitioners, individuals who will have some relationship to the practice as they perceive it. These individuals will develop and use interpretations to make sense of the practice, to give it meaning, to justify it to themselves, and to justify their involvement in it to themselves. This process of interpretation is constant: It does not happen just once and then remain unchanged, it undergoes continual review. The review is a reaction to the continued development of shared meanings in and about the practice. There is a need, therefore, to show how the shared meanings are generated through language and discourse, and how these latter also allow changes in conceptions.

Taylor claimed that the test of the interpretive case is the change it produces in practice. He claimed that the practitioners, by ever widening their horizons, achieve greater insight and a more clairvoyant practice. This change in practice is, Taylor claimed, the interpreter's equivalent of the empiricist's verification. In interpretation we do not verify or falsify, we improve through greater understanding. The argument behind this is that all theories and accounts in the social sciences are historical, ex post facto explanations that can only serve to increase our understanding of ourselves. There is, in any situation, a dual process whereby we are both interpreter of our environment and the objects in it and we are also interpreting ourselves. Thus, in any situation we are in the process of improving our self-identity. Therefore, a better interpretation that leads to more insightful practice also improves our self-interpretation and our sense of ourselves. We have, therefore, an important investment in our practices; they relate closely to our sense of self-esteem.

We must be clear about what constitutes a practice and how it affects our sense of itself and ourselves. Practice is not just something we happen to do everyday or a haphazard sequence of behavior. It is a more coherent set of actions and beliefs that we conform to along with the other people in our profession, and it has its own internal logic and ethic. MacIntyre (1981) defined a practice as follows:

> By a "practice" I am going to mean any coherent and complex form of socially established co-operative human activity through which goods internal to that form of activity are realised in the course of trying to achieve those standards of excellence which are appropriate to, and partially definitive of, that form of activity, with the result that human powers to achieve excellence, and human conceptions of the ends and goods involved, are systematically extended. (p. 175)

He went on to describe the idea of internal goods by giving the example of a child who is being taught chess, and who is offered sweets if he wins, and who initially plays to get the sweets, but who finally comes to like chess for itself. In this case cheating, which he might have done initially to get the sweets, comes eventually to defeat the child's love of the game, so he ceases to cheat and he observes the rules of the game to enjoy its rewards. MacIntyre (1981) went on to identify from this example the rewards that extend from practices in the real world:

> There are thus two kinds of goods possibly to be gained by playing chess. On the one hand there are those goods externally and contingently attached to chess-playing and to other practices by the accidents of social circumstance—in the case of the imaginary child candy, in the case of real adults such goods as prestige, status, and money. There are always alternative ways for achieving such goods,

and their achievement is never to be had *only* by engaging in some particular kind of practice. On the other hand there are the goods internal to the practice of chess which cannot be had in any way but by playing chess or some other game of that specific kind. We call them internal for two reasons: first, as I have suggested, because we can only specify them in terms of chess or some other game of that specific kind and by means of examples from such games . . . ; and secondly because they can only be identified and recognised by the experience of participating in the practice in question. Those who lack the relevant experience are incompetent thereby as judges of internal goods. (p. 176)

Thus, in our professional world we can recognize the internal rewards that stem from our practice, and we can recognize as fellow professionals those who conform to the constitutive rules of that practice. MacIntyre (1981) continued:

A practice involves standards of excellence and obedience to rules as well as the achievement of goods. To enter into a practice is to accept the authority of those standards and the inadequacy of my own performance as judged by them. It is to subject my own attitudes, choices, preferences and tastes to the standards which currently and partially define the practice. Practices of course . . . have a history. . . . Thus the standards are not themselves immune from criticism, but none the less we cannot be initiated into a practice without accepting the authority of the best standards realised so far. (p. 177)

MacIntyre emphasized that changes or improvements in a practice, even if they are the work of only one person, can be shared and enjoyed by all engaged in the practice:

External goods are therefore characteristically objects of competition in which there must be losers as well as winners. Internal goods are indeed the outcome of competition to excel, but it is characteristic of them that their achievement is good for the whole community who participate in the practice. So when Turner transformed the seascape in painting or W. G. Grace advanced the art of batting in cricket in quite a new way their achievement enriched the whole relevant community. (p. 178)

Put another way, our engagement in a practice is always subject to a historical review, which constantly judges the present situation by reference to the past and to the prospects for the future. These assessments or judgments are our way of making sense of a practice and our participation in it, our way of giving meaning to the practice and our own lives by interpretation. So, we may leave a practice because we feel disgraced by association with it, or we may leave it because we are not getting the recognition we want, or because its internal rewards are meaningless for us: Whatever our decision, it is one we make about our lives and reflects the intertwined interpretation of our own self-identity and the practice that concerns us. If we are cricketers, or even just followers of the game, we will know not only that Grace was a great batsman, but in what his greatness lies, and just as when we were newcomers to cricket we were told about Grace, so latterly we accept and understand what we were told, and tell others. However, our telling does not stop there: We are constantly engaged in talk and discussion that reveals to us who is knowledgeable about the game, who is good at the game and who can make good judgments about playing the game or picking the players, and we in turn may receive recognition from others about particular skills we may have, and will become part of the discourse of the game or practice.

In this description of any practice, I emphasize not only its highly personal aspects, but also intellectual aspects of anyone's relationship to it. We have to be reflective persons, to be able to do more than merely perform the mechanical functions of the practice in order to interpret it. In this sense a practice is a more complex activity than some simple physical task like using a shovel or working at a repetitive job in a factory. Learning the language of a practice is much more than learning its technical vocabulary, and participating in its discourse will require use of the technical vocabulary, but also much more besides. The technical vocabulary is in effect a shared shorthand about particular aspects of the practice, the AACR are no more used as a language for discourse about library and information studies than the rules of cricket are for the discourse of the game. The discourse of a practice is a complex net of language and language games that allows participants to show that they are participants and to make decisions about themselves and the practice, and as such it (as Gadamer so grandly put it) recaptures for anyone their noblest task, decision making according to their own responsibility rather than leaving it to experts (Bernstein, 1983).

The development of any discourse, any language, for a practice is performed in a gyrating context of changing times and disciplines. I claim that for the library and information field the current context of meaning is the information culture. This frames the discourse for the field and supports two languages for the context—one utopian and optimistic, the other skeptical and pessimistic. The field is simultaneously developing or maintaining its discourse amidst the strong swirling currents of other disciplines. This is not a position unique to the library and information field: Law, for example, must always consider philosophy, criminology, sociology, psychology, and maybe more. Other disciplines will similarly be affected by near neighbors. In such a situation, our languages of discourse are constantly being tested as the changing and widening context broadens the possibility of language. Pocock (1985) made a similar point when describing the situation of an author whose intentions must be expressed in language available to him, because that language gives him the means of expressing those intentions. However, he goes on to put the possible actions open to any author into a wider context, which opens up the possibilities for language and for a changed or alternative discourse. The richer and more complex the language context, the greater the range of things one can say, and the greater the chance of modifying the context by saying them. It is through such modifications and changes that we build through our discourse a new conception or expression of meaning for the field we are in. Our understanding of our practice will vary, or has the chance of being varied, the more the possibilities of language available to us are varied.

Conceptions change as we come to share a dominant or inspirational or leading language with its own use of technical vocabulary. For example, the attempt within the library and information field to appropriate information management to itself as "what we have been doing all along" represents the acceptance of a new and dominant language with its changed technical vocabulary—emphasizing some of the old vocabulary, forgetting the rest, and adding some more (e.g., the idea of the information audit). As newcomers to the field are inducted into one or another of the extant conceptions of the field, they may change to another (if that is necessary) if the language or the context of the first conception allows them to (or alternatively they may leave). Our purposive strategy—what we are doing—is similarly conditioned and restrained. As we make sense, impute meaning, and interpret our profession and its practice, we are theorizing about it, usually unconsciously. Busha (1983) reflected the feelings of many in the profession when he demanded that "theory and practice should not be compartmentalized into mutually exclusive areas. In our service profession, practice should derive from theory and theory should nourish on practice" (p. 1). However, this call for a closer integration of theory and practice, although heartfelt and desirable, does not explicitly recognize that all practitioners (if they are professional about it) are constantly theorizing about their profession, and that theory is based on the meanings they come to share about that practice through discourse with other practitioners and their own reflection on their own lives. The theory Busha referred to is the kind of positivist theory many researchers have long striven to produce and many practitioners have long failed to comprehend as something that can be subsumed into their general internalized statements of the field that make sense of it for them. The intelligent, experienced, decision-making, educated practitioner, applying some practical reason to his or her situation, demands the kind of theory that an interpretive approach can give. Taylor (1985) explained the relationship between conceptions and practices thus:

> The relationship between practices and conceptions can be put this way: the notion of myself as an individual is constitutive of these practices, is presupposed in them. A social practice is a rule or norm-governed activity. It is defined by certain notions of failure and success, of honesty and turpitude, of excellence and mediocrity, etc. A certain conception of the human person is presupposed in a practice if it is essential to understanding the norms which define it. (p. 189)

What conclusions can be drawn from this discussion of practice, and how does it fit into the general picture? There are two main points to make. First, nobody performs merely at the level of technical performance. We constantly review our situation as we perform the most mechanical of tasks, not only to ask if we are doing it correctly, but also to question its relevance to our own individual sense of purpose, and to ask whether we are the kind of person who really wants to spend our time like this. Thus to reap the internal rewards of any activity we have to participate in it fully, to the point of self-identification—where I say to myself "this is boring, but it is necessary, and I know that doing it shows something about me and I want the satisfaction of seeing it done correctly." Put simply, we take pride in our work, and that pride comes from having a sense of individual purpose that reflects both our need for self-esteem and our need for some external recognition. Support for this comes from Jani, Parekh, and Sen (1990), who found that:

> Better understanding of professional work, greater proficiency in use of professional skills, a greater range of professional experience, the acquisition of new knowledge/skills and improved professional qualifications were the most highly rated indicators constituting professional advancement. These factors all relate to the personal or internal development and growth of the practitioner. (p. 186–187)

Advancement, they concluded, was also perceived to be supported more by personal drive and initiative and family and work environment. Management appreciation, higher salaries, and greater responsibilities were less important, and recognition in a peer community of librarians (professional associations) was given an even lower rating.

PRACTICE AND THEORIES

The second point is that technical performance is never enough as a measure either of individual performance or of professional practice. We always employ a level of judgment in practice, the right of others to use their judgment is respected, and we expect to be assessed on the way we use our own judgment, not purely on technical performance. For example, when a library decides its policy on cataloging, it may judge that full bibliographic entries are not required, that the catalog is just a finding device, that full bibliographic information is available elsewhere if it is needed, and that the library's resources would be misused if full AACR standards were implemented. It might be judged that the library was mistaken in this policy, but it would be on the grounds that the policy was inappropriate for that library, not merely because the full AACR provisions have not been followed. If practice were to demand full technical implementation on all points, there would probably be a problem about managing resources. A choice would have to be made between two things, one only of which the library could afford in full, and so another judgment must be made as to which will be chosen. Either way, technical standards and performance are not a sufficient guide to good practice.

It must be the case that resources beyond the technical are required for professional practice, and this suggests something like a shared background that would prepare practitioners for making professional judgments. Such a provision obviously demands that for judgments to be mutually understood and respected, all participants must share the same universe of discourse. They must share a high degree of understanding and also share the means of changing their judgments. The interpretive approach offers the opportunity to recognize this process.

How does this sense of personal identity, professional pride, and involvement in discourse actually manifest itself in mutually understood theories and views of what the practice is? This can be answered by considering the second question posed at the start of this chapter.

THEORY AND LEVELS OF THEORY

The interpretive approach can be seen as involving several levels of theory, and some parallel theoretical processes. Any participant is theorizing simultaneously about his or her own sense of self-identity, and also, in constant dialogue with that, about the practice he or she is participating in. The process of dialogue inducts someone into a realm come to subscribe to a view of what the practice is, and through discourse may modify that view, may even develop a new view that may of discourse that they may, in time, come (to a greater or lesser extent) to define (think of a Dewey, or a Grace). Through discourse, participants come to be widely shared as a metaphor for, or model of, what the practice is about, or what the participants in it are doing. Furthermore, the current frame or context in which this discourse takes place and takes its meaning is the information culture, and that any metaphor for the field may change if that context of meaning changes, with consequences for the current discourse.

These metaphors are the conceptions Dworkin proposed, and I henceforth use the term *conception* exclusively. A metaphor is a theory, a conception is a view of or a theory about a concept. Participants come to see themselves as "doing" information studies by "doing" information management, or whatever. They have, literally, a conception of what the practice is, and that conception is their interpretation of the practice: It gives them their purposive strategy and shapes and directs the discourse in the field. The conceptions are simply middle-level theories about the field, and are given effect by lower level theories about the way, say, information management, is effected through the use of relevant professional techniques and theories about daily practical problems and tasks. There is a higher level theory, that of interpretation, that gives us our understanding of all this teeming intellectual activity by grass-roots participants who themselves interpret to generate understanding of the processes that make the field what it currently is. There is also a parallel theoretical structure of understanding about evidence and about the way participant activity is to be viewed within the interpretive approach. All this takes place within the highest level of theory that determines the cultural value placed on library and information services. None of this is to be confused with any directive sense of mission or higher purpose a participant may have.

CONCEPTIONS, PARADIGMS, AND KNOWLEDGE

Two other issues about the use of the language of conceptions must be clarified to remove the possibility of terminological confusion. First, what is the relationship between Dworkin's conceptions and Kuhn's paradigms? Second, how does the library and information field stake its claim to an area of knowledge for it to have conceptions about? This is critical for maintaining the field's claim to some kind of believability among a wider community.

Conceptions and Paradigms

The conceptions of the field are to make sense of the field of objects, for a group of subjects. The meaning should be separable from its expression. There must be some underlying consistency in the meaning that reaffirms the original concept. Two questions, one internal and one external, spring from this. First, might it not be that these conceptions so called are, in fact, different concepts for which we can find several illustrative and developed conceptions for each? I claim that the generic nature of the discipline can be reasserted more confidently by the use of the interpretive approach, which allows the existence of separate and seemingly incompatible expressions. The distance between analytical bibliography and automatic information retrieval could be cited as evidence of the lack of any underlying unity. If there is this gap, this plurality of concepts, then it will become apparent with each conception. It is the closeness of fit of each conception to some basic concept of the whole field, like the chapters of Dworkin's chain novel, that is the critical test, and incompatibilities between conceptions may merely be illustrations of Taylor's perspicuous contrast. Even if they are not, if there is nothing common or shared between one conception and another, this may still not invalidate the general thesis if the relationship to a basic concept of the field can be sustained.

The conceptions examined are considered in relation to Dworkin's constructive interpretation, one that connects with purpose, rather than creative interpretation (which would be concerned with rediscovery of an original intention). Therefore, the basic concept need not be an original concept so long as it is true to the purpose of the field.

The second external question is to ask if these different conceptions are not better seen as paradigms in the schema of scientific development outlined by Kuhn. There is much in Kuhn's schema that is attractive to any historian of information studies. There are, however, serious differences that make it difficult to regard the library and information field as a suitable candidate for his theories. These differences make use of his idea of paradigms rather difficult, except in the most general sense: This allows the use of the terminology of conceptions developed here, and the use of the interpretive approach.

Kuhn's belief in the incommensurability of scientific theories is obviously attractive. Barnes (1985) summarized the position:

> Kuhn goes on to show that the comparative evaluation of competing theories remains a formally intractable problem. There is no common measure for the merits of competing theories, no clear and incontrovertible basis upon which to make a rational choice between them. Success in problem solving will not do, since reasonable men may differ on what is to count as a problem . . . Success in theoretical explanation will not do, since men have always disagreed . . . upon what is in need of explanation. (p. 93)

However, the conceptions developed in this work are not scientific theories. They are not to be seen in the same light, and the field of information studies considered broadly is not a science. Unlike the rational scientific tradition that Kuhn dissected, the activity in the profession that is included in this framework of explanation is not a continuous thread of development. Although the library tradition has produced its grand theorists, most of its revolutions have come about not by the detection of anomaly from within and the consequent loosening of intellectual grip of one particular paradigm, but by the intrusion of externally successful systems and methodologies into the field. So although Kuhn can also appeal to the model of law and suggest that paradigms, representing some scientific achievement, can and are applied like legal precedents, and become the inherited knowledge of each generation of scientists, we cannot really accept the whole apparatus of his explanation of scientific revolutions. Although, say, information management or bibliography as paradigm or conception may represent some professional achievement, the process of moving from one to another is not the same in science as it might be in the humanities. (But it might be legitimate to consider paradigms as concepts, so all conceptions operate within one paradigm). It is explicitly the accommodation of various possible legitimate alternative sets of explanations or conceptions of the field that allows an interpretive approach to consider the two subsets of the field mentioned earlier as contemporaries.

Kuhn was faced with the development of an alternative explanation of science to the rationalist one, and he seized on the sociological explanation. Science is what the scientific group allows to be believed: "What better criterion than the decision of the scientific group could there be?" (Kuhn, 1970, p. 170). This seems very close to the interpretive case for shared meanings, but in fact cannot be used to replace it, because what can be maintained as dogma in science or in the development of scientific research cannot be maintained in a profession based on practice and on the experiences of human subjects who are developing human responses. This forces consideration of the second problem already mentioned: How is communal knowledge (about the field) developed?

Communal Knowledge

People have grouped themselves loosely in professional and academic communities where they collectively share some knowledge that is labeled information studies, yet even in the subgroupings that represent the alternative conceptions in the field, there is no obvious overall agreement or obvious means of developing what is called knowledge. Kuhn pointed to the need to understand not only scientific communities, but also the need for the wider communities of which they form part to be considered in seeking the basis of knowledge (Barnes, 1985). So when we describe ourselves as information managers, or bibliographers, or whatever, we do so with one eye on maintaining the discourse within the field and among the participants and with one eye on the wider social community that will, if it shares our view of what we are and can do, come to us for services and give us, directly, the external rewards of which MacIntyre spoke as well as the rewards internal to our practice as we enjoy our success. This is where we look to see if we are maintaining our believability.

Kuhnian perspectives may be considered illuminating, but because they are primarily concerned with science, they cannot be imported wholesale. What needs to be considered is the wider question of knowledge and power in communities and how that relates to the work of librarians and information managers whose professional claim it is to organize that knowledge. The library and information field in general, as the main professional interface between a society and the stored record of its past, has a special position in consideration of its power over knowledge.

The ideology of the profession emphasizes the importance of access to knowledge, but this does not diminish the power of knowledge, which has been of major importance in Western thought. Classification, one of the profession's major weapons in organizing knowledge, remains a problem in the professional field of library and information studies, both because of the difficulties in meeting the practical needs of libraries and because of the constant need to accommodate new branches of knowledge within the structures of existing schemes. This latter problem has two dimensions: how to devise a classification that will express the new field, and how to integrate this with a general classification of all knowledge.

The point is that not only the classification schemes but also the ways of thought that make them possible can be questioned. What are the rules, and how are they derived, which allow the construction of models or classificatory systems? What rules allow the identification of certain people as authors, and the investment in that label with all that is customarily given to it? Foucault (1970) has addressed these questions and found his answer in the use of discourse analysis. Foucault saw the discourse as "a system of possibility for knowledge"—it is what allows the production of statements that will be true or false—a field of knowledge.

Foucault maintained, as Philp (1985) summarized, that:

> [the] rules of a discourse are not rules which individuals consciously follow; a discourse is not a method or a canon of enquiry. Rather, these rules provide the necessary preconditions for the

formation of statements, and as such they operate "behind the backs" of speakers of a discourse. Indeed, the place, function and character of the "knowers," authors and audiences of a discourse are also a function of these discursive rules. (p. 69)

Citing classification as an example, Foucault claimed that we can never claim that one system is absolutely better than another. As Philp explained:

> Truth for Foucault is simply the effect of the rules of a discourse—we cannot claim that our classificatory systems mirror certain enduring features of the natural world which previous classifications distorted. There can be no question of the overall truth or falsity of a classification or of a discourse—the relationship between words and things is always partial and rooted in discursive rules and commitments which cannot themselves be rationally justified. (p. 70)

Foucault claimed that power is an integral component of truth. Power grows from human relations, and certain powers available in our age (the last two centuries) have allowed the construction of the human sciences, which have structured the fields of possibility for those who have to act within them (Philp, 1985). These comments can be seen more obviously to relate to psychiatry or criminology or social work, but they apply equally well to the more academic disciplines of economics, political science, and sociology, all of which advance knowledge claims that are then employed to police normality. Information studies is in indirect relationship to this process, making available information (which includes the contemporary statements of truth or fact for each field) by acquiring organizing and storing and distributing both the information and the metainformation about each field. All these observations suggest that the library and information field is constructed from a complex of discourses—including those of other fields.

What is the relationship between Foucault's discourse and the shared meanings of the interpretive approach? In fact they operate at different points in the process of producing knowledge. The discourse operates according to the hidden rules that, Foucault claimed, can be discovered by discourse analysis. He was concerned with the preconditions of power and knowledge in society as a whole, and although his later work shows a close concern with intellectual regulatory agencies in society, he has no immediate brief for even the broad field of information studies. The interpretive approach, which builds group meanings from perceived shared meanings, can offer insight into the position of that field. However, Foucault's broad idea, especially as it relates to the generation and advancement of knowledge claims and classificatory systems, can be instructively used to help place library and information studies. As the library and information field claims a metaknowledge that will reflect (at best) current knowledge in all fields, its claim to organize knowledge is limited to its claim to do so in a way that best fits others' requirements—in other words, coincides with their own knowledge claims. The librarians' own knowledge claims are in the form of the data structures of the universal classification schemes, which not only place fields (Foucault's disciplines) in relation to one another, but also dictate the character of representation—linear, hierarchic, or enumerative.

The relationship between information studies in general and the generation of knowledge in society is therefore seen most clearly in the generation and use of classification schemes. The same process is at work in reference or information work. A simple example is where a bibliography of a burgeoning new field is compiled as an (entirely legitimate) aid to its students. Such a work claims to encompass the field, maybe even to subdivide and organize it conceptually. The success of the new bibliography will indicate how successful its compiler has been in matching the knowledge claims dominant in the field. In both the case of classification and reference or information work, we can say that they may be considered as tests of those conceptions where attitudes to their character and use are critical. They may be critical in establishing consistency and integrity throughout the field, and in testing whether each conception is in fact that alone and not a new separate concept of the field, as well as being considered in its own right.

CONCLUSION

Two questions remain: What limits can be placed on the range of conceptions used? How can we determine that one conception is better than another? This work does not pretend to exhaust the range of conceptions—obviously new conceptions may be developed in time, may even be developing now. Nor is it claimed that those chosen represent the only ones known so far, or that those chosen have been completely and exhaustively examined. My claim is simply that these offer a chance to test the interpretive approach on a number of known versions of the field, of widely varying practice. They not only test the interpretive approach in themselves but can also test its power in generating a view of the field that is widely hospitable and at the same time enforces or encourages professional and disciplinary common feeling, if not common purpose.

What can be considered a test of the ideas about conceptions advanced here? Obviously, there may be a need to know how this or that conception relates to ideas about the context of meaning, or to other conceptions, and how it related to the self-identity (and self-esteem) of individual practitioners. There would also be a relationship to some or all of the established techniques of the field. There could also be an expectation that a conception would, in the sense of Dworkin's chain novel, offer something for the development of the field; it should be progressive in some way. It could similarly be expected to maintain some narrative unity for the subject, by offering a new view of the past ("information management is what we have been doing all along"), picking up an old point and making it more salient for the field by making it more generalizable. What we have to consider is not only a test of some view being a conception, but also a test of how a conception gives way to a new one.

Transforming Conceptions

The argument so far has deliberately avoided any suggestion of how one conception might be transformed into another. Apart from the views of Dworkin about the evolution of practices as interpretations of them change, I have offered no mark of how we might say one conception is an improvement on another, other than to follow Taylor and say that it will be clearer than a previous interpretation. It is possible to add to the picture of theory building about conceptions and interpretations some view of how we might measure or indicate the significant characteristics of change in interpretation. We have models of how we can measure progress toward a better conception or interpretation in literary theory, in law, and in architecture. Hubbard (1986) built an apparatus for testing movements in architecture on examples of the evolution of taste in poetry and the evolution of judgment in law. Hubbard used the same material on the evolution of legal judgment as did Dworkin, and he adapted to his purposes in describing movement in architectural taste the literary theory of Bloom (1973), retaining the structure and categories, but changing the names. I have imported these into the range of resources for interpretation as indicators of the character of the change in any interpretation. I must emphasize that these are not part of the process of interpretation, but a test or measure of changes in interpretation.

Hubbard (1986) considering the way judges changed interpretation of the law, observed that, "The judges made their opinions plausible by showing how they submitted to the wisdom of their predecessors, but they made their opinions convincing by showing how they exceeded their predecessors" (p. 121). Similarly, as Hubbard remarked, Bloom pointed out that new poetry only becomes acceptable to us not merely because it is similar to previous poetry. Although that helps, it can only make new work a lesser restatement of past work: What new poetry demands is that we reread previous work, in a new light and improved understanding. In rereading, Bloom identified six strategies: Here I list Hubbard's (1986) terms, with Bloom's terms in parentheses.

1. Swerving (Clinamen).
2. Completion (Tessera).
3. Focusing (Daemonization).
4. Self-Limitation (Askesis).
5. Refilling (Kenosis).
6. Becoming the Essence (Apophrades).

These six ratios describe the processes by which our attention is captured by a more convincing and more insightful interpretation. In *swerving*, new interpretations (of poetry, architectural designs, or information studies) follow the old course up to a point, but then swerve away from them in a way that in the new interpretation, is seen as a corrective, not a departure, and makes the new interpretation seem more correct. In *completion*, the older style of interpretation is now seen as incomplete, and the new is seen as completing the interpretation, carrying ideas to their logical conclusion, and developing further and new implications. In *focusing*, the new interpretation shows older interpretations as unfocused, too general, and unspecific to our concerns. The new interpretation is more incisive and definitive—using widely applicable principles to address specific concerns directly and precisely. Following this, in *self-limitation* the new interpretation cuts away the superfluous and concentrates on the essential. Thus in *refilling*, the main import of the older interpretation is replaced with a new inner core. Finally, this new import seizes our mind as being not just something implicit in the earlier interpretation, but it *becomes the essence* of the interpretation: The interpretation has changed. Hubbard's (1986) conclusion (he was considering law) on this process is twofold:

> First, the public needed law that had enough believability so that they could accept it—that is, could accept it restricting their freedom because of the good sense it made. But (and this is often overlooked) the judges who made the law, being, after all, human themselves, needed a system that would let them have self-esteem. (p. 126)

So, interpretation is related both to self-identity and to external reference, and the process of moving from one conception to another is closely connected to the need for practitioners to maintain both their own sense of themselves and their sense of their practice in the wider world.

This allows us to round off the picture of the process of interpretation, and to understand what happens when we develop an improved interpretation of any practice—when we apply a rereading of our theorizing about our own identities and that of the practice we are in to the practice itself.

How far the language of interpretation and conceptions that has been developed here can do the things outlined in this chapter becomes apparent in the following chapters. A note of caution is proper here about the transformation of conceptions, because the conceptions chosen for examination are chosen primarily because they are hard cases that could pose severe tests for the interpretive position. The point of including the conceptions examined next is to show that interpretation can overcome the difficulties they presented. These cases are not presented as a natural series, and I do not wish to be drawn into showing how one evolved into another, as Hubbard proposed, particularly as the interpretive argument maintains that several interpretations can be extant and valid simultaneously.

Part III
Conceptions of Information Studies

This part examines the possibility of applying the interpretive approach to three different conceptions of the library and information field. The range of possible conceptions of the field of information studies is not limited. Further conceptions can arise, flourish, decline, and be replaced, or they may indeed go through some process of change and become dominant again. This exploratory work reviews three of the obvious candidates. These are all hard cases and in dealing with them, I show how the difficulties they pose are overcome: If difficulties with respect to these three can be cleared away, then the claims for an interpretive approach to the field are stronger. The treatment of bibliography (Chapter 8) clearly rests on its relationship to library and information materials, and the revised version of bibliography, even in its new name of the sociology of texts, does little to change this in fundamentals. Other conceptions of the field can reflect basic concerns with clients (actual and potential), with systems, or with services. Information science is given extended treatment as a conception that relates all of these. Information management is examined as a new and burgeoning conception. In all three cases, I have been concerned to show only that the apparent difficulties of applying the interpretive approach melt away: In no sense am I offering any definitive account of any of these areas of practice, not least because the disagreements that exist within them could only mean that the criticism such an account would attract could only serve to distract attention from my main purpose.

Some major areas of professional interest have been excluded: Management, for example, claims a large slice of the professional educational curriculum and is the prime task of senior personnel. It has been excluded from consideration here because if the field of information studies was held to be solely management, then it would have departed too far from the original concept to be considered (from the interpretive perspective) still in existence.

Collection building is another major area of professional activity that I have found trouble in regarding as a conception of the field. This is an important activity in reference and information work, in most of the conceptions previously mentioned, and in a general sense in professional consciousness. However, I have not found it sufficiently independent to count as a separate conception, and it could also be seen more properly as a technique, or set of techniques, than as a conception. Other areas that might, in some eyes, warrant consideration have been omitted from this work either because they do not fit immediate requirements or because they represent marginal viewpoints. The arguments of special interest groups have also been disregarded, alongside broad-based reconceptualizations of the whole field (as communication, or knowledge engineering, or whatever). Other points of view about the field have been ignored where they represent a sense of either mission or higher moral purpose, which I have indicated earlier are not the same as conceptions, and can not be seen as interpretations of what the field is or what the purposive strategy of its participants might be.

One other preliminary point needs to be made. In the library and information field, individual conceptions are rarely so dominant that they express the whole of the field. It would be an unexpected discovery that, say, bibliography or information management was an interpretation or a conception that could be applied to the whole of the profession. My claim is rather that each conception is intellectually significant, to varying degrees, and expresses an intellectual purpose of the profession and characterizes its social structure and its ambitions. I suggest that at certain times a particular conception, say bibliography or information management, held rather more sway than others, rather than claiming that all librarians and information managers saw themselves as bibliographers and lost their sense of self-identity if they felt they failed to match the model.

8
Bibliography

This case is immediately among the most challenging and simultaneously the most interesting. It is the area commonly centred around historical bibliography, but I extend it to include all historical studies in the field, and because there is some confusion about terminology (Bowers, 1975), I use the simple term *bibliography* to avoid the narrower connotations sometimes understood by the label historical bibliography. Although broader aspects of library (or information science) history could be included, they can also be overlooked in this argument without making any case for their exclusion. In recent years there has been a surge of interest in library history paralleled by impressive scholarship in the area, but despite this record, the essential nature of such work is to evoke the history of, let us say, library science, whereas the point is better served by some examples that show people at work with some particular view of its character. Furthermore, library or information history centers clearly on its subject, whereas many of the conceptions of the field exhibit the influence of external developments that are brought to bear on attitudes, practices, theories and interpretations within our field.

So, although broad areas of traditional humanities scholarship are included within this conception, I want to place the emphasis squarely on bibliography and the attitudes and practices of bibliographers. Bibliography can be viewed from two directions: For librarians it was long a measure of scholarly attainment, the bridge between library work and a broader world of scholarship, and the access route to true professional and academic recognition. For bibliographers working in university departments it was an under-laborers task, applying huge inductive and deductive powers based on vast accumulations of wisdom that could be acquired only by painstaking and often inconvenient study, in order to provide historians and literary critics with the real text of the works they studied and used. For library curators and keepers there was and is an obvious circle of interest between bibliography, which concerned itself broadly with the production and studying the circumstances of production of texts, and collection building, which gathered those texts. This would be particularly true of major scholarly libraries where the importance of older materials and the generation of new published texts of the literary heritage would be critical for collection building. Similarly, a knowledge of the history of publications and collections would be critical in the sale room. For the librarian who aspired to be the keeper of a great collection, in times before administration or mechanized processes had acquired their modern allure, bibliography would be an obvious point of reference.

Sadly, there is now little room for bibliographers in libraries, or even in academic departments. However, the impressive literature of bibliographical scholarship reveals the application of acute reasoning powers, highly developed methodology, sensitive judgment, and a rigorous critical assessment of the efforts of fellow bibliographers. Making available the real text of our literary and historical legacy has been an honorable duty, and one academic presses have eagerly embraced. Bibliography was firmly established as a humanistic discipline with a scientific method and concern for accuracy. Yet the comments of leading figures reveal certain difficulties with this self-image. These can be added to the difficulties to be faced when confronting this area as a conception of library science. (It is probably better to consider bibliography as a conception that predates the translation of library science into library and information studies. It may be that an examination of bibliography as a conception of the field reveals why a change in conception became necessary.) My concern here is to address certain difficulties facing an interpretation of bibliography as a conception of library and information studies, first by considering some aspects of the nature of the bibliographical enterprise, to recover its essentially humanistic and social nature, and second, to consider one claim about the character of bibliography that could be seen as an attempt to recapture library and information studies as bibliography.

The difficulties are numerous. They can be summarized as:

1. The relationship to the context of meaning, the information culture, seems remote.
2. If the work of the bibliographer is reminiscent of an interpretive style, it seems far closer to the older hermeneutic approach of revealing authorial intention rather than discovering current purpose.
3. Bibliography is not normally described as a social science.
4. There is little evidence that bibliographers view themselves or their field as having any relationship with other aspects of the broader library and information field, most particularly information science and information management.
5. There is evidence that bibliographers consider themselves and their discipline to be quite separate and different from librarianship.

6. If bibliography has an existence outside of information studies, how can it be regarded merely as a conception of this field, rather than a concept in its own right?

This last problem is one that must also be tackled in other conceptions. It is a point central to this work that external disciplines that have to varying degrees colonized the library and information field can still be regarded as being consistent with the broader tradition of the field, even though they are thriving independent disciplines. The other difficulties are, I believe, also surmountable.

A brief review of some historical developments in the library and bibliographical world in the United Kingdom will show how bibliography grew to be a major influence within the library world, and then shrunk back to a subsidiary position. Bibliographers were in a leading, maybe dominant, position at the heart of the British library profession. The main United Kingdom journal in bibliography is *The Library*. The history of this journal shows that what was once a close connection with librarianship has become weaker over the course of this century. The journal began publication in 1889 as *The Library: A Magazine of Bibliography and Literature*. An emblem on the title page proclaimed it to be "The Official Organ of the Library Association of the United Kingdom." It was edited initially by J. Y. W. MacAlister. After 10 years the journal was recast and a new series began. MacAlister was joined by some collaborating editors, including Melvil Dewey and Richard Garnett. Up to that time the *Library Association Record* had been a part of *The Library*, but it then began an independent career. MacAlister (1898) in the final article in Volume 10, disclosed that he had been dissuaded from his original intention of closing the journal and that it would continue in a new form. He declared:

> The Library in its new form will have three distinct sides—Practical Librarianship in its modern and best sense, Bibliography both archaic and modern, and Literature, in the shape of careful notices of books suitable for libraries. . . . It is not intended, however, that the bibliography of THE LIBRARY should be exclusively or mainly antiquarian. The history and art of books of the nineteenth century are as worthy of study as those of the fifteenth, and arrangements are already being made for papers to illustrate them, as well as for others on interesting points of bibliography in its wider sense. (p. 399)

A. W. Pollard, editor of *Bibliographia*, joined MacAlister as editor, the subtitle of the journal changed to *A Quarterly Review of Bibliography and*

Library Lore, and the increasingly bibliographical nature of the journal is apparent from its contents pages. In the first volume of the new series in 1900, 20 out of a total of 46 items were on bibliographical subjects. Ten years later in the 1909 volume, 17 of 24 items were bibliographical or historical and only one—by Pollard—on the arrangement of bibliographies, was obviously connected with practical librarianship. MacAlister's intention in 1898 to produce a good quarterly—"The new LIBRARY will be a *Quarterly*, and I think enough *good* stuff can be got together to make a respectable number every three months" (p. 398)—had meant that within 10 years he was producing, effectively, a journal of bibliography. Ten years on, in 1919, Dewey had disappeared from the title page, although he and others remained on an advisory committee, and of 17 articles, 14 were bibliographical.

In 1920 another change took place. The annual report presented to the 27th annual meeting of the Bibliographical Society disclosed that:

> The only important change now to be announced is that in order to print the papers read before the Society much more quickly . . . , our *transactions* will henceforth be published in quarterly parts. . . . It is hoped, also, that *The Library*, founded by Sir John MacAlister in 1888, which has already enjoyed a longer life than any other British periodical of the kind, may be brought into the scheme, and that the quarterly numbers may be gradually worked up into a full bibliographical magazine.
>
> As a result of the projected quarterly publication of our Transactions the Society's *News Sheet*, started by Mr Pollard, . . . will shortly cease to appear. (*The Library*, 4th. series, vol. 1, 1920, p. 41–42).

That year *The Library* appeared in a new fourth series, edited by Pollard. The title page now had as a header *Transactions of the Bibliographical Society: Second Series. Volume 1*, and although the main title remained, and has remained, THE LIBRARY, the subtitle lost its reference to anything other than bibliography.

Bibliography seemed to be colonizing successfully. Moreover, the senior bibliographers were also senior national librarians. As MacAlister, an administrator, gave way to Pollard, a bibliographer and senior official in the British Museum Library, so in time a new young bibliographer arose to assume an amazing array of offices in the library, bibliographic, and information worlds. Sir Frank Francis edited *The Library* from 1936 until 1953; he was successively Secretary to the British Museum Library, Keeper of Printed Books, 1948–1959, and Director and Principal Librarian 1959–1968. He lectured in Bibliography at London University from 1945–1959; he was President of Aslib 1957–1958, of IFLA 1963–

1969; Honorary Secretary of The Bibliographical Society 1938–1964 (1938–1940 jointly with R. B. McKerrow), and, more surprisingly, joint editor of the *Journal of Documentation*, 1947–1968, the foremost academic journal for information science in the United Kingdom. His career seemed to span a move over 30 years from a time when bibliography was the senior conception in the field to a time when information science was on the verge of contending for that role. He was the last bibliographer to fill the post of Director and Principal Librarian of the British Museum. Indeed, the title itself disappeared within 5 years of his retirement.

Francis was probably exceptional in combining so many roles and straddling so many fields. Subsequently, although bibliography may not have commanded the attention of the senior figures in the field—or perhaps it should be said that bibliographers did not command the senior posts—there has remained a close connection between librarians and bibliography. A check of recent volumes of *The Book Collector* shows that about one third of contributions are from librarians or lecturers in library schools.

THE CHARACTER OF BIBLIOGRAPHY

I want to take statements from two leading figures in bibliography to show that bibliography is in its concerns close to being a social science, that it is concerned with current purpose and not just authorial intention, and that it now shows a concern to relate to the information society. These points meet the first three difficulties mentioned earlier. First let us consider some of the views of Bowers, the overwhelmingly dominant figure in bibliography for the last 40 years and more. Bowers' (1975) views seem to offer little help. In reviewing the history of bibliography, he identified "two major tenets that have developed from the particular spurt of energy in bibliographical inquiry for which we may chiefly credit both the theories and practices of three giants in Scholarship : Pollard, McKerrow, and Greg" (p. 152). Bowers' own name must be added to the list, and perhaps the names of one or two others. Bowers described the end of bibliography, following Greg, as literary study, and derived the suggestion that its main purpose is to illuminate the processes of printing production. However, the function of bibliography he saw in more narrow terms:

> Accordingly, the function of analytical bibliography is to treat these imprinted shapes, their selection and arrangement, without primary concern for their symbolic value as conceptual organisms but,

instead, as impersonal and non-conceptual inked prints. Thus the general laws governing the selection and arrangement of the pieces of metal and their transfer of tangible inked impressions to paper are the concern of bibliography. (p. 56)

and "to determine the exact details of the mechanical process . . . a mechanical explanation for all phenomena whenever such an explanation can be arrived at on the available evidence." He went on to say, "Bibliography has its own laws of evidence that must be observed, else its way is being violated" (p. 56).

Analytical bibliography, whose rigorous method he summarized, he saw as the foundation for both descriptive and textual bibliography, both of which "serve as intermediaries between the book and the literary critic" (Bowers, 1975, p. 55). Although Bowers was confident about bibliography as a method and as an essential part of humanistic study, he was less confident about its reception in the university outside the library and, maybe, departments of English. He enjoined:

Do everything in your power to encourage all forms of bibliography as reputable and indeed necessary parts of post-graduate liberal arts training. Do not make the mistake of unconsciously trying to confine bibliography to the libraries, simply because it is always welcome there, and appreciated. (p. 107)

Although dependent on libraries as the repositories of his raw material, Bowers did not always reciprocate the level of appreciation he enjoyed there. In his essay on bibliography and modern librarianship, there are many strictures on the inadequacies of libraries, librarians, poorly educated rare book room curators, and chief librarians whose interest and origins are among the more mechanical divisions of the library. Even libraries instituting training programs for rare book specialists did not escape criticism (Bowers, 1975). His complaint was that students were grounded more in managerial aspects of running a rare book room than in the process of becoming descriptive bibliographers. Bowers' complaint against the (U.S.) library profession of his time makes intriguing reading. Bibliography, he claimed, is the modern 20th-century discipline, using the most advanced methods of scholarship, which preserves the written record of our culture in "whatever medium of communication has been used," and:

Modern librarians have sadly neglected this . . . , which in the end rests on bibliographical investigation, chiefly because they have made too little effort to acquaint themselves with the demands of this new and peculiarly twentieth-century scholarly discipline, which is far removed from the enumerative bibliography taught in their profession. (p. 92)

Yet it is often in using the skills of enumerative bibliography that the librarian serves the bibliographic and rare book community. Compiling accurate and adequate records of the works of the past, now so expensively gathered in the greater libraries, is not a frivolous task, nor an unappreciated one. The dedication of resources to such projects as the Eighteenth Century Short-Title Catalogue (ESTC) shows this. Without denying the importance of this side of bibliographical and curatorial work, I want to concentrate on Bowers' ideas, especially those about method, because his work can serve to test the claim that bibliography is a suitable subject for interpretation.

He concluded his case against the librarians by claiming that the "tendency of librarians not brought up in the humane tradition to become managers and technicians . . . has had a most unfortunate effect," and:

> The results of the American tradition are already apparent in the failure of rare-book libraries to rouse themselves from their sixteenth, seventeenth, and eighteenth century somnolence and to adjust to the demands of modern scholars, working bibliographically, and thence textually or historically, especially with the machine-printed books of the present or indeed of the nineteenth century. When *Studies in Bibliography* or *The Library*—to name the two most analytically minded bibliographical journals now being published—are as popular reading in library circles as *The Antiquarian Bookman*, then we shall know that the future will not cry out against us who suffered our librarians, in direct contrast with the past, to fall behind our practising scholars in erudition but chiefly in the understanding of what books are collected for and how they are to be used as something other than sterile artifacts under glass in an exhibition case. (Bowers, 1975, pp. 92–93)

Bowers' language is strong, but it also makes clear that his struggle is with the purposes of libraries and librarians, and that the present (the paper was delivered in 1966) position represents some falling away from the past, which Bowers suggested saw some identity of interest and purpose between the bibliographical and the library community. What can be detected here is that (whether Bowers was right or wrong about the idealized past) there was a sense of there being, or having been, shared meanings and purposes, and also that there had been, as Bowers detected, some parting of the ways as librarians began to reinterpret their practice toward technical and managerial concerns and away from purely scholarly pursuits. The parting of the ways may have been in earnest by the 1960s, by which time library schools were reducing their commitment to historical bibliography. Courses in historical bibliography were compulsory in the London University School of Librarianship as late as 1969, and they remain as options in other schools and departments. Rather like similar optional courses in archives, they serve as a reminder that knowledge about, and of how to deal with, precious materials was at least notionally part of the education of the librarian. It seems then that bibliography was once closely connected to library and information studies, and the evidence from McKenzie shows that there is an aspiration to recover that closeness.

Libraries, librarians, and bibliography were closely connected, particularly in the major collections, possibly as late as the 1950s. Put in this context, the conception of bibliography can certainly be fitted into the development of the understanding of library and information studies as suggested in this work. But how did bibliography fare as a conception of library science, (rather than vice versa) and how did bibliography relate to concepts such as the information society and technology and the social sciences?

In its relationship to social science, bibliography, at least in some of its guises, is rather akin to history, and it can be seriously considered as a discipline studying aspects of human behavior, largely on the evidence of its own practitioners. For it is clear that bibliography is a practice, with a method, and there are trenchantly adamant statements about adherence to the method and practice in all serious commentators, none more so than Bowers (1975). Thus:

> Impersonal judgement is to be preferred to personal judgement. The mechanical interpretation of analytical bibliography based on physical fact is always to be preferred to the interpretation of the critical judgment from values. When bibliography and critical judgment clash, the critic must accept the bibliographical findings and somehow come to terms with them. Critical assumption can never be so valid as strict bibliographical evidence. Indeed, this is not a question of degree: when a clash develops, strict bibliography must be right since step by step it rests on the impersonal interpretation of physical facts according to rigorous laws of evidence; and, correspondingly, criticism must be wrong since its interpretation of evidence can rest only on opinion. (p. 64)

Bibliography, therefore, is not grounded on values or aesthetics, but on careful reconstruction of historical events, based on the elaborate examination of men in printing offices and their practices, working on specific rather than general knowledge of such practices:

> General hypotheses about printing practices must always be tested by the specific evidence of any book under examination. The bibliographical way is inductive, not deductive; when properly employed.
> Moreover, there is a hidden danger . . . of bad bibliography. This danger may come from insufficient general examination of evidence as well as from the misinterpretation of specific evidence. (Bowers, 1975, p. 65)

Thus bibliography is closely tied to technique and so to a rigor and thoroughness that seems quite scientific. Yet the basic data on which bibliographical interpretation is based is not quite the brute data of pure science. This evidence of the printing press is evidence about the actions of men at work—authors, editors, compositors, pressmen: "What a bibliographical fact is needs constant testing . . . the assumption of normality that is basic to bibliographical reasoning can be very dangerous if too little information has been recovered about the variety of procedure possible in the printing process" (Bowers, 1975, p. 65). The basic facts of bibliography are therefore really preinterpretations, and their meaning becomes apparent only in relation to the meaning gleaned from other basic facts, just as the purpose of bibliography is, ultimately, a purpose shared with the general study of historical materials for literary or other purposes, and one shared also with librarians and the concerns of librarianship.

If there is an emphasis in Bowers on rigor and the correct application of the technique, how do more recent authorities view this field?

BIBLIOGRAPHY AND THE RESPONSE TO THE INFORMATION CULTURE

The most recent excursion into a general statement about bibliography came from McKenzie, in the 1985 Panizzi lectures. Another strand of development comes from the entirely different work of continental scholars, particularly French, working in the tradition of "L'Histoire du Livre."

The Sociology of Texts

McKenzie's (1985) views support my claim that the difficulties listed earlier can be overcome. In particular he showed a concern to relate bibliography to the circumstances of the modern information age, to attach bibliography to a concern with current purposes and not just with authorial intention, and implicitly, to relate bibliography to social science interests. McKenzie's Panizzi lectures show both that bibliography is adapting to changed times and conditions, and that some of its practitioners, at least, appreciate that library science has been through a process of adaptation at an earlier date. McKenzie (1985) saw the challenge:

> To sketch an extended role for bibliography at a time when traditional book forms must share with many new media their prime function of recording and transmitting texts. Professional librarians, under pressure from irresistible social changes, are redefining their discipline to describe, house and access sounds, static and moving images with or without words, and a flow of computer-stored information. (p. ix)

McKenzie went on to invert the normal hierarchy of bibliographic subfields and placed historical bibliography in a more important position, whereas Bowers relegated it to an addendum. Why should this be so? McKenzie saw this partial but significant shift as one away "from questions of authorial intention and textual authority to those of dissemination and readership as matters of economic and political motive and of the interaction of text and society as an important source of cultural history" (pp. ix–x). This move, then, signals a shift away from mere mechanical rigor to a process of interpretation with an entirely different focus, and one Bowers might abhor. The earlier mentioned difficulty that bibliographers were more concerned with authorial intention than current purpose is overcome.

This change represents, we can say, a shift in the interpretation of bibliography. In the language of Hubbard, we can observe a swerving away from the older interpretation, a new completion as the older version fails to take account of modern materials, and a focusing. If bibliography is on the move (and by no measure does McKenzie's work attract universal admiration or acceptance among bibliographers; see McKenzie (1992) and Tanselle (1992) for different views on the state of bibliography), then it is shifting to a new base that gives meaning to the field by association with a different set of disciplines and objectives. McKenzie was keen to re-establish the believability of bibliography, and the self-esteem and self-identity of its practitioners, and to orient bibliography more toward some of the basic techniques and other conceptions of the field of information studies. He was also offering a way forward, a progressive view of bibliography, and one based on a broader generalization of bibliography that brings forth a revised view of what it is. McKenzie's lectures have all the signs of a new interpretation of the field, which meet the fourth problem mentioned earlier, that bibliography saw little relationship between itself and other aspects of library and information studies. Whether the other components of Hubbard's tests are present—self-limitation as superfluous ideas are cut away, refilling of the interpretation, and thus becoming the essence of the tradition of bibliography, yet remains to be seen.

McKenzie (1985) saw bibliography as a "sociology of texts" (p. 5), the discipline that "studies texts as recorded forms." (p. 4) His concept of a text was broad, and his definition of bibliography was interestingly broad, too:

> If . . . we were to delineate the field in a merely pragmatic way, take a panoptic view and describe what we severally *do* as bibliographers, we should note rather, that it is the only discipline which has consistently studied the composition, formal design and transmission of texts by writers, printers, and publishers; their distribution through different communities by wholesalers, retailers, and teachers; their collection and classification by librarians; their meaning for, and—I must add—their creative regeneration by, readers. However we define it, no part of that series of human and institutional interactions is alien to bibliography as we have traditionally practised it.
>
> But . . . the accretion of subjects . . . demands that we also seek a new principle by which to order them. Recent changes in critical theory, subsuming linguistics, semiotics, and the psychology of reading and writing, in information theory and communication studies, in the status of texts and the forms of their transmission, represent a formidable challenge to traditional practice, but they may also, I believe, give to bibliographical principle a quite new centrality. (p. 4)

As McKenzie also included verbal, visual, oral, and numeric data within his definition of text, he gave an extremely changed and broadened view of bibliography. Such a new conception of bibliography might compete again as a possible conception for the field of information studies, and it also changes bibliography in other ways.

First, the relation to the current context of meaning for information studies, the information age or society, no longer seems so remote. Indeed McKenzie seemed to be suggesting that it is now a central concern for bibliography. Second, bibliography adopts a changed attitude to the construction of meaning, making it purposive for the reader, the subject, rather than solely concerned with authorial meaning. Third, it seems to be moving more clearly toward the social sciences.

McKenzie's bibliography, his sociology of texts, brings bibliography back closer to library science and information studies than Bowers would have it, and reveals that despite Bowers' strictures, the two share much in expression and meaning. Whereas Bowers referred to libraries as storehouses of the materials needed by the bibliographer, McKenzie related the objectives of bibliographer and librarian much more closely—relating the comprehensive and indiscriminate commitment of bibliography to describe all texts to the more formally librarianly objective of universal bibliographic control. (McKenzie, 1985). This seems to meet the fourth problem, about bibliography's relationship to broader aspects of library and information studies, and also fits neatly with a requirement of an interpretive discipline that meanings are established not of things in themselves but only by relation to other objects. "It . . . enables the discovery of any possible relationship there might be between any one text and any other text . . . bibliography is the means by which we establish the uniqueness of any single text as well as the means by which we are able to uncover all its inter-textual dimensions" (p. 51).

In an age of full text online retrieval and relational databases, this looks like a bid for the current center ground in the library and information field. Moreover, bibliography:

> impartially accepts the construction of new texts and their forms. The conflation of versions, or the writing of new books out of old ones, is the most obvious case. But the construction of systems, such as archives, libraries, and databanks is another. In every case, the elements from which they are constructed are bibliographical objects. A test case would be the sale and dispersal of, say, the library of a seventeenth-century scholar: we become acutely aware at such moments of a library's status as a text or a meta-text, and of its biographical and intellectual meaning. (p. 51)

McKenzie's reiteration that bibliography "of its nature, and not merely as a partial effect" (pp. 51–52) is concerned with texts as social products shows that he not only abandoned the concentration on authorial intention but explicitly allowed the creative construction of meaning at any time (rather like Dworkin's lawyers and legal texts): "Bibliography as a sociology of texts has an unrivalled power to resurrect authors in their own time and their readers at any time" (p. 19). In giving access to social motives, bibliography also "testifies to the fact that new readers of course make new texts, and that their new meanings are a function of their new forms. The claim then is no longer for their truth as one might seek to define that by an authorial intention, but for their testimony, as defined by their historical use" (pp. 19–20).

McKenzie's bibliography is an interpretive discipline, and one that clearly develops an interpretation of the purposes of library and information studies. The McKenzie view of bibliography is more clairvoyant than Bowers'. Whether the older bibliography, under the influence of Bowers (still, as editor of *Studies in Bibliography* a major influence in bibliographic studies until his death in 1991) ever had a hold, or a claim to a hold, on a conception of librarianship, it is clear that a certain limitation of purpose and departure from the other concerns of librarians left it unable to retain its position, either with respect to the doctrines of the field or the appointment of its senior officers. Whether a newer expression informing a broader practice of bibliography can recover that position is not our concern here.

Histoire du Livre

Whereas McKenzie placed more emphasis on the sociological, and in his reference to critical theory, linguistics, McLuhan, and so on, implied a concern with broad general theory, the French view is more explicitly historical, albeit a social history owing much to the pre-Annaliste historian Lucien Febvre. Martin's (Martin & Febvre, 1984) account explained the purpose of the book:

> The story is about something other than the history of a technique. It has to do with the effect on European culture of a new means of communicating ideas within a society that was essentially aristocratic, a society that accepted and was long to accept a culture and a tradition of learning which was restricted to certain social groups. (p. 12)

Chronologically, the Febvre and Martin approach long predates McKenzie. However, the leading journals in bibliography are still dominated by the work of analytic and textual bibliographers. The new bibliography does not yet have a strong hold over Anglo-American work, despite appeals for such a shift. Feather (1980) stated:

> We have accumulated a great corpus of invaluable technical knowledge from our detailed studies of the making of books. If we can also adopt and adapt the historical and cultural approach of our French colleagues, and blend it with our own techniques of analysis

and description, we shall not merely broaden the definition of bibliography, we shall deepen its scholarly significance and intellectual excitement. (p. 15)

Such a synthesis, which McKenzie also called for from a different position, would also bring bibliography closer to some of the other conceptions of the library and information field.

CONCLUSION

No attempt has been made to address the topic of rare book librarianship: This has been deliberate. To try to equate rare book librarianship and bibliography would be, effectively, to marginalize bibliography as a conception, whereas it gathers its power only by serving as a conception for the field overall. Six problems were cited with respect to bibliography: We have answers to them all. Additionally, with respect to the fifth problem, the independence of bibliography, we can note that McKenzie's (1985) concern is with the transmission and reception of texts and he saw the consequences of current social and technological forces. He quite explicitly renewed the case for bibliography as the central guiding conception of library service:

> Bibliographers . . . may of course continue to insist on making a rigorous distinction between books as we commonly know them and non-book forms, and on the restriction of "pure" bibliography to description and analysis of the book as a physical object. But libraries . . . are under significant pressure to evolve systems which accommodate these new forms of text in a rational, coherent, stable, and yet socially accessible way.
>
> The pattern is already pragmatically there in the transformation of our personal and city libraries. Some of us still buy books, of course; but we also borrow them . . . We are beginning to store information at home in our own computer files, or to buy access to other systems. That principle of buying access is simply an extension of the old idea of the lending library: we do not buy the book so much as the time in which to read it . . . the technical capacity most consumers now command . . . (to copy texts on T.V. programmes or cassettes) has also in part transformed the notion of purchase as a form of acquisition and the ways in which—some of us at least—form our personal libraries.
>
> My concern . . . is to find the continuity of these forms with past forms, of our new libraries with past libraries in their traditional

function as collectors, conservators, classifiers, and communicators. (pp. 59–60)

Continuing his argument for the copyright deposit, adequate storage, and public access to all forms of texts, including many that are machine specific, McKenzie concluded that "only a traditional, bibliographically informed concept of library service, dedicated to the public interest as a matter of principle and not of profit, will effect the preservation of such texts, guarantee their authenticity, and ensure access to them" (p. 63).

There is, therefore, a renewed appeal for a conception of librarianship as bibliography. In advancing his claims and putting forth his appeal, McKenzie may have ignored, in a formal sense, the context of meaning of the information culture (which may cost him success), but he did, in concentrating on older library functions, take account of the effects of new technology, and in fact he strove to downgrade the significance of the computer as a tool, emphasizing its limited memory, its concentration on retrieval of content and the "essential consonance of its functions . . . with the traditional purpose of libraries" (p. 61).

McKenzie's bibliography as a conception of librarianship has taken account of many recent developments and has shifted bibliography (slightly) into the social sciences, but his interpretation is based on an older conception of the field—as a storage center—that may mean his arguments are, finally, unpersuasive to librarians, however much they may regenerate bibliographers. However, his work does show that there is a conception of library and information studies that is bibliography, and it does match the requirements of an interpretive approach.

Strangely, we find further support for this in Feather's observation that rare book libraries themselves change their practices, moving away from an exclusive concern with bibliographers to provide a service for all users of older material—a change of interpretation of role that the theory of bibliography may only now be matching, in its new conception that meets the challenge of new media and changed library practice (Feather, 1980, 1982).

There is also a change in the character of the rare book librarian. Earlier in this chapter the connection between bibliography and collection building was noticed: The position has changed, almost in line with changes in other parts of the library and information field. Traister (1987) noted:

> Different sorts of personalities have been recruited into or attracted by the field [of rare book librarianship]. On the whole they are not collection builders. Their budgets do not permit them to be. They are instead people who see their task as trying to manage the collec-

tions they have inherited, ordering them, cataloguing them, publicizing them, making them function in their libraries.... In cooperation with their colleagues in technical services and systems, their task is not simply to put books on the shelves but also to put cards into the catalog or records into the database and to worry about service to the readers whom these records attract. (pp. 144–145)

Although McKenzie's appeal may rejuvenate bibliography, on the ground and in the libraries, chief librarians of major libraries are no longer bibliographers and collection builders. Bibliographers now, in their rare book libraries, are more likely to be like other librarians.

9
Information Science

When visiting schools of information science . . . I have often been introduced to the faculty members in the following terms: "Here is Dr. A, he teaches linguistics for information science. And here is Prof. B who gives courses in computer science for the information scientists. Dr. C here is a statistician who has a course on statistics for information science." And so it goes on until I am compelled to ask: "And who teaches information science?" The usual answer is that information science is a peculiar mix of linguistics, communication, computer science, statistics, research methods, together with some techniques from library science such as indexing and classification. Any integration of these elements has to be achieved, if that is possible at all, by the students themselves. (Brookes, 1980a, p. 128)

It is by no means certain that information science exists: but it is clear that information processes need scientific study. (Jones, 1981, p. 1)

This chapter considers the general position of information science, and three problem areas: the philosophy of information science associated with Brookes, the bibliometrics associated with de Solla Price, and experimental information retrieval. All three cases present problems for an interpretive approach, and they are discussed to show that these problems can be overcome. Each case is discussed to show that as a driving force for ideas in information science, it contributed to the development of the interpretation of the library and information field and helped develop a conception of the practice of the field. The discussion is mainly confined to developments within the English-speaking world.

INTRODUCTION AND BACKGROUND

The literature of information science is extensive, coming from researchers, theorists, practitioners, and outside observers. The earlier examination, comparing the proposed treatment in this work with the more traditional division into library science on the one hand and information science on the other, revealed some division of opinion as to what constituted information science. It is a somewhat battered and in some ways disoriented field. Schrader (1986) noted a conceptual chaos, which:

> issues from a variety of problems in the definitional literature of information science: uncritical citing of previous definitions; conflation of study and practice; obsessive claims to scientific status; a narrow view of technology; disregard for literature without the science or technology label; inappropriate analogies; circular definition; and, the multiplicity of vague, contradictory, and sometimes bizarre notions of the nature of the term "information." (p. 192)

Some of this confusion may spring from Griffith's (1980) finding that, in the United Kingdom and the United States, the beginnings of information science were marked in the 1950s by the migration of a number of natural scientists, behavioral scientists, and applied mathematicians into problem areas dealing with information. The vast majority were, however, natural scientists, and despite the great contributions of these pioneers, major mismatches of approaches and subject matter resulted.

What Griffith did not mention is that these migrants descended into problem areas already populated with documentalists trying to resolve those problems with tools generated from within another tradition, the library tradition. The consequences of this cross-cultural movement are still apparent. Even a cursory review of the literature will reveal that whereas librarians seem well aware of something called information science, for other academic disciplines the identification process is not so easy. For those coming to the field from a library orientation there is a view of it that emphasizes, above all, automated information retrieval, and to a lesser extent other automated processes and a systematic study of literatures and literature users.[1] There is also a confusion about the driving power in the field of practice, empirical research, and theoretical foundations and formations. Machlup and Mansfield (1983) observed that "Information Science is not involved in any such methodological controversy" (between formal and empirical sciences), "chiefly because no agreement exists about its object or objects. By and large, information scientists deal with practical matters and, therefore, with the world of experience" (p. 16). They detected four main uses of the term infor-

---

[1] See for example the work of de Solla Price, and some of the comments on course orientation in Dudley, Clough, Bryant, and Moore (1983).

mation science in the literature, one embracing the other three. These others concerned a broad sense covering the systematic study of information, and two more specialized senses related to computer science and library science, where it "indicates a concern with the application of new tasks and new technology to the traditional practices of librarianship" (Machlup & Mansfield, 1983, p. 18).

In this work I use information studies as the more general term. The idea of information science used here is more closely related to research than to everyday information work, and accordingly concentrates more on the research problems of such areas as automatic information retrieval.

Antecedents and Development

The antecedents of information science lie early in this century, although Davis and Rush (1979) did mention that through library science it can trace its roots to Nineveh and King Ashurbanipal. More seriously, they claimed its identity and image were set in the post-World War II period, citing Bush's (1945) *As We May Think* article as the earliest and most influential work signaling the beginning of that period. In institutional terms, the roots can be found in the Special Libraries Association, founded in 1909, and the American Documentation Institute (ADI), founded in 1937, and in the United Kingdom and Ireland in Aslib, which dates from 1925, and the Institute of Information Scientists (IIS), founded in 1958. Other international roots starting with Otlet and La Fontaine's International Institute of Bibliography, later to become the Federation Internationale de Documentation (FID), in 1938, were closely associated with research and development in classification schemes and bibliographic control. In the United States, research in the 1940s set the tone for future trends in information science, and research gradually fed through to education programs: In 1955 the first course in machine literature searching was taught at Case Western Reserve University, and later in the 1950s the National Science Foundation in the United States set up its Division of Science Information (Miski, 1986; Williams, 1990).

In the United Kingdom there was also significant development in the 1940s and 1950s. The great landmark was the Royal Society's 1948 Conference on Scientific Information, although another 1952 conference, on communication theory, should also be mentioned. By the late 1950s, documentation was losing favor as a term in the English-speaking world, as Farkas-Conn (1990) recalled: "*'Documentation'* projected an old-fashioned image: the people working in the field were by now concentrating on information and its retrieval and on representation of information" (p. 191).

From 1958 through 1968, another major series of changes finally set information science in its present tracks. In 1958, a major Washington International Conference on Scientific Information coincided with the annual FID meeting, and in the United Kingdom the Institute of Information Scientists was set up. The ADI slowly escaped from documentation and became, in 1968, the American Society for Information Science (ASIS). Apparently the Association for Computing Machinery (ACM), still so called, had also wanted that title, to indicate a concern with more than hardware (Farkas-Conn, 1990).

Publications and Associations

In 1966, the ADI had together with the Chemical Literature Division of the American Chemical Society and the Documentation Division of the Special Libraries Association established *Documentation Abstracts* (soon to become *Information Science Abstracts*), and the first volume of ARIST (*Annual Review of Information Science and Technology*) appeared. By that year the institutional framework of information science was settled, its publication vehicles were largely established, and its first heroes were in place. Price (1986) had produced the first edition his seminal work *Little Science, Big Science* in 1963, and the first textbook (Becker and Hayes) also appeared that year.

The journal literature reflects the gradual movement away from a librarian-documentation accent to one centered on science and technology. In the first issue of *The Journal of Documentation*, in June 1945, Theodore Besterman, the editor, declared "[A]nything in which knowledge is recorded is a document, and documentation is any process which serves to make a document available to the seeker after knowledge. This process will be the chief concern of the *Journal*" (p. 1). Of 22 articles in the first volume, only 7 were on topics obviously scientific or technological. In Volume 11 (1955), 6 of 9 articles were so, and by Volume 20 (1964) 12 of 17 were recognizably connected with such topics. In Volume 31 (1975), 18 of 22 were on topics associated with computer applications or statistical analysis of documents. As was seen in an earlier chapter with *The Library*, there has been a gradual takeover by particular interests that now effectively define the character of documentation or information science for the library and information community.

There are separate professional associations, for both librarians and information scientists, both in the United Kingdom and Ireland, although the degree of overlapping membership confuses the relationship between the two groups. In the United States, the Special Libraries

Association caters to the same kind of professional in practice as is catered to by Aslib in the United Kingdom and the Institute of Information Scientists in the United Kingdom and Ireland. The research community is unlikely to gather in these bodies: Its meeting places are the annual conferences of ASIS, the ACM-SIGIR (Association for Computing Machinery Special Interest Group in Information Retrieval), and the Information Retrieval Group of the British Computer Society.

Practitioners gather at annual conferences of the Special Libraries Association, the Institute of Information Scientists, and Aslib. There is a third component to this information science world, that of the information system producers and information service suppliers, strongly associated with the two annual online conferences in New York and London. Practitioners may attend these and similar conferences, where they will encounter, sample, and buy new products and services, the intellectual input for which was provided by the information science research community, often several years before.

The research community will publish in journals run both by research and by practitioner groups. The leading United Kingdom research journal, the *Journal of Documentation*, is published by Aslib (a group straddling research and practitioner interests). Another British research journal, the *Journal of Information Science*, is published for the Institute of Information Scientists. In the United States, a major research journal is published by ASIS; the other major international journal in the field, *Information Processing and Management*, does not have any institutional affiliation. There are, it seems, greater divisions between practitioners who call themselves information scientists and researchers and theorists whose field is information science, than there are between librarians and practicing information scientists. A strange situation exists where the research community defines information science, but membership of the practitioners' professional associations defines who is an information scientist. What, then, defines the practice of information science?

DEFINITIONS OF INFORMATION SCIENCE

There are several available sources for information science. Unfortunately some of the major collections[2] are short on overall discussions of the field,[3] preferring to include more technical material exemplifying

---

[2] See, for example, Machlup and Mansfield (1983), Griffith (1980), Davis and Rush (1979), and Saracevic (1970). Machlup and Mansfield did discuss information science with library science (see Chapter 6), but they considered this the least satisfactory section of their work (U. Mansfield, personal communication, 1986).

[3] Heilprin (1985) is, in part at least, an exception to this general rule.

work in the field. Machlup and Mansfield (1983) included much about information science, but it comes mainly within chapters on, and from the viewpoint of, cognitive science and computer science.

Griffith (1980) provided a different and useful starting point. He concluded from an analysis of citations that:

> Evidently, authors in library and information science and technologies cite works in seven principal areas. These areas nearly completely capture the principal processes involving information.
>
> 1. Retrieval theory, methods, and evaluation: the retrieval, interpretation, "transformation" and analysis of information.
> 2. Statistical studies of literature: the organization of information.
> 3. Communication and information exchange in, principally, science: the generation, dissemination and use of information.
> 4. The impact of information and communication on technology: the use of information.
> 5. Design and evaluation of information systems and products: the applied science of information services and products.
> 6. Specific information products and services.
> 7. Oddments and miscellaneous: apparently, one paper fields generated by the specific application of theory or method of analysis to a particular problem. (p. 6)

In his dedication he specifically mentioned, all "who have, over the period covered by this volume, instructed most of the rest of us—especially, Bertram Brookes, Robert A. Fairthorne, Manfred Kochen, Derek J de Solla Price" (p. viii).

Brookes is used in this chapter because of the volume of comment his work has aroused, particularly with respect to his ideas on the philosophical foundations of information science. Brookes gives a firm, positivist, Popperian basis for information science that is immediately a challenge to the interpretive position. I suggest that his views can be decomposed to show that they do not, despite the Popperian orientation, form an impediment to an interpretation of the field.

Price's work on quantitative measures and bibliometrics is used here similarly to show that, despite an apparent incompatibility, his work is also dependent on interpretation and is not a barrier to the views advanced in this work. Two views of information retrieval are also used to argue that information science, even those components normally seen as a hard science, are compatible with social science explanations. These three cases (Brookes, Price, and automated information retrieval) are used to show, rather as Dworkin used legal cases, that their contributions to judgments about what information science is, or what problems should be analyzed, are matters of constructive interpretation. Griffith (1980) held that:

> Information science is soft because people with all their glorious flexibility and petty fickleness are intrinsic to the systems we study, whether as users, producers, operators, decision makers or as the ultimate, apparently unanalyzable, language processing devices. Immediately, this introduces the possibility of a variety of approaches: theories are not clearly right or wrong; results are rarely the final answer. Both research problems and concepts linger on, as the literature of many social sciences makes clear. (p. 2)

Just as Griffith seems to be backing ideas that reflect those behind the interpretive approach, there is further support for the sociological role in information science from Garfield (1971), Roberts (1976), Shera (1971), Wersig and Windel (1985), and Wilson (1980). There is, however, some creeping psychologism to overcome. Farradane (1980) produced a picture of the scope of information science that is heavily based on linguistic analysis and psychological work on information handling and that concentrates entirely on the information-seeking operations of an atomistic individual, who apparently does not need any sense of meaning.

Brookes' emphasis on the scientific character of information science is found elsewhere. Borko (1968), for example, gave a definition centered on the two phenomena of information and its use:

> *Information science* is that discipline that investigates the properties and behaviour of information, the forces governing the flow of information, and the means of processing information for optimum accessibility and usability . . . It has both a pure science component which inquires into the subject without regard to its application and an applied science component, which develops services and products. (cited in Tenopir, 1985, p. 5)

Other definitions cited by Tenopir (1985) include the ASIS definition, which also emphasizes similar characteristics: "Information science is the study of the characteristics of information and how it is transferred or handled. It is concerned with the way people create, collect, organize, label, store, find, analyze, send, receive and use information in making decisions" (p. 5). There is another definition from Swanson (1978) that stresses communication:

[Information Science is] concerned with how man communicates with man. It is the study of how information is transferred—from the point of generation to the point of use—and all the intermediate steps of collecting, organizing, interpreting, storing, retrieving, disseminating and transforming information. As a discipline information science stresses the application of modern technologies to the handling of information. (p. 148)

Tenopir took from Saracevic the observation that the major departmental home of information science courses was in library schools, with computer science and management or business schools further behind in the list. She also took an observation from Fosdick (1978), who identified information science courses in library schools as nontraditional courses or "courses that would not have been offered in library schools prior to the interest in and awareness of information science as a field in its own right in the 1960s. Implicit in this definition is that such courses relate to the relatively new practice of the manipulation of data by computer" (p. 101). From these last two observations there would seem to have been a tug and pull relationship between library schools and information science. These definitions, together with the historical background, form the backdrop against which the problems identified for this chapter can be tackled.

THE PROBLEMS

Just as bibliography presented its difficulties for this work, so too does information science. There is in this case no problem about accepting the idea of the information society as a context of meaning. However, information science offers us problems in other areas, notably:

1. Of all the possible conceptions examined here this seems most firmly and securely rooted in a positivist epistemology.
2. There is some difficulty in identifying information science as a social science.
3. It seems (and in some cases claims) to be a fully fledged separate discipline and profession in its own right.
4. What is to be taken as representative of the practice of information science? Theory, empirical research, or professional employment?

These problems are addressed *inter alia* in the rest of this chapter.

Information Science, Interpretation, and Independence

Whether or not information science is an independent field is not a problem. The task is to present it as a conception of the practice of the library and information field. The existence of an altogether unfamiliar information science as put forward by Kochen (see Chapter 6) is not a problem. Because a spokesman for this view, Kochen, was apparently able to be in dialogue with the library and information community, there seems to be no difficulty in considering information science to exist within a wide range, some part of which is within or coextensive with some part of the library and information field.

The task faced in asking the question, "Can information science be viewed as one conception of the field of library and information studies?" is to show partly that a changing conception of the broad field could result in a view of information science—and perhaps abandon it at a later stage, and that information science thus seen is a social science and meets other criteria of the interpretive position. There is no direct assault on positivist explanations of information science: All that the interpretive position requires is that under analysis information science *qua* a conception of information studies is shown in its methods to be an interpretation of primitive data, leading to the construction of shared intersubjective meanings, and not a construction from objective value-free brute data.

It is clear that in the 1960s what was then known as library education suffered a methodological crisis. Despite its strengths and successes, the mismatch between resources and techniques in providing the necessary metainformation about library holdings forced library practice to review its current conceptions of both the scope of the discipline and the proper preparation of its practitioners. The range of solutions included improved management, reduced or transformed standards, more limited objectives, and new technology. Currently management and technology have both claimed large slices of the time available for professional preparation. Clearly, a practicing profession looked more to the applied science side of information science—the products and services—but there is another significant aspect to be considered, which makes Borko's claim for information science to be, also, a pure science, more significant.

In generating the new theory, the pure science, which according to Borko inquires into the subject without regard for its application, is significant. It is intellectually impossible to apply the products and services of the applied science component without having the necessary conception of the field that called for the existence of such products and understood the manner and purpose of their application. If you do not have the concept of a hammer, you do not know when you need one, and you cannot express a need for any tool or service or product unless you have a conceptual framework, a conception that conditions meaning and tells you what you need.

The definitions of information science quoted earlier, all used the words " . . . is the study of" or " . . . is the discipline that." Yet we are arguing that information science can be a conception that makes sense to practitioners. In two of the definitions (those of ASIS and Swanson, given earlier) a host of activities connected with the study or discipline are listed (collecting, organizing, interpreting, or to collect, create, organize, label). The definitions are broad enough to include what would previously have been called librarianship or library science. This suggests both that there was a need within the library and information field for a redefinition, a new interpretation, a new conception that broadened the disciplinary and professional horizons to allow the practicing professionals to deal with new and testing phenomena, and that this kept close to the original concept. We can identify this need as a need for swerving and focusing in the language of Hubbard. Yet the definitions of information science rarely speak of practice, emphasizing more the idea of a discipline. This has had confusing consequences, including the suggestion that information science was the theory for the practice of librarianship. However, from the existence of professional bodies we know that there are practitioners who consider themselves information scientists (and who frequently consider themselves not to be librarians).

The interpretive approach as laid out by Dworkin and Taylor requires that interpretation can only be by a participant. This does not mean, necessarily, someone working in a library or information service, any more than an interpretation of law need be by a practicing lawyer. A participant can be anyone within the field—a judge or a qualified academic commentator. The legal example also shows that the interpretation is of the practice of law—not daily activities, or even what the doers of those activities make of them, but some overall view of what the practice is about. This might come about by the development of superior generalizations that offer an understanding of a broader range of actions, for example, in a way that the active participants themselves then had to build into their own understanding of how they understood their practice. Clearly the interpretation of practice is not what practitioners think or do. It is the generation of new shared intersubjective understandings or meanings among participants of or for the practice. In this respect, the interpretation of the practice of information science must come from its theory and research (which extends theory), and not solely or predominantly from its practitioners' daily occupational experience.

PROFESSIONAL PREPARATION

Looking at the educational preparation for information science, we find an emphasis on subjects that support the claim that, as a conception of the library and information field, information science provided a broadening perspective, a better introduction to analytical tools, an interaction with a range of other disciplines, and a concern with new media and modern technologies that together could help the individual practitioner cope with the changed working environment. For example, the (British) Institute of Information Scientists in 1988 published revised criteria for information science. These criteria are used by the Institute to assess professional educational courses in information science and to assess applicants for corporate membership of the Institute. The criteria are arranged in four sections, as follows (the headings are instructive):

Section 1 Information Science

1. Information and its users
2. Information sources
3. Information storage and retrieval
4. Analysis of information
5. Dissemination of information
6. Theory of information science

Section 2 Information Management

1. Planning
2. Communications
3. Management information and control systems
4. Human resource management
5. Financial management
6. Economics and marketing of information systems

Section 3 Information Technology

1. Computer systems
2. Communications (technical)
3. Computer applications
4. Environment

Section 4 Ancillary Skills

1. Research methods
2. Linguistics
3. Foreign languages

The introduction to the Criteria states that "information science is concerned with the principles and practice of the provision of information. To this end it includes the study of information from its generation to its exploitation, and its transmission in a variety of forms through a variety of channels" (Institute of Information Scientists, 1988, p. 1). The introduction clearly links theory (principles) and practice, and is broader than some of the earlier definitions, which concentrated on information science as a study or discipline. It can be inferred that the IIS (Institute of Information Scientists) statement implicitly demands an interpretive account that will link the principles to the practice. As the proposed criteria are a revision, it would also seem that there is a development of understanding of the field that is finding an alternative expression. Furthermore, the criteria for information science include not only information science itself but also two other expressions: information management and information technology.

The IIS criteria state that for an educational program (course) to be recognized it must cover a lot of any of Sections 1, 2, or 3, plus some at least of the other two sections. This seems to be explicit recognition in practice that there are equally viable alternative expressions of meaning of what information science is. Courses with a larger technological component are akin to the model of information retrieval that is later rejected as false for the specific field of library and information studies. I claim that the broader Artificial Intelligence/Information Retrieval (AI/IR) model of information retrieval discussed later in this chapter, which gives greater attention to areas that are included in the information management and ancillary skills section of the IIS proposals, really contributes more to the conception of the overall field that the IIS seems to presuppose. The range of subjects covered suggests that the field of information science is still searching for a settled curriculum. Tenopir (1985) supported this. She reported that her findings "reinforce the general feeling voiced by many writers that Information Science is a field that still is not mature and that has no clear definition or focus in practice" (p. 23).

Such a situation suggests that the process of interpretation for the discipline is still incomplete, especially so for that version of information science that serves as a conception for the broad library and information field.

It is questionable how much a knowledge of database structure, or inferential statistics, or linear programming, form part of the necessary equipment for the daily, or even the annual, round of the librarian or information scientist, but they may indeed be useful in the process of study of information in all its aspects. Thus the emphasis that shows in the leading journals within what we might call the library tradition of information science—the *Journal of the American Society for Information Science, Information Processing & Management,* and *The Journal of Documentation*—on two or three specialized aspects of the field could be held to reflect a reorientation of the whole field toward a new conception. The areas given most significant coverage, as Griffith identified, are experimental automatic information retrieval, and quantitative studies of the generation, storage, and use of literature. I consider them after a review of the theoretical work of Brookes.

BROOKES

An examination of some of the work of Brookes, who was identified by Griffith as one of the most significant influences in the field, will help to resolve the question of whether or not information science is a social science. The relationship of information science to one variant of positivist epistemology can also be clarified. Brookes' starting point is familiar and often repeated in all the literature of the field: "Information science floats in a philosophical limbo. It has no theoretical foundations" (Brookes, 1980a, p. 125). He added, "Information science is now regarded both by the public and by most of its proponents as an essentially practical activity concerned to exploit the computer" (p. 126).

Conveniently, Brookes (1980a) also placed information science firmly among the social sciences: "Of all the social sciences, information science is most intimately concerned with the interactions between mental and physical processes or between subjective and objective modes of thought" (p. 126). Brookes proceeded from this starting position to a representation of information science as an outgrowth of Popper's World 3. Unfortunately, he chose Popper on rather cavalier grounds[4] and never offered any better justification.

Brookes' reading of Popper[5] leads to a convenient formulation that takes him immediately to the world of brute data. He argued that physical scientists and technologists, working in the physical environment (World 1), and social scientists and humanists working in a world of subjective human knowledge or mental states (World 2), all deposit their records and artefacts in World 3, which is apparently "The world of objective knowledge, the products of the human mind as recorded in

---

[4] On page 126 we read "of modern philosophers I find Sir Karl Popper much the most congenial, precisely for the reason that most professional philosophers of our time disapprove of his ideas."

[5] Brookes' reading of Popper has been severely criticized (see Neill, 1982, and Rudd, 1983).

languages, the arts, the sciences, the technologies—in all the artefacts humans have stored or scattered around the earth" (Brookes, 1980a, p. 127). For Brookes, the practical working task of library and information scientists is clear.[6] He went on to claim that "the *theoretical* task is to study the interactions between World 2 and 3, to describe and explain them if they can and so to help in organizing knowledge rather than documents for more effective use" (p. 128).

The distinction between knowledge and documents is a difficulty he did not satisfactorily examine. Is knowledge separate and unconnected to the documents, or is it entirely drawn from the documents—in which case documents must be synonymous with artefacts? These artefacts seem to be, by Brookes' account, meaningfully stable: "The artefacts which record human knowledge exosomatically become independent of the knowing subjects who created them. These artefacts are no longer subjective and inaccessible but objective and accessible to all who care to study them" (p. 128).

Brookes (1980a) claimed that Popper's World 3 allows the objective study of knowledge, and that this is the justification for a new science:

> This approach thus enables us to escape from the subjectivities of the 2000-year old approach to theories of knowledge and from subjective psychology as well as from traditional philosophy. Furthermore, in adopting the interaction between worlds 2 and 3 as our field of study we are laying claim to territory which no other discipline has already claimed. (p. 128)

This claim depends on us not being concerned with meaning, or with the purposes of the users of this objective knowledge. Brookes later identified objective knowledge (World 3 knowledge) with the current consensus—a kind of intergroup subjectivity that might seem to invalidate his claim to it being objective, but that is more amenable to the position of the interpretive approach. However, as Taylor (1978) argued, this consensus is really an argument for convergence of beliefs. This can suggest to us that Brookes' objective knowledge is really a product of a common language rather than of any Popperian World 3. Brookes (1980a)

---

[6] We might question his terminology here. His expansion of the definition of World 3 would seem to have to include libraries, museums, art galleries, and so on, and so he might legitimately speak of library and information science, although his initial project is restricted to information science alone. If he really means the broader field, then our task of arguing for information science as a conception of library and information studies is made easier, but we still have to grapple with his fascination with objective knowledge.

claimed that, of the objective knowledge of World 3, "Only the first steps—the classification of the artefacts—has so far been attempted" (p. 130).

Following Taylor, it can be claimed first that, whatever the advantages or relevance of World 3 and Popper, this is really a set of intersubjective meanings derived from the constitutive practice in any field, and that the classification of the artefacts is really an exercise conducted, as a practice, with the same intersubjective meanings. Further evidence of this comes from Brookes (1981) when he concluded that although information is embedded in documents, or in the minds of knowing subjects (such as experts), it is in every case contained within a discernible knowledge structure that is familiar to the reader, who "is . . . reassured to find the information in a context to which he can relate" (p. 9). Brookes concluded from this that "information offered to others must be presented within a relevant cognitive structure because that is the only way in which the users can perceive its warrant or authority" (p. 9).

Brookes' (1981) own general conclusion to his review of the foundations of information science reiterates the importance of a *science* of information, and that the paradigm of information science is changing. In particular he called for recognition that information and knowledge exist only in cognitive spaces (rather than in books, physical objects) and that "That techniques of quantitative analysis derived from the physical sciences be adapted for use in cognitive space, that human individuality be taken into account and that we make better use of the empirical data available in the social sciences in developing our theories" (p. 11). Finally, therefore, information science does become a social science with a humanistic core, albeit one with quantitative methods and empirical data. The incompatibility of these with "human individuality" does not seem to have assailed him, but once he has been rescued from Popper's World 3 and strange ideas about objective knowledge, Brookes' information science is not incompatible with a social science of library and information studies, nor with an interpretive approach to it. Brookes' interpretation of the nature of information science, and, implicitly, the knowledge claims he made about its task and methods, rest on fundamentally different bases to the strongly empirical studies of Price and researchers in experimental information retrieval. Brookes' attempt to reach the philosophical high ground does offer a foundation for studies about information that rest on a broader generalization, and thus might explain a wider range of experience than purely empirical studies, or even many philosophical approaches to librarianship. In that sense he offered a conception of the field that can fit into the interpretive pattern developed by Dworkin.

QUANTITATIVE STUDIES OF INFORMATION: PRICE AND BIBLIOMETRICS

Price is another of the heroes of information science identified by Griffith in his dedication. Price's work is examined here as a seminal work in bibliometrics and as prime example of the application of quantitative methods. Bibliometrics is successfully established as a scientific study within the field, based on examination of observable hard or brute data. This obviously defies the requirement that, for interpretation, the field be seen as a social and not as a natural science. This position can be turned. I show that his work is dependent on interpretation and that his data cannot stand without interpretation. His work has a sociological thrust, giving another dimension to the understanding of what comprises information science. Very interestingly, he builds his case on the construction of a narrative of the development of the field, a point I return to in the final chapter. I claim that analysis of his work, and the knowledge claims it makes, adds to the range of understanding available about information science. This also embellishes information science's claim to offer a superior interpretation of information studies, and thus assists its claim to offer an improved conception of the practice. In Hubbard's terms, this offers us examples of completion, focusing, and refilling.

Price (1986) claimed starkly, "My approach will be to deal statistically, in a not very mathematical fashion, with general problems of the shape and size of science and the ground rules governing growth and behaviour of science-in-the-large" (p. xvi). Price's principal work in this field, *Little Science, Big Science*, cannot alone be regarded as a sufficient statement of the field, but it is a seminal work and can be regarded as a sensible starting point for any discussion. Price set the agenda, and almost alone defined the scope and purpose, of bibliometrics, and in the 1986 reprint of *Little Science, Big Science*, his original work is repackaged with nine of his other papers.

Price linked scientific manpower, scientific literature, expenditure on science, and the influence of science and scientists in the political sphere. He treated the sociology of science, and although he did not specifically discuss information science, his comments on the social role of the literature in science and his discussion—or invention—of the techniques of measurement and analysis of the literature, clearly treat the subject matter of information science even if the subject itself is not covered. His work has given bibliometrics much of its method and purpose and also its standing as a serious scientific study. This is not to diminish the earlier work of Bradford, or, going further back, of Hulme or Fremont Rider.

Price built on the work of these earlier pioneers and placed it in a wider, more modern, and more urgent framework.

Immediately, several observations can be made about the context for the work and about the contribution the work made to information studies. First, Price gave a clear formulation to the idea of an "information explosion," and gave it in a form that demonstrated the dynamic character of the problem, and implicitly stated the need for a problem-solving profession of knowledge or document management. Second, he linked this information explosion to the similar growth in scientific manpower and expenditure, and thence to political structures and the role of scientific knowledge in society and the problems societies face when seeking to expand the quantity of knowledge they produce. In short, Price's context is the information society. In fact, Price's work was probably the first to define problems of knowledge output in terms with political implications.

Uniquely, Price also, it seems, both clarified a problem and produced the tools that might provide a solution. By linking literature output to manpower, or rather to the possible available manpower, and to historical evidence about the output of scientists, Price was able to suggest how large an increase in total manpower would be required to produce a stated increase in good scientists. In short, to double the number of good scientists, it might be necessary to increase the total by a factor of five. Such observations have similar (although not exactly the same) consequences for the literature. A problem for the management of a working scientist is how to ensure that the scientist reads only the best, and of that no more than will still allow time for his own work, of the available literature. Librarians do not make qualitative judgments about material on the shelves: The only qualitative assessment is made at the point of selection. The problem facing the librarian or information officer parallels that of the scientist—how to assess quality when only a moiety can be acquired.

Price provided answers that are social in character. He examined the social linkages between scientists, as shown by their citation practices and the development of invisible colleges (the international conference circuit). He claimed to be able to do this using unambiguous and quantifiable data, and to be able to present a set of observable regularities (or laws) about the behavior of science, scientists, and the literature. Others, notably Line (1981), have applied similar techniques to larger bodies of literature. Price, it could be said, was supplying the pure science for which the products and services of the applied science could be devised. Yet, strangely, Price's ability to conduct his studies owed much to the data already collected by Garfield and others through the use of an applied product—the ISI's science citation index. There is an interesting circularity in the close working of the theorist and the practitioner here that supports an interpretive reading of what actually happens in the progress of practice and theory.

What is the character of the data Price used? There is a close parallel between the hard facts of citation studies and the brute data of political science. Similarly, an interpretive approach is necessary in order to preserve meaning—or, to construct meaning. In giving information studies the technical armory of bibliometrics, Price provided tools that changed the conception of the job to be done. How close was this changed conception to the original conception of the field, and how much did the new conception change the character of the profession and the discipline? In other terms, can this new development be seen as maintaining the integrity of the field?

As political scientists will still use the brute data of voting figures or intentions, in the field of information studies brute data are employed, even when, overtly or surreptitiously, the real work is being done by a process of interpretation dependent on the use of intersubjective meanings. Indeed, this is very close to the central point of the interpretive position: the notion that brute data alone, in the social and human sciences, are grossly inadequate for the construction of any incontrovertible theory or knowledge. So, just as the act of raising one's hand or marking a name on a piece of paper does not objectively constitute anything, and must be placed in its cultural context, the data of bibliometrics are already culturally constructed data.

Price used many indices of scientific output, and manipulated these using some mathematical techniques. For example, he calculated growth rates of scientific manpower, and the saturation point of such manpower on the basis of the number of doctorates earned each year in the United States. (More strictly, he borrowed the work of Harmon and others.) These figures he correlated with intelligence test scores. Elsewhere he used statistics on the output of literature—per author, per field, per country, per century—and correlated these with the representation of authors in measures of social success like biographical dictionaries. Yet all these are of little significance without an understanding of what they mean. So scholarship and science cannot be merely counted, they have to be described in nonquantitative terms:

> Essentially, scholarship is a conspiracy to pool the capabilities of many men, and science is an even more radical conspiracy that structures this pooling so that the totality of this sort of knowledge can grow more rapidly than any individual can move by himself. The humanities, by resting with the capability of the individual,

eschew this growth rate and certainty. As we find ways of being certain through impersonality and mathematics, so the humanities are left with fewer of the problems. It is in this way that natural philosophy was transformed into science, and, in general, it is in this way that the different substantive contents have erected different social apparatuses of information pooling and exchange. (Price, 1986, pp. 159–160)

So, variations in citation practices are understood by reference to a statement about the generally understood nature or purpose of science and scholarship, rather than vice versa. If scholarship is not generally understood as a conspiracy, but the metaphor makes sense to those who wish to understand it, then it becomes a shared meaning. It is difficult to represent a conspiracy quantitatively, but such evidence of citation linkages that can be presented that both supports the technical practice of information work, and can also suggest conspiracy have that latter connotation not of themselves, objectively apparent to any observer, but because that idea and construction has been suggested. Conspiracy as a label explains the citation linkages and practices as much as it gives us understanding of the process of scholarship. Interpretation, therefore, plays a large part in developing any picture of the literature of science or scholarship. This is true not just at the global level of the whole field but also at the more microscopic level of the individual datum. As voters and constituencies are for politics, so references (citations) and individual works are for the study of literature. The brute datum of the journal article also requires nonquantitative explanation, as Price (1986) explained: "A scholarly publication is not a piece of information but an expression of the state of a scholar or group of scholars at a particular time. We do not, contrary to superstition, publish a fact, a theory, or a finding, but some complex of these" (p. 160). Price went on to explain that from papers we can learn—through citation linkages, about the working relations of people. Yet even this requires explicit interpretation beyond what the brute data can reveal: "My own sociological analyses indicate also that collaboration arises more from economic than from intellectual dependence . . . the amount of collaborative authorship measures no more than the economic value accorded to each field by society" (p. 160).

All these interpretations alone do not meet Taylor's criteria for an interpretive discipline. The point in relation to Price's work on citation as a measure of science is that the expression does vary according to the manner of the interpretation. Citation studies are of interest to the historian or sociologist of science, and to the librarian, albeit in markedly different ways. Price made clear that his index (the proportion of articles cited that were published in the last 5 years) should have direct application to information services, and we can construct the kind of sense of bibliometric data that someone building an information service would have.

It is in this special sense that there is a bibliometric interpretation of the library and information field. The particular expression of meaning that arises from the bibliometric orientation is obviously very different from that in the case of bibliography. Even the reinterpreted bibliographic perspective of McKenzie looked for completeness of collection, whereas the bibliometric interpretation has a focus on the needs of particular users, and although of obvious application in collection building, it is more precisely aimed at developing criteria that will improve selection criteria and processes so that information services will acquire the most significant material. Collection building becomes predicated on the behavior or anticipated behavior of the user, rather than on the intrinsic merit of published works in themselves.

Citation studies and other studies of the size of literatures that ignore their substantive content and concentrate on the characteristics of the form find quantitative expression and mathematical manipulation convenient tools, yet these are insufficient to convey the meaning of even the changing form of material. Price rightly linked all his quantitative observations to other analyses that provide a context for meaning and indeed the meaning itself: The quantitative studies merely provide an accessory to the analysis. However, in being used they also change the profession's perception of practice—they take us through one phase of interpretation to another. A library faced with the economic impossibility of collecting all material, and possibly realizing that such a course could be considered undesirable on other grounds, might seek to use its purchasing power to acquire the largest possible percentage of significant literature, and seek also to utilize shelf space to store only the most useful material. Scientometric or bibliometric studies (which include studies of invisible colleges) would provide an answer that would change the perception, among information practitioners, of the literature. Substantive content would be perceived through traceable linkages in the literature, the professional behavior of scientists would reveal the current state of the literature in any field and the current state of the subject, and the technical task of the practitioner would be restated along appropriate lines. As in Dworkin's constructive interpretation, Price moved us away from the intention of those generating or producing the material—the authors, publishers, and booksellers who want us to buy what is produced because it is there—to some constructive intention of the participants in the practice.

The bibliometric argument is based on social data—the raw material is the actions of human subjects, and is dependent on external frameworks of explanation, which may vary according to the perspective of the perceiving subject. It is therefore correct to present this as a social science, and to suggest an interpretive approach as more profitable than the administration of quantitative laws. The literature on Bradford's law is extensive: More important probably than an exact formulation (which few will know how to apply) was the original idea that changed professional understanding and theorizing about the raw material, the literature.

The bibliometric interpretation is powerful, but it is incomplete. The changed complexion of selection also demands an attention to the processes of retrieval, which also incidentally supply the means to conduct the large-scale bibliometric analyses on which much of the bibliometric case depends. Although incomplete, the picture of information science that bibliometrics helps to build has shifted the interpretation substantially from an older position. The particular kinds of judgment that Price's work helped to develop added to the armory of the practicing information professional ways of understanding the character of information and its use by its generators and users. These in turn helped to transform professional objectives and practices in collection building and in the development of information services such as the ISI's, and offered an understanding of the information explosion and a way of coping with it. Price's work in bibliometrics added to information science's claims to be a successful conception of the library and information field.

INFORMATION RETRIEVAL (IR)

Experimental information retrieval has successfully established itself as hard scientific study in the field. Many of the researchers work outside university departments of information studies, and few people employed in libraries participate in this type of research. They may never see its results, which may only appear in information services and products many years after the research work, and even then only in an invisible form. This area of information science, like bibliometrics, seems to defy the requirement that, for interpretation, the field be seen as a social and not as a natural science. This position, too, can be turned. Shera (1971) put information retrieval in a necessary perspective: "what we have failed to perceive is that information retrieval is a child of Information Science, not an independent discipline in its own right, and that Information Science itself is an aspect of the communication process and communication is a social phenomenon" (p. 77).

In this section, two forms of research in automated information retrieval are considered. They are shown to represent stages as IR research develops and progresses to offer more complete definition of information science and to contribute substantially to an information-science-based conception of practice in the library and information field. The existence of two models of information retrieval demands that our picture of the development of conceptions be elaborated. In cases examined so far, we have seen that something can be considered as a conception of information studies, even where there is also clear evidence for the case to be considered as a conception of something else as well, or as a separate discipline. Beyond the situation of a simple conception, there are two other possibilities. First there is the case where some body of theory or practice, although showing something in common with the early patterns of development of other conceptions, never actually attains the status of a conception. This failure could be because of simple inability to supersede a prior conception, or failure to offer a sufficiently broad conception to cover the field, or by being overtaken by another more virile conception before actually realizing its own potential. Failure could also be represented in terms of Hubbard's six strategies for measuring a rereading of architecture. Second, there is the case of the false conception.

The idea of the false conception requires some explication. The argument with respect to information retrieval is that what has been the mainstream of automated information retrieval until recently is for many practitioners an inaccessible area of professional activity. As such, it cannot contribute toward the construction of any conception of the practice, and so does not assist in the construction of an interpretation of information studies as information science, and would have remained a false conception for the field. The change in the character of IR research has increased the power of information science and its appeal as a conception of the field. Since the mid-1980s, there has been a changed emphasis within the field of information retrieval, switching some attention from logic and computation to more humanistic and sociological issues centered around questions about the nature of any interaction between human subjects and information systems. This latter, a far broader universe of inquiry than the older focus on collections of document surrogates and the means of interrogating them, individually and collectively, is a basis for constructing a legitimate conception of the field of library and information studies.

In adopting this division, I am fitting in with but not following Ingwersen's (1992) tripartite categorization of IR research. My schema conflates his final two stages, the last of which integrates previous stages. He divided the field into "the system components and processes (the *traditional* approach . . .); the human participants and their information requirements (the *user-oriented* approach . . .); the integration of all the interaction processes taking place in IR (the *cognitive* approach . . .)" (p. ix). Three benefits flow from categorizing IR research like this. First, the power and range of the interpretive account are extended by expanding the available language of interpretation. Second, insight is gained into the character of conceptions as dynamic ideas, and of their relationship to the original concept. Third, the descriptive language of what librarians do can be enhanced by adding to it a description of the impact on practice of a false conception.

One other question about false conceptions demands attention. Bibliography was discussed as a conception that had been superseded and might now be attempting a comeback. Would it not be legitimate to consider bibliography as becoming a false conception as it faded from central relevance to the field? The answer is no, because bibliography became superseded because of its diminished relevance to the field when it had failed to change. Information retrieval can be shown to have undergone a change in emphasis that, for the field of information studies, transformed its plausibility as a basis for a conception of the field.

Information Retrieval As Computer Science

My argument here is that this type of research work, although attractive to part of the library and information research community, remained unsuccessful as a conception of practice. To see why it can be considered in this light we can look at two works by Salton, and review some of the earlier discussion about the relationship between library science and information science. It becomes clear that for most practitioners this kind of computer-science-based information retrieval, although highly relevant, remained arcane and intellectually inaccessible. As such, it could never truly inform practice, even though it became incorporated into the systems practitioners used. Thus it failed as an interpretation because the cycle of interpretation advancing understanding, as the interpretation sways from theory to practice, cannot be completed. This view might be contested by those in the chemical information business, for whom this kind of information retrieval forms an essential part of practice, and for them and those like them the power of information science as information retrieval will have been longer established. Although this work had an obvious appeal to a purely information science community, it would not have been able to generate enough shared meanings shared among a wide enough body of people to count as, or as assisting toward the construction of, a conception of the broad field of information studies.

This point can be illustrated by reference to a few key publications (Jones, 1981; Salton, 1985; Salton & McGill, 1983). Salton and McGill's (1983) standard introductory work on information retrieval is written for both computer science and library science and information science students. They claimed that "a direct link exists between information retrieval and computer science. On the other hand, information retrieval also takes on aspects of behavioural science, since retrieval systems are designed to aid human activities" (pp. xi–xii). The authors made no attempt to cover the behavioral science aspects, even though they claimed that:

> [The book] covers the basic aspects of information retrieval theory and practice, and also relates the various techniques to the design and evaluation of complete retrieval systems. . . . The text concentrates in particular on the description of the concepts, functions and processes of interest in retrieval rather than on the detailed operation of any one existing retrieval system.
>
> The text should thus be accessible to students with only a cursory knowledge of the operations of digital computers and only a superficial exposure to computer programming. (p. xii)

The collection edited by Jones (1981), in which only one of the contributions (Belkin, on ineffable concepts in information retrieval) eschews empirical study, shows a similar concentration, with more emphasis on experimental work in the field. Jones summarized the work record of experimental information retrieval thus:

> Unfortunately, though many retrieval experiments and investigations have been carried out in the last twenty years, much of the experience in the conduct of tests which has been gained is not very accessible. Published papers tend to be cleaned up accounts of objectives, general methods, and results. Project reports may be much fuller, but even here it is often extremely difficult to find out exactly what was done, or why it was done. Though an improvement in the quality of experiments is detectable, far too many of those reported are defective, and in many cases defective in recognized ways, for which remedies are available. As all but the most limited test is a major enterprise, it is a pity that so much effort

should be wasted. The best that can be said about many reported studies is that even if they are individually dubious they may collectively point in the same direction. This is perhaps something, but it is not much. (p. 3)

So there was a scientific enterprise that barely conformed to the scientific image of carefully controlled cumulative research, expressed in a language that most practitioners in the field could not readily comprehend, dedicated to the solution of problems those same practitioners would rarely encounter directly. This does not offer a good prospect for an interpretive account, for it does not have a meaning for the group of subjects outside the research community in IR. It cannot therefore fit into a cycle of preinterpretation, interpretation, and postinterpretation (except for a very limited sector of the profession). It is difficult to speak of the subject matter of experimental information retrieval as a field of objects that have some coherence without reference to the broader world of documentation or information, for which information retrieval cannot act as an interpretation because its concern is too narrow.

What then can be said about experimental IR? Salton (1985) responded to the precise criticism raised in a previous issue by Keren that "only very rarely does useful and nontrivial information emanate from the published research" (p. 268). Salton's response concurred with criticism that much IR work was not worth doing and ought to be forgotten, but claimed that there is work that offers "interesting perspectives to researchers and practitioners alike" (p. 269) and that lies in the area of "text analysis, storage and retrieval." There can be no question that research in this area is of interest to practitioners in library and information studies. What is not clear, however, is that the topics Salton discussed are actually meaningful to those practitioners. Salton picked 10 areas:

- Vector processing
- Probabilistic retrieval
- Inverted file procedures
- Relevance feedback
- Boolean query formulations/fuzzy sets
- Front-end procedures/expert systems
- Citation network
- Text passage retrieval
- Linguistic analysis.
- Character matching (simulation methods/mixed search and retrieval systems)

Salton (1985) concluded that "All the forgoing research areas are directly relevant to information retrieval practice in that they point the way to the construction of flexible, interactive retrieval systems which should substantially simplify the collection search and retrieval processes for future generations of information seekers" (p. 270). This may be true, but two crucial factors separate this from the conception of information studies found in bibliography. First, as has been stated, the relevance is limited, and cannot be generalized across the field. IR research is best seen as technical, relating more directly to the technology than to the substantive issues facing the profession. This may seem a contradiction of the analysis of the information culture, but although there is a technological dimension to the information culture, its ultimate orientation, although conditioned by the potential of technology, is still toward society, social questions, and social interaction. This makes information retrieval markedly different from bibliography as a conception, in a way that can best be expressed by describing bibliography as a craft, with direct application to the materials a librarian would handle, whereas information retrieval is more indirect with less obvious application to the physical or social attributes of materials.

Second, the research is separated, in time, from practice. There has to be an intervening phase of technological development before practitioners encounter the fruits of research, and what they must encounter is the characteristics of a particular commercial product, rather than direct application of the research literature, and this further divorces the research from the practice, and makes interpretation more difficult.

There is another approach to information retrieval that has become necessary as expert systems have become real possibilities in information work. Designing expert systems has forced attention to focus more on intellectual than technical issues, and has therefore refocused some research attention on more cognitive rather than computer science.

Information Retrieval as Cognitive Science

This alternative, or developed image of information retrieval, has been developing alongside the more technical model discussed earlier, and the technical work continues to be critically important. The difference is in the attention being given to human information activities, and the way these can be modeled, particularly in reference to conversation or dialogue analysis and human–computer interaction.

Croft (1987) described the state of IR in terms that confirm the views of Salton and Sparck Jones, and indicates why this second model of IR is potentially more successful and more realistically considered as a conception of the field:

> It has been thirty years since H.P. Luhn suggested using statistical information for the identification of content-bearing portions of document texts. There have been many advances in the field of information retrieval (IR) since that time, but some fundamental issues remain unsolved. To put it simply, we do not know the best way of representing the content of text documents and the users' information needs so that they can be compared and the relevant documents retrieved. We cannot even agree on a definition of relevance. Statistical approaches to the analysis of text and retrieval of documents have significant advantages in terms of efficiency and performance relative to other techniques, but one need only look at the absolute performance levels measured in terms of recall and precision to see their limitations. Dissatisfaction with the current state of affairs is one of the two major factors in the recent upsurge of interest in intelligent IR. The other factor is the increasing awareness of the importance of IR as an application area, brought about by the proliferation of systems that handle text and multimedia documents.
>   Intelligent IR . . . deals with the overlap of research in artificial intelligence (AI) and IR. The projects in this area generally fall into two categories: (1) basic research in such areas of AI as natural language processing, knowledge representation, and reasoning that use IR as an application and (2) research that concentrates on the development of systems that blend traditional IR techniques and techniques developed in AI research. Both approaches contribute to the goal of building significantly more effective systems. (p. 249)

Croft, writing as a computer scientist and designer of an expert system, emphasized the technical aspect of this changed model of IR. He identified the key new element as the marriage with work in artificial intelligence. For the library and information field, the significance lies not merely in the development of more effective systems, but also in the shift in research emphasis away from purely technical concerns to a broader interest in the whole information-seeking and using process.

The availability of more effective systems will itself be a significant instrument in the reconceptualization of the library and information field. A more powerful tool, which may well become widely diffused in a way that research is not, will rapidly reorient the profession in its practice, and will lead to redefinition of what that practice can and should attain.

A critical feature of AI-oriented IR is its interactive nature. This means that the user is much more closely involved in the working of the technology, and indeed enters into a dialogue with it. This in turn means that the practitioner has a closer interest in formulating the expertise and contributing to the understanding of dialogue or conversation analysis with which a system is loaded. Practitioners in the field are much more able to contribute to such debates than they are to the IR technical processes. Belkin and Vickery (1985) summarized this position:

> In recent years research in information retrieval has begun to experience a shift in emphasis from the study of document or text representation and associated search techniques, to study of the users of IR systems, characteristics of the questions of problems they bring to them, and interactions of users with intermediaries and with other aspects of the IR mechanism, including evaluation of its success. In general one might characterize this shift as an explicit recognition of the integrated nature of the information system as a whole, and especially of the importance of understanding and dealing with the entire information search process, even if emphasis in any study is to be placed on only one aspect. This shift has lagged behind, but is roughly coincident with, the increasing importance of interactive systems for IR, which we feel have been a major impetus to this wider understanding of IR. (p. 1)

This more developed interactive or intelligent IR is potentially a good basis for constructing a successful conception of the field. How it can contribute to the development of an interpretation of the library and information field is shown next by considering it within the broad context of information science.

INFORMATION SCIENCE: CONCLUSION

The point is not that information science is comprehensible only from an interpretive position, but to suggest that such an approach is possible, legitimate, and potentially profitable. The examination of the IIS criteria and the AI/IR research from such a standpoint does show that it would be legitimate to form a conception of the field based on an idea of information science that capitalized on that later form of information retrieval. Such a conception would make the field more intelligible, especially to those coming from the broader and less technological traditions of information studies. It would also inform that broad tradition with the idea of an information culture, as discussed in Chapter 4, which would make the layout of the world view of information science in the IIS criteria more accessible and comprehensible to the generality of library and information practitioners.

One final interpretive observation will draw a closer tie between AI-based IR research work and the practicing professional. Within expert systems, there has been a development toward explanation-based learning programming, which is based on the observation that the most complex professional learning is done in an apprenticeship situation—watching the experts at work—rather like hospital interns or indeed the kind of pre- and postcourse experience currently required by the United Kingdom Library Association for professional recognition. The point here is that knowing the rules, in chess for example, is not sufficient to guide chess play or work performance. Successful chess play is based on an understanding of more general and abstract principles, which in a profession can only come from learning the set of shared meanings, and contributing to their development, which contact with practitioners alone can give. As expert IR systems come to include such learning processes so they will more closely match the normal world of retrieving knowledge and will more closely fit into the interpretive picture.

So, it is possible to consider these hard aspects of information science in the same way as other aspects of the broad field of library and information studies. There is no conclusive evidence that either bibliometrics or information retrieval lie outside the range of activities that can be considered by the interpretive approach. It is quite legitimate to proceed, as Brookes suggested, as if information science lies within the social sciences, at least for the purposes of this study.

Interpreting Information Science

In Chapter 7, I outlined a picture where there are several levels of theory in operation, and parallel theoretical processes. I suggested that participants theorize simultaneously about their practice and about their own self-identity, as they engage in dialogue and discourse that they eventually help to define, and through which they subscribe to a view of what the practice is, what they are doing. This discourse may lead them to develop a new view of what the practice is (what they are doing), a new conception. All this takes place, currently, within a context of meaning called the information culture.

A number of test questions were identified that might be asked of any practice. How does the conception relate to this context of meaning?

How does it relate to other conceptions? How does it relate to the self-esteem and self-identity of the practitioner? How does this interpretation of what the field is, this conception, relate to the central techniques of the field? What does it offer for the development of the field? Is it progressive, does it maintain the narrative unity of the subject, maybe by picking up some point and making it more salient?

Quite clearly, information science predates any ideas about information culture, but equally clearly there is in the work of Price an explicit attempt to offer a systematic view of how the information explosion has affected the task of librarians or information managers (to cease collecting everything, and to collect the moiety of literature relevant to good science), and the review of automated information retrieval revealed a view, expressed variously, about the way information technology was to affect the processes of information retrieval. Earlier in this work Vickery and Vickery's (1987) preface was cited, where they explicitly linked their work to an information society. For them at least, information science has become "a scientific understanding of the process of information transfer" and seems to have very close links with, and could be said to derive some authority from the needs of, the information society.

In respect to other conceptions, there is in the development of information science, expressed in some of the definitions cited earlier in this chapter, a move to a more generalized concern for information than had been expressed earlier by those concentrating on the traditional concerns of libraries. This has been accomplished in part by the expansion of the range of information science and a consequent increase in its knowledge claims. There has been a widening of disciplinary and professional horizons. Information science has sustained some of the narrative unity that Dworkin's view of interpretation demands, but has emphasized different aspects of the task, making some concerns more peripheral, some others more central. It is still using the same techniques, although it has taken many in hand and may not give them all the same emphasis. Collection building is something the work of de Solla Price has subjected to a sea change: Cataloging has also experienced pressures, and in some accounts now becomes knowledge representation, or developing document surrogates. The practice of information science has effected these changes, altered the working vocabulary, the dialogue, and the discourse, and in so doing has expanded the range of possibilities open to the practitioner. These developments collectively offer us several of the strategic tests of rereading taken from Hubbard and Bloom. The practice is offering some possibility of progress, some opportunity for development of the field. In presenting the practitioner with more urgently relevant tasks, more technologically immediate solutions, and more scientifically respectable methods, the practice is also upholding the self-esteem of its practitioners, allowing a significant subset of them to maintain a self-identity that earlier library-based conceptions, or even McKenzie's bibliography might not. In that sense, to be doing information science is to have a conception of what it is, and is recognizably an interpretation of library and information studies.

10
Information Management

The final conception to be considered is information management, an example of a conception in the earlier stages of growth. The treatment is illustrative rather than critical, and information management will not be given the extensive attention accorded to bibliography or information science. It is included here as an indicator of the richness of alternative conceptions available in the field. The profusion of conceptions, if viewed as such within the interpretive tradition, is a sign of disciplinary and professional strength, flexibility, and responsiveness rather than weakness and uncertainty. Once seen within the interpretive tradition that accommodates pluralist expression, this further variation or conception can be seen as extending the range of the field rather than prejudicing its integrity.

INTRODUCTION

> IRM is an integrated management technique. Deriving mostly from data processing, it has increasingly encompassed management and information areas as well. Further growth of IRM should draw on professional expertise in the information studies disciplines by bringing information professionals into the IRM area. Conversely, IRM may provide the most promising frontier for expansion of information studies. (Lytle, 1986, p. 327)

Lytle's bibliography includes 130 items, to which can be added the 202 included in the 1982 bibliography of Levitan (1982), and countless more since. Information management, or information resources management, had by the 1980s, established itself as the coming model for the information disciplines. Within the library and information field its influence has already been widely felt, with hortatory messages, changes in names of professional bodies and educational programs and institutions, and even some indication of changes in practice among some professionals. It is clear that information resource management (IRM) has a serious claim to be treated as a conception of the field, at least in the minds of its innovators. What kind of conception is it? Information management is at present on the way up. How far it is allowed to go may depend on the pace of change in the library and information field and the degree of conservatism of its practitioners. It is a burgeoning conception, and it is a good example of a conception whose current appeal is closer to being a potential model, rather than an actual practice, than any other available.

Definitions

Information resource management can be understood within a century-long process of development for information management strategies and techniques. It can also be tied quite specifically to the increase in the information flow within large bureaucracies, in particular the U.S. federal bureaucracy. Lytle (1980) claimed that:

> IRM is fundamentally a management activity. It is applied to organizations, not to individual, national, and international levels of society. It is concerned with information assets, or the content of information, as well as with information resources, or the equipment, supplies, and people through which an organization handles its information. (p. 310)

This emphasis on the content of information is intellectually challenging for the library and information profession. It places IRM close to the more traditional area of reference and information work, and switches emphasis from service to entrepreneurial considerations. In these respects, IRM as a concept contradicts much of the traditional philosophy of the library and information profession, and its acceptance as a conception of the field would indicate an inversion of some historic values. A construction can be put on this development that maintains the integrity of the field while opening to the information practitioner more areas for the employment of his or her expertise. Interestingly, this development comes from an allegedly theory-free examination of information practice in large bureaucracies, and as such can be seen as a prime example of practice informing theory, as the interpretive case proposed by Dworkin and Taylor demands.

Like both bibliography and information science, information management is not a home grown development from within information studies. It is a separate development, threatening to develop a separate profession, which the library and information field has grasped in the hope of making it its own. Some of the problems that surfaced in the treatment of the other conceptions recur here, in particular the problem of accepting as a conception a practice that has an independent existence. The arguments that can be employed are intrinsically the same in this case, although there are two distinctive factors that distinguish information management. First, the renaming exercises among the library and information institutions are obviously a bold attempt to capture the whole information management business as the legitimate business of the library and information field. This view might be challenged by those who would argue that the process is not one of capture but of transformation, whereby the older discipline and profession is seeking a new identity and is sloughing off its old persona, rather than merely being hospitable to the new development. Second, information management is itself a field whose definition is unsettled. There is a broad field called information management that has some subsidiary elements, including IRM. Whether the information studies interest is with the whole or the part is unclear. A loose definition of information management that accommodates at any time any or all of the material that is relevant suits my purposes best. This approach seems easiest because some of the literature treats IRM as incorporating information management—being in fact the highest stage of that older topic. This view conveniently suggests an implicit acceptance of a development of information management through various stages of interpretation, IRM being the current stage. The earlier stages were periods dominated first by the management of paperwork and paperwork-based systems, and latterly the addition of the management of the information technologies that emerged in the 1960s and 1970s. The third (IRM) stage, according to Lytle (1986):

> addresses a major organizational concern: applying information resources to achieve strategic objectives. It uses as a primary means to this end the integrated management of information technologies ... further stages of information management progressively integrate information into the business of the organization. (p. 311)

This development would herald a major change in the character of the library and information field if it were ever to grasp a monopolistic position as the only conception of that field. I have argued that an advantage of the interpretive approach is to allow simultaneous variant conceptions, and that hitherto no single conception has ever established such a monopoly within the field: It seems historically unlikely that such a situation would arise, and epistemologically irrelevant if it did. Even where there has been a period of consistent interpretation in, say, law, there has always been a subsequent change that has forced a change in the dominant conception. Indeed, this is a key component of the interpretive case as advanced by Dworkin, that interpretation moves, and conceptions change, as preinterpretations are confronted by the reality of practice, which in turn forces the change to the interpretive stage, and thus again on to the mature interpretive position.

The critical questions relate therefore not to whether information management will undermine the interpretive case by taking over the library and information field, but whether such a development can be considered consistent with the already established character of that field. That is to say, using Dworkin's vocabulary, is the integrity of the field maintained? If it is not, then information management is not a legitimate conception of it. If it is, and can be regarded as simply another face of the field, then there are no difficulties.

Unfortunately, the information management spectrum forces us to confront some very basic problems in relation to the library and information field. These can be encapsulated in the business orientation of information management. The older appeal of firstly librarianship and latterly information studies, through bibliography and through information science, to some academic foundation and claim to existence as an academic discipline is severely shaken by this new business orientation. In professional education, too, several university departments of information studies or information science have begun to link their courses to business studies programs and some departments are formally gathered into faculties of business studies, underlining the importance of management and business considerations for the library and information field. There is in information management little appeal to any firm epistemology or claim for an academic base. Such use as there is of academic disciplines is limited to more practical and professional fields like management or the more practical side of information technology. Sutherland (1991) was unapologetically explicit about this lack of theory:

> Information management is about the application of practical arts and sciences, involving pragmatism and coping with very rapid change; it is a long way from any theory.
> Information management is weak on hypotheses and theories. The speed of past and impending decisions makes it unattractive, if not impossible, to wait for an opinion to be formulated as an hypothesis, tested and turned into a theory. It is more pragmatic to do something, before circumstances change out of all recognition. (p. 101)

The second problem is more directly concerned with the values of information management. Within the information professions it has been a key article of faith for many practitioners that information should be free and freely available to all and, by extension, accessible to all. Although the practice of commercial online information systems has dented this principle and it carries less weight in company information units, it has survived largely intact in much of professional practice. Information management is founded in part on a directly contradictory principle, one that maintains that "the organization can no longer afford to treat data and information as a free good" (Horton, 1982, p. 47). The information profession would have to desire to turn its face away from an academic orientation and toward a business profile if it were to adopt wholesale the principles and tenets of information management. This statement, and the conflicting situations already mentioned, suggest that the two fields are at present some distance apart. This may be true, but it is not fair to the information management/IRM field to suggest that the provision of free information to the public is in that view to be dropped. Horton (1985) stated quite explicitly that he was discussing information management within organizations, and that "while information in some contexts can and should be viewed as an economic (private) product, yet in still other (sociopolitical) contexts it must also be viewed as a human right (public good)" (p. 31). It is worth quoting Horton at length on this point, which is quite critical for the values of information professionals. He continued:

> For example, in a democracy can a government afford to take the posture that all of the information it produces in order to keep citizens informed must be sold at a fully competitive market price, knowing that the economically disadvantaged will not be able to afford it? Hardly. Both legal and common sense arguments can be made against taking such a position where information carries a dual role. There is a tension, then, between looking at information in an economic commodity sense and looking at information as a human right. A government's relationship with its citizens in a democracy is a case in point where information carries a dual role. Totalitarian states obviously fare much better in this regard. (p. 31)

Unfortunately, the action of some governments in cutting back substantially on what information they provide in regular published form seems to suggest that only the new, economic arguments advanced by IRM about information have caught on and that the caveats about democracy and personal information may have been ignored. This would induce caution among library and information practitioners in accepting the values of information management, despite Horton's explicit recognition of the need for freely accessible information. Horton's remarks also suggest that there may be two different kinds of information practice—an observation that is comfortably accommodated within an interpretive framework but poses difficulties for any monopolistic claims within the library and information field for information management. The sense of caution is reinforced by the relative absence from the literature (until the late 1980s) of library and information studies of seminal literature on information management (IM) or IRM. There was some publication in this area, but mostly it described the application of IM/IRM to the library and information field. We know that the term information management does occur with increasing frequency in the literature of the last few years.[1]

This is evidence of interest and the character of the library and information literature may be to introduce the idea and characteristics of IM/IRM to the field so that the most appropriate form of IRM be developed for the library or information practitioner. In this case, there is no difference from the situation in both bibliography and information science, where entirely legitimate conceptions of library and information studies were in existence alongside separate disciplines, with their own professionals, in both cases.

Such a situation, being almost the norm for the library and information field, may therefore be accepted as unremarkable, and attention should focus on what makes information management an attractive conception for the field, and on what IM/IRM is.

THE FOCUS OF INFORMATION MANAGEMENT

Information management is in principle firmly rooted in the arguments developed in the United States for the idea of the information society. Machlup, Bell, and Porat are cited as key figures in the portrayal of the information management worldview. In this, the library and information field must find the relationship comfortable, and the prospect of a closer integration of our field into a general structure of information disciplines very encouraging. Lytle (1986) found that information management has focused on six critical areas:

1. Managing the content of information or information assets.
2. Managing information as an integral part of the organization's strategic planning.
3. Managing information through information policies.

---

[1] See also Beatty (1982), Cronin (1985), Estabrook (1986), Herring (1991), Lane (1985), Roberts and Wilson (1987), Trauth (1988), and Wilson (1989).

4. Measuring the cost and value of information in order to manage it.
5. Managing the impact of information on organizations.
6. Managing the converging information technologies of data processing, telecommunications, and office automation.

Herring (1991) provided a more recent list with a British and work-related orientation, listing key responsibilities of information managers in healthcare. Information managers will:

1. Develop and implement strategies to provide the information required to support the achievement of the business objectives.
2. Identify the systems required to meet these information requirements and determine the priorities for their introduction.
3. Specify in detail these systems and to coordinate their development or procurement and implementation.
4. Organize and manage the operational support required to maintain these information systems.
5. Provide and manage an information reporting and analysis service to support clinicians, operational managers and general managers.
6. Organize appropriate training and development for nonspecialist managers and health professionals in the field of information and computing.

Herring added to this nine appropriate skills required of an information manager:

1. Business analysis
2. Systems analysis and design
3. Networks and communications
4. Specific operational computing
5. Information analysis
6. Data management
7. Project management
8. Presentation, training, and human interaction
9. Data and information sources awareness

Herring's list gives greater emphasis to technical skills, closely related to management and technology. The best comprehensive treatments of IRM are by Horton (1985) and Horton and Marchand (1982). Horton (1985) provided a basic text for IM/IRM.

The great promotion for information management came with the U.S. government's Paperwork Reduction Act of 1980 and subsequent legislation. This legislation concentrated on the information problems of a large bureaucracy, and the subsequent thrust of information management has been to treat information as a real economic good and to concentrate on getting the right information to the person who needs it, without excessive cost and without drowning information users in mountains of irrelevant material. Horton (1985) identified seven basic concepts and principles (they are really more like precepts and axioms, but I have accepted his terminology):

1. Information is a critical organization resource.
2. Users of information must be held accountable for effective and efficient management of information.
3. Information resource needs must be integrally linked with the fundamental organizational management processes such as strategic planning and management control.
4. Information technologies must be integrated.
5. Information is a resource that has a life cycle.
6. Shift attention from technology to information content.
7. Using information to rethink the company's business.

To his list, Horton (1985) appended five other key concepts, which give a further insight into the worldview of information management. First, information is owned and used by and for the organization, and the senior information official is "entrusted in a stewardship role for the efficient, effective, and economic procurement, development (i.e. as in an information system), enhancement, operation, and disposition of the organization's information assets and information resources" (p. 23). There is here a correspondence in part with what librarians and information scientists do with information resources (acquisition, collection development, circulation), but the focus is rather different, as Horton went on to make plain when covering the "rights and obligations of the information handler; for example a library or computer center within an organization. Sometimes information handlers are given the job of systems managers or operating managers. That is, they act as intermediaries between the end-user and information suppliers" (p. 23). Here Horton made plain that the traditional library role is only one aspect of information management, but that in some circumstances (as the information community is apparently keen to exploit) they may take on a larger information management role. Is there any conflict between that role and the traditional professionally ascribed role of the librarian or information professional?[2]

---

[2] See on this point Estabrook (1986) and Ellis (1986).

Second, Horton differentiated between data, documents, and literature. He observed that "in short, we are witness to the decomposition of literature down to the data element level as our knowledge creation and diffusion machinery becomes increasingly machine-assisted" (p. 25). This point is one independent of any theory or principles of information management, and is really just a comment on the changing character of information life as advanced information technologies become easier and cheaper to use compared with traditional paperwork. This point applies equally to the library and information work environment, and is a powerful incentive to regard the two fields as concerned with the same problems. He observed that data, documents, and literature are tending to converge and that as more and more information is being captured automatically, within structured programs, intermediate stages like the creation of documents are beginning to disappear. If this is connected with the increasing facilities for nontraditional publishing (the creation of grey literature that removes literature from the realm of the traditional library, be it formal library or information center), then the more traditional library or information professional is obviously under pressure to adapt to the changed circumstances. This point makes the appeal of information management as a conception of library and information work stronger, as the conditions of practice enforce a re-examination of the meanings shared among the practicing professionals.

Third, Horton referred to the information environment as a key concept. He used the term *information environment* in a specific sense, meaning the information component of an enterprise. He tied this to two related terms, *information infrastructure* and *information architecture*, the former referring to all the information components (hardware, software, data, other resources) and the way they are linked, the latter referring to the design of the total information system of an organization, including all databases and other information facilities and the way the blueprint for the organization's information system structures the building blocks of the total system. Information architecture is then "a global depiction of information flow that supports the organization's essential functions" (Lytle, 1986, p. 315).

This notion must seem strange to the library and information field, but it is a good example of what IM/IRM offers to that field as an increment to the normal practice. What is seen in bibliography and in information science is a preoccupation with the document, either as a physical entity or for its intellectual content or characteristics. IRM does not threaten or reject this, it merely shifts emphasis away from a document- or content-centered world to one of concern for goals and the means necessary for their attainment—an example of swerving in the language of Hubbard. To that end, it also provides some discipline that has hitherto not been a normal part of library and information practice. In this respect, the ideas of information infrastructure and architecture are an increment to the armory of the information professional, wholly consistent with original purposes, to the basic field.

In accepting information as a critical resource, Horton was also accepting the broad arguments about the information society, as advanced by Bell, where information and/or knowledge are regarded as the key wealth-creating resources. This point is one that is also promoted by the professional bodies in the library and information field. In that field, too, the view of Horton that attention should be shifted from the technology to the content is also well established. In some of the other basic concepts, Horton propounded views that are held in a slightly different way within the library and information field. For example, in proposing that users of information be held accountable for effective and efficient management of information, he presented a principle that would be anathema to the shared values of practicing librarians and ordinary users. However, effectively, library selection and collection development policies are devised precisely to that end: All that has changed is the emphasis.

THE INTERPRETATION

Having reviewed some of the correspondence between the best known view of information management and the library and information field, how can it be said that the former is a conception of the latter? Mere correspondence in stance is not enough, and it is plain that accepting IRM would require a reorientation and the acceptance of some novel principles, or at least the application of familiar principles in a novel way.

How would a possible reinterpretation of the field of library and information studies take place? Would IRM offer an acceptable development? We should expect to find some integrity with the original purpose of library and information work and study, and there should be signs of shared meanings being established or being changed to accommodate these new ideas. In other words, is it plausible to suggest that the library and information profession believes it is in the business of information management? Do librarians believe that this is what they are doing?

The Professional Reaction

Lewis (1985) offered a view of how thinking in a key professional organization in library and information work developed the argument for change toward information management. Lewis explained how:

The most significant development, at least from the vantage point of the LIR community, has been the way the new technologies have liberalized access to information by bringing the end-user and information provider into direct (non-mediated) contact. Information is no longer the sole responsibility of librarians and information officers; nor is it only to be found in libraries or information units. Information is pervasive, and information processors no less so.

It was in direct response to challenges of this kind that Aslib, which previously concerned itself exclusively with the problems of special libraries and information units, changed its name to the Association for Information Management. This change is certainly not cosmetic; it constitutes a statement of intent and indicates an awareness of the rapidly-changing nature of the information environment. (p. 17)

Other bodies are also considering name changes, although none have yet made the change. In the United Kingdom, the Institute of Information Scientists has deferred for the moment any decision on a name change (partly because it has taken so long to get information scientist established), but Institute of Information Managers was a well-favored possible change when views were canvassed in 1991. Farkas-Conn (1990) also revealed that the ASIS was not entirely happy with its name, as many members felt their work to be closer to information engineering (managing and planning systems) than science. Although the change of name of a major professional body implies a wide degree of acceptance, or at least acquiescence, it is still clear from Lewis' comments that the change is a signal of what is to come rather than a recognition of what has happened. The change in the last 10 years has been slower than Lewis and others would have wished or expected. Lewis (1985) felt obliged to plead the case for change in attitude among professional librarians and information scientists, and to educate his reader about the need for an increased emphasis on the management function:

There is a nascent awareness of the importance of effective, integrated, corporate information management in organizations, and it is here that the LIR profession has a distinct contribution to make—as *managers* of this resource. There is, I believe, an urgent need for the profession to develop an altered self-perception: to discontinue the idea of putting ourselves into hermetically-sealed boxes labelled "librarian," "information scientist," etc., and to view ourselves as *bona fide* managers—of the information resource. There is a need to broaden the boundaries of our action and our thinking, and in order to do this we must be prepared to offer our unique skills in such a way as to impress on senior management that we, too, are mangers. (p. 14)

This statement from the former director of Aslib, a senior professional at the center of developments, is revealing, both of the way in which leaders in the profession envisaged the future and of the extent to which shared meanings along the new lines have not yet emerged in the way an interpretive argument requires them to do. Yet there is other evidence that the currently shared meanings of what library and information work is or is concerned with can be rephrased to suggest a strong continuity with the current interpretation. Cronin (1985) argued for:

> the importance of developing improved strategies for the effective management of information. It is not enough to develop new, more sophisticated, higher-performance information-handling systems. Technology *per se* is not the answer . . . There is a need to understand how individuals (lay and professional) use information, and how their information seeking and utilization behaviours could be better supported by "bespoke" systems for generating, capturing, retrieving, and massaging information and data. . . . It will call for the development of a new sensitivity (to contexts, organizational cultures and human behaviours) and a conceptually-integrated approach to information policy planning. (p. 7)

This is evidence of a belief that although there had to be a substantial reorientation of the profession, the basic job in information management is one for which the practicing background of library and information work is appropriate and necessary, and that the character or being of the profession is best protected by accepting the need for this change, which is partly forced by changes in society and is partly an opportunity to expand the range of the natural working environments of information professionals.

Wilson (1989) seemed to accept this situation, in which there is a two-way process of colonization:

> The information management concept is applicable not only to business and industry, but also to public sector and voluntary agencies, and to public and academic libraries. . . . The idea of information management has become accepted to such a degree that librarians, records managers and information scientists may need to *become* information managers if they are to have their deserved impact upon the organization they serve to a greater extent than in the past. (p. 208)

Effectively, it would seem, librarians and others will become information managers, and will colonize new areas of activity (libraries, information units) for information management. What is being offered in exchange is less clear. Wiggins (1988) concluded that all the occupational groups being drawn into information management are forced to do so because of other threats to their status:

> There is no doubt that IM/IRM is here to stay, if only to provide a "new territory" into which computer managers, librarians, information scientists, office managers, etc. can try and expand their influence and areas of responsibility away from their own patches which are increasingly threatened with "takeover" by others. (p. 11)

This search for a new ground, rather reminiscent of some of the claims of Brookes, hints at the rest of the exchange whereby librarians and others are offered the chance to influence the form and direction the emerging field of information management will take. What then can be identified as central to the knowledge claims advanced on behalf of information management that make it attractive as a conception of the library and information field?

From Corbishley (1986), we can identify key activities for information managers that indicate how this question can be answered. In her description of information management in a district health authority in the United Kingdom, she showed that through the 1980s a series of inquiries focused attention on the complex information requirements of the authority and the need to manage them effectively. Her list of typical information needs includes:

1. Activity data
2. Epidemiological information
3. Demographic information
4. Strategic plans
5. Administrative and procedural information
6. Legislation
7. Financial information
8. Technical information
9. Clinical data
10. Bibliographic information
11. Directories
12. Maps
13. Press cuttings

Corbishley indicated this list is not exhaustive. The information needs can be related to the terms of reference of the United Kingdom Steering Group on Health Services Information, and to the brief of the District Information Steering Group set up in May 1985. She summarized the terms of reference of the Steering Group on Health Services Information (chaired by Korner and commonly known as the Korner Report) as to:

1. Agree, implement and review principles and procedures to guide the future development of health service information systems.
2. Identify and resolve health service information issues requiring a coordinated approach.
3. Review existing health service information systems.
4. Consider proposals for changes to, and developments in, health service information systems arising from elsewhere and if acceptable to assess priorities for their development and implementation.

The brief of the District Information Steering Group embraced several information issues, including the following:

1. The implementation of the Data Protection Act.
2. Confidentiality of records.
3. Implementation of the Korner recommendations.
4. Further development of integrated information systems. (p. 309)

The introduction of such integrated information services poses a challenge to the library and information community. By relating these developments to the comments of Wilson and Wiggins about the personnel in the field, it can be seen that information management makes certain knowledge claims about the field that could appeal strongly to the practice.

These claims appeal because they extend the range or horizon of the field, and they extend the power of the field to generate shared meanings and a sense of what the practice is in a more acutely information-conscious environment. They correspond to Hubbard's tests of change in interpretation. The focus of information management identified by Lytle and Herring, together with the areas of work identified by Corbishley, indicate three salient characteristics to these claims, which are in part given definition by new language and new skills. First, they establish the practice's concern with a wider range of information and information formats (swerving and completion). Second, although they maintain the professional concern with information technology, they allow a changed emphasis. This has two linked aspects: other information professionals are recognized as being most concerned with technological components of information systems, but an interest in these systems is retained, and greater recognition is given to the information content (focusing and self-limitation). This also allows closer connection with other information professionals. Third, and probably most important, the conception of the library and information field as information management integrates practicing professionals into the structure of their organizations, partly through emphasis on the need to manage information, and stresses the involvement of the practice in the management process and structure of the organization.

These attributes and effects seem to come as additions to practice in the library and information field, albeit with changed emphases. In consequence the interpretation of the field is being changed and extended. The processes of refilling and becoming the essence are completed. The shared meanings are being developed, the subject (the library or information worker) remains the same, and the means of expression are still varied. Information management can reasonably be considered as a conception of the library and information field, and it does maintain the integrity of the field, being largely an outgrowth of practice, both within the profession and in the wider working environment. It is almost a natural case within the Dworkinian argument for a conception of the field.

11
Summary and Conclusion

THE ARGUMENT

This work began with several propositions about the field of library and information studies. In brief these were:

1. Since the 1960s at the latest, the discipline and profession have been so disparate that is difficult to see how all its practitioners can share a sense of belonging to the same field.
2. The field currently lacks an understanding of its origin or its direction, so much so that it is impossible to state confidently what practitioners do.
3. The task of uncovering what librarians or information workers do is a theoretical one.
4. The profession is a practical one, and research, theory, and practice should be more closely related.
5. The way the field is viewed should be consonant with thinking in other social sciences and should consider practice and theory in all aspects of the field.

Four tasks were then identified for this work:

1. To show how the powerful intellectual and professional influences that have strongly affected the recent development of the field can be accommodated within the library and information tradition, even when they seem to be in conflict.
2. To explain how professional practice allows the gradual, serial replacement of one conception of the field by another but still accommodates all conceptions within the tradition.
3. To show how practice demands a different and more inclusive approach to theory that relates to what those in practice do as much as it does to research.
4. To show how the information culture now acts as a context of meaning for the field.

It was claimed that the grounds for building a theory for the library and information field could be identified as the approach known as hermeneutics or interpretation. By using this approach, and by rejecting the traditional positivist approach these tasks can be tackled successfully.

I want to conclude by reviewing what the construction of the field through the interpretive approach provides, and by identifying some implications that follow from using that approach.

THE INTERPRETIVE ARGUMENT

In building an interpretive case, we are concerned with the common sense of everyday understanding and language that allows understanding of what people do, what their purposive strategy is. This is accomplished by understanding the meanings available to them and the opportunities open to them to clarify meaning and advance understanding of their situation and of the practice they find themselves in. My claim is that we can only really understand what librarians or information managers do by following this approach. Because this builds on the common everyday sense of practice, and because it would be a reflection of what is done in research and theorizing and practice anyway, we already have the resources we need to apply this approach. What is required is the framework that emphasizes the basic shared understandings, the intersubjectivities that form the building blocks of practice and of the identity of practitioners, and allows the construction of conceptions or explanations of the practice without destroying its narrative.

This task involves the process of constructing a new text of the field that uncovers the shared meanings, which also means uncovering the shared language. The claim is that the world is understood and interpreted through the generation and learning of these shared meanings; it is not just an agglomeration of the views of individuals. Following Outhwaite, I am accepting that all social inquiry must begin with the everyday language that allows intersubjective meanings to develop and is the medium of communication and the root of all concepts of all participants in any practice.

One of the basic claims for interpretation is that meaning that is unclear can be clarified, and that clearer meanings than those hitherto available can be constructed. The superiority of a meaning becomes apparent when we attain a more clairvoyant or insightful understanding of the practice, which leads to a new theory and an improved practice.

The appeal to a clearer meaning is through the language of expression. This requirement to see through the language itself requires that the language is a shared set of meanings. We can only avail of this

SUMMARY AND CONCLUSION 205

language if it is available to us, and our recourse if it fails is to other attempts to explain or to read the phenomenon or text whose meaning is unclear. This is done by widening the framework to include other readings, so that eventually the appeal is to some common understanding, and it is within this hermeneutic circle that we must exist and seek all meanings.

Components of Meaning

Following Taylor, meaning is accepted as having three components: First, it is for a subject, a person; second, it is about something (i.e., the meaning of something can be separated from the thing itself); third, it exists only in relation to other meanings, so all meanings in a field are interrelated, and each part of the field is defined by its relation to the whole discipline.

Requirements of a Hermeneutic Science

Following Taylor, to be able to construct an interpretive account requires a field of objects about which there is some sense or meaning, and some coherence. Second, it must be possible to distinguish between different expressions of the meaning. Third, the meanings must exist for a (human) subject. In consequence, the structure and the interpretation of meaning are not independent of each other. Additionally, the interpreting human subject is then seen as a self-interpreting animal, an important point when considering the meaning of practice for a participant.

Interpretation and Validation

Hermeneutics appeals to insight to clarify differences of interpretation, rather than the style of validation familiar to empiricists. The validation of social theory in the interpretive account lies in its ability to change social practice for the better, so a better theory can challenge self-understandings about practice and may lead to an improved practice: This has obvious appeal to a practical profession.

Self-Identity and Interpretation

The idea of self-identity is quite critical in the hermeneutic account of basic material of the social sciences. Every participant in a social practice is always involved in a dual process of interpretation, interpreting objects and events around themselves, and also themselves. We are constantly reviewing our self-identity, and a better interpretation that produces more insightful practice also improves our sense of ourselves. Our practices become an important part of our self-definition.

Fusing Horizons and the Language of Perspicuous Contrast

How are conflicts between interpretations resolved? Gadamer suggested that we develop a fusion of horizons whereby differing viewpoints come to understand one another by melting into each other through developing a common language. Following this, Taylor maintained that we can indeed develop such a common language by using the obvious differences between practices and interpretations to develop a language of perspicuous contrast, which would be common to both interpretations and would illuminate or offer insight that would develop a broader, inclusive, and more insightful language and interpretation.

PRACTICE

A practice is a

> coherent and complex form of socially established co-operative human activity through which goods internal to that form of activity are realised in the course of trying to achieve those standards of excellence which are appropriate to, and partially definitive of, that form of activity, with the result that human powers to achieve excellence, and human conceptions of the ends and goods involved, are systematically extended. (MacIntyre, 1981, p. 175)

In any practice, we constantly, as individuals, seek to develop some understanding that explains the practice to us, preferably in terms that make sense for our own self-identity. We may initially accept the interpretations made available to us: As neophytes we will be subordinate to some degree to the established authority of the practice. As our understanding develops, so will our interpretation of the practice and we will in time come, by our behavior and our language, to join in the shaping of the shared interpretation of the practice. We may indeed help to change the interpretation as we, with others, embellish or transform the sense of what constitutes the internal goods and rewards of the practice.

In this process, we do not seek to verify or falsify our views: Instead the practice is improved by developing a better, more insightful, more clairvoyant interpretation of the practice. The clairvoyance enables participants to see deeper into, rather than through, the practice: Participants justify their practices by understanding them better. Improved understanding is reflected in improved practice, but we cannot say that changes in understanding determine precisely the change in practice, only that we are aware of having an improved view of the practice when we find the changed practice to be better.

It is through the discourse of any practice, and through the range of possible language contexts open to that practice that we learn about the practice, develop interpretations of it, and come to share its meanings and its rewards. As the range of possible language contexts expands, so the chances of changes in interpretation increase. It is through this theorizing, this constant possibility of reinterpretation and reconceptualization that participants in any social practice come to understand what it is that they do. Seen in this framework, it is obvious that we are not limited by the boundaries of technical competence—in fact, rather the reverse, as technical competence only has meaning within a broader understanding of what it is we are at, what constitutes our purposive strategy.

The Interpretive Argument in Information Studies

For the argument within the field of information studies, I have accepted Dworkin's idea of changing conceptions of a field as mirrors of changing interpretations, and I have also proposed that the current context of meaning is the information culture. The information culture limits the structure of interpretations currently possible for the field, and this is so no matter which view is taken about the desirability or otherwise of an information society. The information culture is all pervasive, and effectively structures the possible vocabularies and contexts within which even those ignorant of or opposed to the idea of an information society must exist.

The range of conceptions is not limited to the traditional division between librarianship and information science, but is potentially limitless, and the traditional, characteristic tools and instruments of the field are not legitimate conceptions nor can they constrain the argument about conceptions and interpretations.

Benefits follow from adopting an interpretive approach. First, understanding of what we do is anchored in what practitioners actually do—or rather, in what they see themselves doing, what they see the practice as being. This means that all participants in a practice are inevitably theorizing about their practice and developing or sharing interpretations of it that reflect what they see the practice as being. Second, there is the possibility of greater understanding between currently unrelated parts of the broad field by allowing all practices and interpretations to be seen as legitimate expressions of the basic concept, and part of a complex and still-developing narrative. Third, this allows further interpretations to develop and be accommodated within the broad tradition. Finally, research and theory are allotted a clear role within the processes of the practicing profession.

Applying Interpretation to Practice

A view of information studies has been built that claims that the interpretive view is a better account than any alternative. In this sense we must appeal, finally, to interpretation as what we all do constantly, in any social practice: It is the way all participants in any practice construct their sense of what the practice is and what they are doing. All that is now required is that it be given formal recognition. In part, this appeal is inevitable, because from the start it has been accepted that for a hermeneutic science the appeal will not be to brute data but to what is insightfully or experientially true, in effect, what gives a truer reading of the text.

This work has offered a view of how a narrative can be constructed, which through redescription offers an alternative and hopefully more insightful text of the field. Ultimately, it is through narrative that the new historical exigency is constructed, and through building narratives that we interpret our world, our profession, our practice, and ourselves.

The Conceptions

Three conceptions of the library and information field were examined. They were chosen partly because they illustrate some development within the field through time, and partly because they all individually posed serious problems for anyone constructing an interpretive account. The treatment of them showed that the problems dissolve. The interpretive approach reveals that the basic data is not brute or objective data, but really conforms to Taylor's category of primitive data because it is, ultimately, social or linguistic data, and the character of the field is confirmed as being consistent with the social sciences or humanities. Thus, the data is itself an interpretation, and reflects theories held about it. Furthermore, each of the three cases allowed extension of our understanding of the field. By using an interpretive approach, it became pos-

SUMMARY AND CONCLUSION 209

sible to see how each of the conceptions extended the kinds of claims being made about and for the library and information field, and how each offered improved interpretations of the context of practice. Similarly, through the development of conceptions such as bibliography or information management and the consequential development of new languages expressing the new concerns, new contexts, and new standards, shared meanings are developed and participants in the practice are inducted into theories of the practice. Participants may help to revise these conceptions as their own self-identity and the language contexts in which they operate change.

Bibliography. In the case of bibliography, it was seen that a redefinition of the field as the sociology of texts (a notion that has yet to win widespread acceptance among bibliographers) did offer an example of an attempt to recover lost ground. In this case, a conception that at some point lost its grip on the attention of the library profession as an explanation of what the field was about was redefined by one of its participants in an attempt, among other things, to relate bibliography to a more modern information-conscious environment.

Information Science. Information science was given detailed consideration, especially with respect to the development of new types of knowledge claims about the library and information field. The contributions of Brookes, Price, and the research community in experimental information retrieval were considered, and their impact on the language, instruments, and interpretation of the field examined. The language of interpretation was extended by using the notion of a false conception. Information science was shown to have a powerful impact on interpretation of the field, but, as with bibliography, the existence of an information science separate from and outside the library and information field was seen not to be a difficulty.

Information Management. Information management was considered as a new and burgeoning conception of the field. Like information science, it was said not yet to be finally settled in form, and also existed as a conception of the library and information field alongside other, less well defined, practices of information management. A review of typical concerns of information management in health care disclosed indications of the kind of new claims being advanced by information management for the library and information field that would extend the power and language of that practice and give a new clarification, wider horizons, and firmer purpose to the practice.

Transforming Conceptions

It is possible to incorporate into the picture of theory building about conceptions and interpretations some view of how we might measure or indicate the significant characteristics of change in interpretation. Using the work of Bloom and Hubbard, we can identify strategies for measuring the change from one interpretation to another. It should be noted that this is an addendum to the process of interpretation; it is not part of that process itself.

This allows us to round off the picture of the process of interpretation, and to understand what happens when we develop an improved interpretation of any practice—when we apply a rereading of our theorizing about our own identities and that of the practice we are in to the practice itself.

Interpreting the Practice

We live and find our identity in a practice that is wide ranging and successful in its search for definition and relevance. The use of conceptions within interpretation of the practice shows how a field can develop powerful measures of understanding that can exist simultaneously and add to the richness of the resources available to the field. Each conception offers its own insights into what constitutes the field and each new conception deepens and embellishes, as well as changes, our understanding of the field. Rather than being indicative of intellectual weakness or of inadequate organizational definition, the acceptance of several expressions of what the field is about shows a subtlety and suppleness in the field. This in turn attracts a broad spectrum of participants who, in finding their own identity in the shared meanings of their practice, in whatever conception of the practice they choose, attest to its vitality.

There are probably other conceptions that could be examined which might allow further extension of the language of interpretation, and more will emerge as the context of meaning changes. At present, the conceptions available to us, which reflect the meaning of the field for its participants, also reflect the powerful influence of various explanations of the information culture as the current context of meaning for the field.

IMPLICATIONS

If the views advanced here are a better way of interpreting information studies, then there are implications for the way in which researchers and practitioners do their work. There are four areas in which some review of present understanding of our practices is required.

Practice, Theory, and Society

This project has examined internal aspects of the field and perceptions of it, yet these must be placed in a wider context of the society in which we live. We have to establish what gives us our believability, what makes society willing to continue paying us money or giving us resources, and in particular what makes it recognize our claim to organize and store its knowledge. The job we have to do is also dependent on people wanting us to do it, so we are looking for what justifies us to society. Simultaneously, it is convenient for the wider society to recognize a community that will perform these tasks for it: Society not only needs a job done, it needs a community of people who can say what that job is. This is the point at which members of the wider community become participants in the information practice, but also the information community similarly participates in the society. In seeking believability and confidence, we offer justification for ourselves as a community. This is not just a relationship between the practice and the society: Each individual's sense of personal identity and commitment to the practice will be entwined with the social recognition of the practice.

One of the main problems for information studies has been to articulate a sense of itself that ties together its past, present, and future as a recognized practice with an academic disciplinary component. The problem may be represented as a matter of how to model the disciplinary and community identity of the social practice.

In the face of the disparate activities that the field has always embraced and the initial appearance of the professional information community as a de facto accidental collection of people from different backgrounds, it is no surprise that the first drive for identity should have been to represent the field as scientific. Many of the now established social sciences have so represented themselves in their infancy in an effort to get academic respectability. Political science and social science as labels carry the mark of this early drive for recognition, even though few people would now argue that these terms refer to studies that can or do conform to the paradigm of the natural sciences. Information studies as a field is still somewhat insecure as a member of the social sciences, but clinging to a positivist model of science hinders the construction of a secure identity for the field and a confident theoretical basis that will stall any attempts to usurp the information community's role in society, or dissolve the field into mere technical training.

The problem of disciplinary and community identity shows up in Brookes' response (Chapter 9) to the list of things taught in departments of information science he visited: "But who teaches information science?" Information studies is a practice embracing a number of specific activities, and it is a mistake to look for some extra activity that somehow connects them all together. However, we do have to ask; what holds all the activities that go on in information studies together in one practice? The implication of what I have been arguing in this book is that community identity across the field, both over time and across the various activities that at any one time constitute the practice, is given by the point of the practice as seen not just by its participants but by the society in which the practice makes sense.

The sense or meaning of the practice is not completely internal to it, but is part of a wider social understanding of the importance of knowledge, of the dissemination of knowledge, of building current culture on past cultural achievements, and consequently of the need for an institution that stores knowledge in an accessible form and a field that understands, reconstructs, and executes this institutional role. The identity of the community of information workers comes not from there being one thing that they all do, but from their special institutional role in providing for the transmission and dissemination of knowledge in society. All the activities of the information community are not the same, but they have the same overall point: to fulfill wider social understandings and expectations about knowledge.

The information studies community draws its integrity from participation in this wider social world. That we have the identity we do as an autonomous identity is due to the fact that our activities have a social meaning that go beyond what we narrowly do in our everyday practice. Thus the internal goods of our practice are permeated by external goods, that is, goods that relate to our membership and role in a wider knowledge and information-sharing society. Our professional identity shares the values that are embedded in this wider idea that knowledge has a certain meaning and value.

Moreover, the value placed on knowledge and access to it historically by the wider society comes to shape our consciousness of our practice. We are heirs to a long tradition. Thus we can see the practices of the past as continuous with our own in this sense of sharing with us an institutional role that exists because of its contribution to wider cultural projects of our society. We are involved in continuing that narrative.

I do not want to suggest that information studies is completely determined by these wider understandings. Our autonomy develops as the field develops and comes to be not the mere thing of the wider society, but an agent that helps determine what the wider society understands by knowledge, and what of it can be stored, organized, and accessed, and how. Society needs the field to be relatively autonomous, because in that way alone can it, from an informed perspective, contribute to shaping and reshaping the wider social perception of our information needs.

We see this aspect of autonomy at work in our construction of interpretive conceptions of the field. These are our best judgments of what the field is about. Each conception has some organizing center, which is the explanation it offers of various things. As we relate our interpretation of our practice to ourselves, and also to the society of which we see ourselves as part, the conception must offer a sense of the value of continuing to do these things. However, it is important to observe that the conceptions are never merely descriptive of the field. They also prescribe what is to be done in the future. The prescriptive element involves judgments about how money should be spent, curricula designed, who is now to be read in and out of the literature, what counts as significant work, and what kind of professional education should take place. All of these embody value judgments about the direction of the discipline that must ultimately show the wider society that the conception is not only the best current interpretation of the field itself, but also is the best current realization of the wider social understandings of the importance of knowledge. Contention between conceptions is not only about their internal purpose, but also about their claims to the attention of the wider community.

As members of the information studies community, we ultimately justify our activities and the demands they make on social resources in terms of our ability to interpret and make practical sense of those wider social understandings of knowledge and our role in it.

Library and Information Theory

The interpretive approach makes possible an integrated theory about practice in the library and information field, and allows the field to grow and change without making that theory invalid. In this respect, interpretation offers what has previously not been available, but in other respects it poses problems for theory building in the field. First, historical reconstructions and narratives become of prime significance, challenging research approaches that would either claim a scientific, value-free objectivity or are based on experimental data or other sources that do not reflect the social practice all participants are engaged in. Second, theory building becomes inseparable from considerations about the interpretations of practice. Third, theory must become closer to what the practice actually is, what the participants' purposive strategy is. Where research or theory is seen as irrelevant, or something distinct from the practice, then its chances of being applied have always been slight. Similarly, when an interpretation of practice, a conception, ceases to make sense of the practice then its claim on the attention of participants in the practice will weaken as will its claim to characterize the practice.

Library and Information Research

The implications for research are similarly fundamental. This work has not addressed research as a separate topic. I have discussed not the research questions (which are internal to each conception) of the field, but a view of what the field is, centered on what its practice is; so we have been discussing not research, but the guiding or regulative principles that help our understanding of what is going on when particular research methods are adopted to deal with particular problems. So far, nothing that has been said can clearly indicate how one "does research" in library or information studies: The comments have not been about interpretation as a research method.

A legitimate question arises about how anyone, even if they accept the interpretive approach and the constructions put forward in this book, should approach the research questions that arise within each conception of the field. This is more poignant because the interpretive approach explicitly denies the validity of the raw data commonly gathered in research on human subjects, because it denies the possibility of there being any objective, value-free observation. Interpretation also presupposes that research will be an integral part of practice and will inform the hermeneutic circle of interpretation between practice and theory. The objectives of research change, the character of research changes to something far more closely allied to practice, and the ways and means of research activity are constrained by what the interpretive approach considers legitimate. This means, for example, that research approaches based on grounded theory are not acceptable, because the interpreter cannot accept that the data can speak for itself and indicate what kind of research method is appropriate. If there is no value-free observation, then also there are no data independent of theories about it: Anything perceived as valid data is valid because it is already part of a process of interpretation; it has already been used by subjects in a practice in an early phase of preinterpretation. Similarly, the position sometimes called pluralist, which will allow a variety of research methods, maybe even for the same question, to be applied to a research inquiry is also unacceptable, because for human subjects there can be no equally valid methods, only equally valid interpretations, conforming to the practice of inter-

SUMMARY AND CONCLUSION 215

pretation, even if the result is a variety of expressions. The tradition of interpretation is not a libertarian rejection of all authority in method, equally accepting of all and every approach. Interpretation makes its own demands of the interpreters, in particular that the particular practice be understood, and that the data be understood as being in a process of interpretation. This also requires that we understand that there is a shift in the focus of research to take account of the background ideologies that dictate its agenda. We are not conducting objective, scientific, value-free research: We are operating within the demands and restrictions of a particular conception and against the background of a particular context of meaning. Our research will be a recapitulation of those background ideologies. Recognition of this may lead to different types of questions being formulated, for example, about the sociology of knowledge in information studies, or about which interests a particular conception of the field serves, or how conceptions maintain themselves over time, or what leads to the demise of particular conceptions and outlooks.

What is the upshot of this? Immediately it can be said that narrative becomes more important. Furthermore, we can also say that we are already constructing narratives. Even de Solla Price, when he offered his analysis of the literature of science, was constructing a narrative. Narrative, which is of enhanced utility and importance within a less scientific social science, based on material that can no longer be regarded as objective fact becomes a more important resource in research. It will have a significant role in determining the background against which research and theory are developed. The likely change is that the kinds of tentative judgments made in humanistic work may come to inform other research, coupled with a greater concern to establish how meaning becomes apparent to practitioners in information work and to users of information and information systems. What will change is not the set of research methods and techniques, but the set of questions that will be asked within an interpretation of the practice.

Practice

The interpretive approach offers practitioners the means to recapture research and theory in the field and to harness it to improved practice and enhanced and broader understanding of the whole field of information studies, but this is not available to anyone. Practitioners, to be able to use the resources of interpretation, in particular that insight that gives a certain clairvoyance to the practice, must of course be skilled technically in the demands of their practice. However, they must also, to be considered real members of the practice, be able to share the internal rewards of that practice and most importantly, they must be skilled in the practice of interpretation. Their ability to interpret their involvement with their practice and with their own self-identity is dependent on a well-developed interpretive skill. The interpretive insight is not some simple flash of intuition that conveys instant understanding; it is a deep insight into the practice that allows the construction of better theory that offers more understanding about the practice than other theories. Members of a practice are those who share its internal rewards; interpretation of a practice requires that and more.

Interpretation requires that we broaden our understanding of practice to be more inclusive: The processes of theory building are inextricably intertwined with our practices, and all that we do to make sense of the practice, including much of our research, must be seen as part of that practice and not as a separate endeavor. What then of those practitioners who are not in what is commonly understood as practice; those teachers, faculty members, researchers, and theorists who do not staff libraries, manage information systems, or direct information businesses? Are they to be considered outside the practice, or in need of some retraining to couple them more closely to normal practice? No; it is the understanding of practice that must be seen to change: As practice is perceived as including a wider range of activities, so we fuse our horizons into a more clairvoyant understanding of what the practice is. Ultimately, we are all in practice: What we call that practice indicates our understanding of what it is that we do.

References

Allen, G. G., Exon, F. C. A. (Eds.). (1986). *Research and the practice of librarianship: An international symposium*. Perth, Australia: The Library, Western Australian Institute of Technology.
Austin, D. (1986). Vocabulary control and information technology. *Aslib Proceedings, 38*, 1–15.
Barnes, B. (1985). Thomas Kuhn. In Q. Skinner (Ed.), *The return of grand theory in the human sciences* (pp. 83–100). Cambridge, UK: Cambridge University Press.
Batty, D., & Bearman. T. C. (1983). Knowledge and practice in library and information services. In F. Machlup & U. Mansfield (Eds.), *The study of information: Interdisciplinary messages* (pp. 365–370). New York: Wiley.
Beagle, D. (1988). Libraries and the 'implicate order': A contextual approach to theory. *Libri, 38*, 26–44.
Beatty, S. B. (1982). The role of professional societies in information resource management. In G. P. Sweeney (Ed.), *Information and the transformation of society* (pp. 297–308). Amsterdam: North-Holland.
Becker, J., & Hayes, R. (1963). *Information storage and retrieval: Tools, elements, theories*. New York: Wiley.
Belkin, N., & Vickery, A. (1985). *Interaction in information systems* (LIR Report No. 35). London: British Library.
Bell, D. (1976). *The coming of post-industrial society: A venture in social forecasting*. Harmondsworth, UK: Penguin.
Bell, D. (1979). The social framework of the information society. In M. L. Dertouzos & J. Moses (Eds.), *The computer age: A twenty year review* (pp. 163–209). Cambridge, MA: MIT Press.
Benediktsson, D. (1989). Hermeneutics: Dimensions toward LIS thinking. *Library and Information Science Research, 11*, 201–234.
Beniger, J. R. (1986). *The control revolution: Technological and economic origins of the information society*. Cambridge, MA: Harvard University Press.
Beniger, J. R. (1988). Information society and global science. In *Annals of the American Academy of Political and Social Science, 495*, 14–28.
Bennett, G. E. (1988). *Librarians in search of science and identity: The elusive profession*. Metuchen, NJ: Scarecrow Press.
Bernstein, R. J. (1983). *Beyond objectivism and relativism: Science, hermeneutics, and praxis*. Oxford, UK: Basil Blackwell.
Besterman, T. (1945). Foreword. *Journal of Documentation, 1*(1), 1.

REFERENCES

Blake, F. (1978). Public access to information in the post-industrial society. In E. L. Josey (Ed.), *The information society: Issues and answers* (pp. 86–93). Phoenix, AZ: Oryx.

Bloom, H. (1973). *The anxiety of influence: A theory of poetry.* New York: Oxford University Press.

Borko, H. (1968). Information science: What is it?" *American Documentation, 19,* 3–5.

Bowers, F. (1975). *Essays in bibliography, text and editing.* Charlottesville: University Press of Virginia.

Bradley, J. (1993). Methodological issues and practices in qualitative research. *Library Quarterly, 63*(4), 431–449.

Bradley, J., & Sutton, B. (Eds.). (1993). Symposium on qualitative research: Theory, methods, and application. *Library Quarterly, 63*(4), 405–527.

Brookes, B. (1980a). Foundations of information science: Part 1, Philosophical aspects. *Journal of Information Science, 2,* 125–133.

Brookes, B. (1980b). Informatics as the fundamental social science. In P. J. Taylor (Ed.), *New trends in documentation and information: Proceedings of the Thirty-ninth FID Congress held in the University of Edinburgh, 25–28 September 1978* (pp. 19–29). London: Aslib for FID.

Brookes, B. (1981). Foundations of information science: Part IV, information science, the changing paradigm. *Journal of Information Science, 3,* 3–12.

Buckland, M. (1983). *Library services in theory and context.* New York: Pergamon.

Bush, V. (1945). As we may think. *Atlantic Monthly,* 176(1): pp. 101–108.

Busha, C. H. (1983). The meaning and value of theory: An introduction. *Drexel Library Quarterly, 19*(2), 1–4.

Busha, C. H., & Harter, S. P. (1980). *Research methods in librarianship: Techniques and interpretation.* New York: Academic Press.

Capurro, R. (1992). What is information science for? A philosophical reflection. In P. Vakkari & B. Cronin (Eds.), *Conceptions of library and information science: Historical, empirical and theoretical perspectives* (pp. 82–96). London: Taylor Graham.

Cawkell, A. E. (1986). The real information society: Present situation and some forecasts. *Journal of Information Science, 12*(3), 87–96.

Cawkell, A. E. (Ed.). (1987). *The Evolution of an information society.* London: Aslib.

Cooper, M. (1983). "The structure and future of the information economy. *Information Processing & Management, 19*(1), 9–26.

Corbishley, H. M. (1986). Information management in a district health authority: Case study 3. *Journal of Information Science, 12,* 307–310.

Croft, W. B. (1987). Approaches to intelligent information retrieval. *Information Processing & Management, 23,* 249–254.

Cronin, B. (1983). Post-industrial society: Some manpower issues for the library/information profession. *Journal of Information Science, 7,* 1–14.

Cronin, B. (Ed.). (1985). *Information management: From strategies to action.* London: Taylor Graham for Aslib.

Cronin, B. (1986). The information society. *Aslib Proceedings, 38*(4), 121–129.

Davies, R. (1987). Outlines of the emerging paradigm in cataloguing. *Information Processing & Management, 23,* 89–98.

Davis, C. H., & Rush, J. E. (1979). *Guide to information science.* Westport, CT: Greenwood.

Dudley, E. P., Clough, E. A., Bryant, E. T., & Moore, N. E. (Eds.). (1983). *Curriculum change for the nineties: A report of the curriculum development project on library and information work* (Library and Information Report No. 14). London: British Library.

Du Mont, R. R. (1989). Bridging the gap between theory and practice: The role of research in librarianship. *Training and Education, 6,* 24–30.

Dupuy, J.-P. (1978). Myths of the information society. In K. Woodward (Ed.), *The myths of information: Technology and post-industrial culture* (pp. 3–17). London: Routledge & Kegan Paul.

Dworkin, R. (1986). *Law's empire.* London: Fontana.

Ellis, D. (1986). Information management and information work. *International Journal of Information Management, 6,* 115–116.

Ellul, J. (1965). *The technological society* (J. Wilkinson, Trans.). London: Jonathan Cape.

Ellul, J. (1980). *The technological system* (J. Neugroschel, Trans.). New York: Continuum.

Estabrook, L. (1986). Librarianship and information resources management: Some questions and contradictions. *Journal of Education for Library and Information Science, 27,* 3–11.

Exon, F. C. A. (1989). In-house library research as an intermediary between theory and practice. *International Journal of Information and Library Research, 1,* 24–39.

Farkas-Conn, I. S. (1990). *From Documentation to information science: The beginnings and early development of the American Documentation Institute-American Society for Information Science* (Contributions in Librarianship and Information Science No. 67). New York: Greenwood.

Farradane, J. (1980). Knowledge, information, and information science. *Journal of Information Science, 2,* 75–80.

Feather, J. (1980). Cross-channel currents: Historical bibliography and *L'Histoire du Livre. The Library* (Sixth Series), *2,* 1–16.

Feather, J. (1982). The rare book librarian and bibliographical scholarship. *Journal of Librarianship, 14*(1), 30–44.

Fidel, R. (1993). Qualitative methods in information retrieval research. *Library and Information Science Research* 15, 219–247.

Fosdick, H. (1978). Library education in information science: Present trends. *Special Libraries, 69,* 100–118.

Foucault, M. (1970). *The order of things: An archaeology of the human sciences.* London: Tavistock.

Frohmann, B. (1990). Rules of indexing: A critique of mentalism in information retrieval theory. *Journal of Documentation, 46,* 81–101.

Gadamer, H.-G. (1975). *Truth and method.* London: Sheed & Ward.

Gadamer, H.-G. (1976). *Philosophical hermenutics.* Berkeley: University of California Press.

Garfield, E. (1971). Information science and the information conscious society. *Journal of the American Society for Information Science, 22,* 71–73.

Giddens, A. (1985). Jurgen Habermas. In Q. Skinner (Ed.), *The return of grand theory in the human sciences* (pp. 121–139). Cambridge, UK: Cambridge University Press.

Griffith, B. C. (Ed.). (1980). *Key papers in information science*. New York: Knowledge Industry Publications.

Guinchat, C., & Menou, M. (1983). *General introduction to the techniques of information and documentation work*. Paris: UNESCO.

Heilprin, L. B. (Ed.). (1985). *Toward foundations of information science*. White Plains, NY: Knowledge Industry Publications.

Herring, J. E. (1991). Information management—The convergence of professions. *International Journal of Information Management, 11*, 144–155.

Hoel, I. A. (1992). Information science and hermeneutics—Should information science be interpreted as a historical and humanistic science? In P. Vakkari & B. Cronin (Eds.), *Conceptions of library and information science: Historical, empirical and theoretical perspectives* (pp. 69–81). London: Taylor Graham.

Hollnagel, E. (1980). Is information science an anomalous state of knowledge? *Journal of Information Science, 2*, 183–187.

Horton, F. W., Jr. (1982). Needed, a new doctrine for information resources management. In F. W. Horton, Jr. & D. Marchand (Eds.), *Information management in public administration* (pp. 45–57). Arlington, VA: Information Resources Press.

Horton, F. W., Jr. (1985). *Information resources management*. Englewood Cliffs, NJ: Prentice-Hall.

Horton, F. W., Jr., & Marchand, D. (Eds.). (1982). *Information management in public administration*. Arlington, Virginia: Information Resources Press.

Hounsell, D., & Winn, V. (1981). Editorial introduction to Qualitative Approaches to the Study of Information Problems: A Symposium. *Social Science Information Studies, 1*, 203–207.

Houser, L., & Schrader, A. M. (1978). *The search for a scientific profession: Library science in the U.S. and Canada*. Metuchen, NJ: Scarecrow.

Hubbard, W. (1986). *Complicity and conviction: Steps toward an architecture of convention*. Cambridge, MA: MIT Press.

Ingwersen, P. (1992). *Information retrieval interaction*. London: Taylor Graham.

Institute of Information Scientists. (1988). *Criteria for information science*. London: Institute for Information Scientists.

Jani, N., Parekh, H., & Sen, B. (1990). Individual perceptions of professional advancement. *Libri, 41*(3), 183–193.

Jones, K. S. (Ed.). (1981). *Information retrieval experiment*. London: Butterworths.

King, A. (1984). *The coming information society* [The Second British Library Annual Research Lecture, 1983]. London: British Library.

Kochen, M. (1983). Library science and information science: Broad or narrow? In F. Machlup & U. Mansfield (Eds.), *The study of information: Interdisciplinary messages* (pp. 371–378). New York: Wiley.

Kuhn, T. S. (1957). *The Copernican revolution*. Cambridge, MA: Harvard University Press.

Kuhn, T. S. (1970). *The structure of scientific revolutions* (2nd ed). Chicago: University of Chicago Press.

Landau, H. B. (1986). The challenge of the emerging information society: Are we ready? In H. Edelman (Ed.), *Libraries and information science in the electronic age* (pp. 36–56). Philadelphia: ISI Press.

Lane, N. (1985). Information management: An Australian photomontage. *Aslib Proceedings, 37,* 31–51.

Lessnoff, M. (1974). *The structure of social science.* London: George Allen & Unwin.

Levitan, K. B. (1982). Information resource(s) management—IRM. *Annual Review of Information Science and Technology, 17,* 227–266.

Lewis, D. A. (1985). Expanding horizons. In B. Cronin (Eds.), *Information management: From strategies to action* (pp. 9–18). London: Taylor Graham.

The Library Association. (1981). Report of the working party on the future of professional qualifications, 1977, revised 1978. In L. J. Taylor (Ed.), *A librarian's handbook* (Vol. 2, pp. 659–678). London: Library Association.

Line, M. (1981). The structure of social science literature as shown by large-scale citation analysis. *Social Science Information Studies, 1,* 67–87.

Lyon, D. (1988). *The information society: Issues and illusions.* London: Polity Press.

Lytle, R. H. (1986). Information resources management 1981–86. *Annual Review of Information Science and Technology, 21,* 309–336.

MacAlister, J. Y. W. (1898). "The Library" redivivus. *The Library, x,* 398–400.

Machlup, F. (1962). *The production and distribution of knowledge in the United States.* Princeton, NJ: Princeton University Press.

Machlup, F. (1980). *Knowledge, its creation, distribution, and economic significance. Vol. 1: Knowledge and knowledge production.* Princeton, NJ: Princeton University Press.

Machlup, F. (1982). *Knowledge, its creation, distribution, and economic significance. Vol. 2: The branches of learning.* Princeton, NJ: Princeton University Press.

Machlup, F. (1984). *Knowledge, its creation, distribution, and economic significance. Vol. 3: The economics of information and human capital.* Princeton, NJ: Princeton University Press.

Machlup, F., & Mansfield, U. (Eds.). (1983). *The study of information: Interdisciplinary messages.* New York: Wiley.

MacIntyre, A. (1981). *After virtue.* London: Duckworth.

Martin, H., & Febvre, L. (1984). *The coming of the book* (D. Gerrard, Trans.). London: Verso.

Martin, W. J. (1988). *The information society.* London: Aslib.

McKenzie, D. F. (1985). *Bibliography and the sociology of texts* (The Panizzi Lectures, 1985). London: British Library.

McKenzie, D. F. (1992). The history of the book. In P. Davison (Ed.), *The book encompassed: Studies in twentieth century bibliography* (pp. 290–301). New York: Cambridge University Press.

Meadow, C. (1979). Information science and scientists in 2001. *Journal of Information Science, 1,* 217–222.

Merton, R. K. (1965). Introduction to *The technological society,* by Jacques Ellul. London: Jonathan Cape.

Miski, A. (1986). Education for information science. In A. Kent (Ed.), *Encyclopedia of library and information science* (Vol. 41, Supplement 6, pp. 47–65). New York: Marcel Dekker.

Natoli, J. P. (1982). Librarianship as a human science: Theory, method and application. *Library Research, 4*, 163–174.

Neill, S. D. (1982). Brookes, Popper, and objective knowledge. *Journal of Information Science, 4*, 33–39.

Olaisen, J. L. (1985). Alternative paradigms in library science: The case for paradigmatic tolerance and pluralism. *Libri, 35*, 129–150.

Oldman, C. (1981). Scientism and academic librarianship. In M. Barnes et. al. (Eds.), *Information and society: A collection of papers presented at meetings of The British Sociological Association Libraries and Information Study Group, 1978–1980* (pp. 15–29). Leeds, UK: School of Librarianship, Leeds Polytechnic.

Outhwaite, W. (1971). *Understanding social life: The method called verstehen.* London: Allen & Unwin.

Outhwaite, W. (1985). Hans-Georg Gadamer. In Q. Skinner (Ed.), *The return of grand theory in the human sciences* (pp. 21–39). Cambridge, UK: Cambridge University Press.

Philp, M. (1985). Michael Foucault. In Q. Skinner (Ed.), *The return of grand theory in the human sciences* (pp. 65–82). Cambridge, UK: Cambridge University Press.

Pocock, J. G. A. (1985). *Virtue, commerce, and history: Essays on political thought and history, chiefly in the eighteenth century.* Cambridge, UK: Cambridge University Press.

Porat, M. U. (1977). *The information economy: Definition and measurement* (Vol. 1). Washington, DC: U.S. Department of Commerce.

Price, D. D. (1986). *Little science, big science . . . and beyond.* New York: Columbia University Press.

Rayward, W. B. (1983). Library and information sciences: Disciplinary differentiation, competition and convergence. In F. Machlup & U. Mansfield (Eds.), *The study of information, interdisciplinary messages* (pp. 343–363). New York: Wiley.

Reynolds, M. M., & Daniel, E. H. (Eds.). (1974). *Reader in library and information services.* Englewood, CO: Microcard Editions Books.

Roberts, N. (1976). Social considerations towards a definition of information science. *Journal of Documentation, 32*, 249–257.

Roberts, N., & Wilson, T. D. (1987). Information resources management: A question of attitudes? *International Journal of Information Management, 7*, 67–76.

Rommetveit, R. (1986). Meaning, context and control: Convergent trends and controversial issues in current social-scientific research on human cognition and communication. *Inquiry, 30*, 77–99.

Rudd, D. (1983). Do we really need world III? Information science with or without Popper. *Journal of Information Science, 7*, 99–105.

Salton, G. (1985). A note about information science research. *Journal of The American Society for Information Science, 36*, 268–271.

Salton, G., & McGill, M. J. (1983). *Introduction to modern information retrieval.* New York: McGraw-Hill.

Saracevic, T. (Ed.). (1970). *Introduction to information science.* New York: Bowker.

Saunders, W. L. (1974). The nature of information science. *Information Scientist*, *8*, 57–70.
Saunders, W. L. (1989). *Towards a unified professional organization for library and information science: A personal view*. London: Library Association Publishing.
Sayers, W. C. B. (1955). *Manual of classification* (3rd rev. ed.). London: Grafton.
Schrader, A. M. (1986). The domain of information science: Problems in conceptualization and consensus-building. *Information Services and Use*, *6*, 169–205.
Shannon, C. E. and Weaver, W. (1963). *The mathematical theory of communication*. Urbana-Champaign, IL: University of Illinois Press.
Shera, J. H. (1971). The sociological relationships of information science. *Journal of The American Society For Information Science*, *22*, 76–80.
Shera, J. H. (1983). Librarianship and information science. In F. Machlup & U. Mansfield (Eds.), *The study of information: Interdisciplinary messages* (pp. 379–388). New York: Wiley.
Simonton, W. (1980). AACR2: Antecedents, assumptions, implementation. *Advances in Librarianship*, *10*, 1–38.
Skinner, Q. (1985). Introduction: The return of grand theory. In Q. Skinner (Ed.), *The return of grand theory in the human sciences* (pp. 3–20). Cambridge, UK: Cambridge University Press.
Suppe, F. (1985). Current epistemological approaches to observation and interpretation. In L. Heilprin (Ed.), *Toward foundations of information science* (pp. 187–192). New York: Knowledge Industry Publications.
Sutherland, E. (1991). Methodologies and models for information management. *Aslib Proceedings*, *43*(2–3), 99–107.
Sutton, B. (1993). The rationale for qualitative research: A review of principles and theoretical foundations. *Library Quarterly*, *63*(4), 411–430.
Swanson, R. W. (1978). Education for information science as a profession. *Journal of the American Society for Information Science*, *29*, 148–155.
Tanselle, T. (1992). Issues in bibliographical studies since 1942. In P. Davison (Ed.), *The book encompassed: Studies in twentieth century bibliography* (pp. 24–36). New York: Cambridge University Press.
Taylor, C. (1978). Interpretation and the sciences of man. In R. Beehler & A. R. Drengson (Eds.), *The Philosophy of society* (pp. 156–200). London: Methuen.
Taylor, C. (1983). *Social theory as practice* [B. N. Ganguli Memorial Lectures, 1981]. Delhi, India: Oxford University Press.
Taylor, C. (1985). Alternative futures: Legitimacy, identity and alienation in late twentieth century Canada. In A. Cairns & C. Williams (Eds.), *Constitutionalism, citizenship and society in Canada* (pp. 183–229). Toronto: University of Toronto Press.
Tenopir, C. (1985). Information science in the United States. *Education for Information*, *3*, 3–28.
Toffler, A. (1973). *Future shock*. London: Pan Books.
Toffler, A. (1981). *The third wave*. London: Pan Books.
Traister, D. (1987). A caucus-race and a long tale: The profession of rare book librarianship in the 1980s. *Library Trends*, *36*(4), 144–145.

Transactions of the Bibliographical Society: Second Series. Volume 1: The Library; A Quarterly Review of Bibliography (1920). 4th Series, 1.

Trauth, E. M. (1988). Information resource management. In A. Kent (Ed.), *Encyclopedia of library and information science* (Vol. 43, Supplement 8, pp. 93–112). New York: Marcel Dekker.

Urquhart, D. (1981). *The principles of librarianship*. Leeds, UK: Wood Green.

van Rijsbergen, C. J. (1986). A new theoretical framework for information retrieval. In American Society for Computing Machinery, *Proceedings of the 1986 ACM Conference on research and development in information retrieval* (pp. 194–200). New York: ACM Press.

Vernon, K. D. C. (Ed.). (1984). *Information sources in management and business* (2nd ed). London: Butterworths.

Vickery, B. C., & Vickery, A. (1987). *Information science in theory and practice*. London: Butterworths.

Wersig, G., & Windel, G. (1985). Information science needs a theory of information actions. *Social Science Information Studies, 4*, 11–23.

Wiggins, R. E. (1988). A conceptual framework for information resources management. *International Journal of Information Management, 8*, 5–11.

Wilkinson, J. (1983). The legitimization of librarianship. *Libri, 33*, 37–44.

Williams, B. (1985). The information society: How different? *Aslib Proceedings, 37*(1), 1–8.

Williams, R. V. (1990). Specialization in the education of information professionals. In A. Kent (Ed.), *Encyclopedia of library and information science* (Vol. 45, Supplement 10, pp. 339–359). New York: Marcel Dekker.

Williamson, N. J. (1984). Subject access in the online environment. *Advances in Librarianship, 13*, 49–97.

Wilson, P. (1983a). Bibliographical R & D. In F. Machlup & U. Mansfield (Eds.), *The study of information, interdisciplinary messages* (pp. 389–398). New York: Wiley.

Wilson, P. (1983b). The catalog as access mechanism: Background and concepts. *Library Resources & Technical Services, 27*(1), 4–17.

Wilson, T. D. (1980). On information science and the social sciences. *Social Science Information Studies, 1*, 5–12.

Wilson, T. D. (1989). Towards an information management curriculum. *Journal of Information Science, 15*, 203–211.

Winograd, T., & Flores, F. (1986). *Understanding computers and cognition: A new foundation for design*. Norwood, NJ: Ablex.

Young, S. (1981). Sociological perspectives in librarianship and information science. In M. Barnes et al. (Eds.), *Information and society: A collection of papers presented at meetings of The British Sociological Association Libraries and Information Study Group, 1978–1980* (pp. 30–39). Leeds, UK: School of Librarianship, Leeds Polytechnic.

Author Index

A
Allen, G. G., 6, *217*
Austin, D., 119, *217*

B
Barnes, B., 15, 131, *217*
Batty, D., 7, 100, 101, 102, *217*
Beagle, D., 8, *217*
Bearman, T. C., 7, 100, 101, 102, *217*
Beatty, S. B., 192, *217*
Becker, J., 158, *217*
Belkin, N., 182, *217*
Bell, D., 11, 64, 66, 67, 68, 69, 76, 79, 81, *217*
Benediktsson, D., 15, 24, 25, *217*
Beniger, J. R., 70, *217*
Bennett, G. E., 15, 16, 24, 37, 101, *217*
Bernstein, R. J., 29, 124, *217*
Besterman, T., *217*
Blake, F., 70, *218*
Bloom, H., 134, *218*
Borko, H., 161, *218*
Bowers, F., 5, 143, 144, 145, 146, 147, *218*
Bradley, J., 9, *218*
Brookes, B., 85, 86, 155, 167, 168, 169, 212, *218*
Bryant, E. T., 156, *219*
Buckland, M., 89, *218*
Bush, V., 157, *218*
Busha, C.H., 9, 10, 125, *218*

C
Capurro, R., 16, 24, *218*
Cawkell, A. E., 59, *218*
Clough, E. A., 156, *219*
Cooper, M., 63, *218*
Corbishley, H. M., 199, 200, *218*

Croft, W. B., 180, 181, *218*
Cronin, B., 59, 192, 198, *218*

D
Daniel, E. H., 109, *222*
Davies, R., 119, *218*
Davis, C. H., 157, 159, *219*
Dudley, E. P., 156, *219*
du Mont, R. R., *219*
Dupuy, J.-P., 70, 71, 72, *219*
Dworkin, R., 24, 25, 42, 43, 44, 45, 46, 47, 48, 49, 50, 92, *219*

E
Ellis, D., 194, *219*
Ellul, J., 73, 74, 75, 76, 79, 81, *219*
Estabrook, L., 192, 194, *219*
Exon, F. C. A., 6, *217*, *219*

F
Farkas-Conn, I. S., 157, 158, 197, *219*
Farradane, J., 161, *219*
Feather, J., 151, 152, 153, *219*
Febvre, L., 151, *221*
Fidel, R., 17, *219*
Flores, F., 17, 88, *224*
Fosdick, H., 162, *219*
Foucault, M., 131, *219*
Frohmann, B., 118, 119, *219*

G
Gadamer, H.-G., 86, *219*
Garfield, E., 161, *219*
Giddens, A., 34, *220*
Griffith, B. C., 156, 159, 160, 161, *220*
Guinchat, C., 108, *220*

H

Harter, S. P., 9, 10
Hayes, R., 158, *217*
Heilprin, L. B., 87, 159, *220*
Herring, J. E., 192, 193, *220*
Hoel, I. A., 16, 24, *220*
Hollnagel, E., 18, *220*
Horton, F. W., Jr., 191, 193, 194, 195, *220*
Hounsell, D., 18, *220*
Houser, L., 109, *220*
Hubbard, W., 134, 135, *220*

I

Ingwersen, P., 176, 177, *220*
Institute of Information Scientists, 165, 166, *220*

J

Jani, N., 126, *220*
Jones, K. S., 155, 178, 179, *220*

K

King, A., 59, *220*
Kochen, M., 98, 100, 163, *220*
Kuhn, T. S., 15, 17, 130, *220*

L

Landau, H. B., 60, *221*
Lane, N., 192, *221*
Lessnoff, M., 34, *221*
Levitan, K. B., 187, *221*
Lewis, D. A., 196, 197, 198, *221*
Library Association, The, *221*
Line, M., 171, *221*
Lyon, D., 62, 63, *221*
Lytle, R. H., 187, 188, 189, 192, 195, *221*

M

MacAlister, J. Y. W., 141, 142, *221*
Machlup, F., 64, 65, 156, 157, 159, 160, *221*
MacIntyre, A., 122, 123, 207, *221*
Mansfield, U., 156, 157, 159, 160, *221*
Marchand, D., 193, *220*
Martin, H., 151, *221*
Martin, W. J., 59, *221*
McGill, M. J., 178, *222*
McKenzie, D. F., 28, 147, 148, 149, 150, 152, 153, *221*
Meadow, C., 7, 8, *221*
Menou, M., 108, *220*

Merton, R. K., 75, *221*
Miski, A., 157, *221*
Moore, N. E., 156, *219*

N

Natoli, J. P., 10, 11, *222*
Neill, S. D., 167, *222*

O

Olaisen, J. L., 10, 17, *222*
Oldman, C., 15, 16, *222*
Outhwaite, W., 22, 23, 24, 32, 86, 93, *222*

P

Parekh, H., 126, *220*
Philp, M., 131, 132, *222*
Pocock, J. G. A., 6, 52, 53, 56, 57, 91, 125, *222*
Porat, M. U., 64, *222*
Price, D. D., 158, 170, 171, 172, 173, *222*

R

Rayward, W. B., 97, 98, 99, 100, *222*
Reynolds, M. M., 109, *222*
Roberts, N., 161, 192, *222*
Rommetveit, R., 88, *222*
Rudd, D., 167, *222*
Rush, J. E., 157, 159, *219*

S

Salton, G., 178, 180, *222*
Saracevic, T., 159, *222*
Saunders, W. L., 99, 102, *223*
Sayers, W. C. B., 87, *223*
Schrader, A. M., 109, 156, *220*, *223*
Sen, B., 126, *220*
Shannon, C. E., 59, *223*
Shera, J. H., 100, 103, 104, 161, 175, *223*
Simonton, W., 119, *223*
Skinner, Q., 13, 14, 15, 52, *223*
Suppe, F., 16, 17, 59, *223*
Sutherland, E., 190, *223*
Sutton, B., 9, *218*, *223*
Swanson, R. W., 161, 162, *223*

T

Tanselle, T., 148, *223*
Taylor, C., 24, 25, 26, 27, 28, 29, 30, 31, 32, 33, 38, 39, 40, 41, 51, 80, 88, 92, 117, 126, 168, *223*
Tenopir, C., 161, 166, *223*

Toffler, A., 59, *223*
Traister, D., 153, 154, *223*
Transactions of the Bibliographical Society, *224*
Trauth, E. M., 192, *224*

U
Urquhart, D., 107, 108, *224*

V
van Rijsbergen, C. J., 17, *224*
Vernon, K. D. C., 11, *224*
Vickery, A., 10, 11, 182, 184, *217*, *224*
Vickery, B. C., 10, 11, 182, 184, *224*

W
Weaver, W., 59, *223*
Wersig, G., 161, *224*
Wiggins, R. E., 199, *224*
Wilkenson, J., 8, *224*
Williams, B., 59, 157, *224*
Williamson, N. J., 119, *224*
Wilson, P., 98, 110, 119, *224*
Wilson, T. D., 161, 192, 198, *222*, *224*
Windel, G., 161, *224*
Winn, V., 18, *220*
Winograd, T., 17, 88, *224*

Y
Young, S., 16, *224*

Subject Index

A
analytical bibliographies, 144
automation, 68
axial principle, 66
   expansion of information economy, 68–69
   growing importance of theoretical knowledge, 67
   libraries as central resources for storage of knowledge, 68
   merging of technologies, 68
   postindustrial society, 67–68
   production of new intellectual technology, 67
   professional services, 66
   proponents and detractors, 69–70

B
bibliography, 209
   adaptations of, 148
   analytical, 144
   character of, 143–146
   closer to library science and information studies, 150
   collection building, 139–140
   context of meaning for information studies, 149
   criticism of libraries, 144–146
   difficulties in interpretation, 140–141
   enumerative, 145
   function of, 143–144
   growth and waning of, 141–143
   historical, 146–148, 151–152
   measure of scholarly attainment, 139
   methods, 146–147
   new conceptions of, 149
   practices, 146–147
   purposive for readers, 149–150
   response to information culture, 147–151
   shift in interpretation, 148–149
   sociology of texts, 149–151
   technique, 147
   under-laborer's task, 139
bibliometrics, 10, 170–175
brute data, 26–27, 30, 167–168, 172
   attack on, 38–40
   empirical science, 38–39
   exactitude of, 33
   historical data, 51
   linguistic labels as, 89
   meaning that can attach, 38
   reduced certainty of, 34
building knowledge, 25–29

C
cataloging
   changes in, 110
   codes, 87
citations, 172–173
classification
   changes in, 110
   power over knowledge, 131–132
   schemes, 87
cognitive science and information retrieval (IR), 180–182
common meanings, 31–32
communal knowledge, 130, 132–133
computer science and information retrieval (IR), 177–180
computerized information retrieval, 10, 69
conceptions, 49, 128
   arguments about, 114–115
   changing, 125

230 SUBJECT INDEX

concept of information studies, 93–94
consistency and integrity, 116
different, 115
excluding some, 116
expression or manifestation of, 110–111
giving definitions to, 112
independent disciplines, 116–117
information studies, 137–138
no requirement for, 114
paradigms and, 128–131
practices, 208–209
relationship to technical skills, 116–117
testing, 133–134
transforming, 134–136
concepts, 49
constructive interpretation, 45–46, 129
constructs open to only one interpretation, 26
context, 20
context of meaning, 55–57, 114
   creating interpretations, 57
   information society, 62
   information studies, 69
   language crucial for interpretation, 56–57
contextual meaning, 87
convergence of beliefs, 41–42
conversational interpretation, 45
creative interpretation, 45, 129

D
development of theory and rules, 113–114
disciplines and practices, 117

E
empirical science and brute data, 38–39
enumerative bibliography, 145
European philosophy, 13–14
evidence, 19–20
experience, 19
experiential meaning, 29
experimental information retrieval. See information retrieval

F
false ally, 31
fusing of horizons method, 14

G
grand theory, 13

H
hermeneutic background, 2
hermeneutic science, principal requirement, 94–95
hermeneutics, 8, 12, 15, 18–19
   changes in information retrieval, 17
   competing strands of, 24–25
   empirical attempt to escape from, 26
   history of, 22–24
   information science, 16
   insight, 30
   interpretation, 22–25
   linked to interpretive approaches, 12
   logical positivism and, 33–35
   meaning, 27–28
   philosophy of, 25
   professional identity, 16
   reputation of, 93
   science requirements, 27–28
   seeking meanings of language, 26
   social theory validation, 30–31
   textual analysis, 23
   theory of, 24
   top-down vs. bottom-up approach, 25
   understanding social sciences, 86
historical bibliography, 146–148
historical data, 51–53
human actions as natural events, 14
human life and observable data, 22
human sciences and brute data, 172
hypothetico-deductive logical positivism, 33

I
IIS (Institute of Information Scientists) statement, 166
indexing, changes in, 110
induction, 26
information
   growth of, 68–69
   infrastructure, 195
   vs. knowledge, 64–65
   postindustrial society, 67–68
   theory, 59
information age, 11, 20, 60. See also information society
   availability of more information, 60
   dependence on intellectual technology and intellectual class, 60
   general trends in society, 61–63
   information studies view of, 57–58

information technology changes, 61
information-related occupations, 60
  need of explanation for, 52
  reaction to phenomena of, 58
  satisfactory account of, 41
  technological way of thinking, 60
  understanding, 34
  wealth based on generation of knowledge, 60
information architecture, 195
information culture, 20, 57–58, 78–81, 94, 114, 119–120, 124
  bibliography response to, 147–151
  definition of, 11–12, 58
  examination of, 20
information economy, 63–66
  assessing worth of services, 65
  automation, 68
  divisions of, 64
  growth of information and information retrieval, 68–69
  information and noninformation products, 65–66
  knowledge vs. information, 64–65
  occupations part of, 64
  who is included in, 64
information environment, 195
information explosion, 171
information management, 209
information managers, 5–7, 63
  describing and defining, 5–7
  organizing view of fields, 49
  theory, research, and practice relationship, 6–7
information research and libraries, 214–215
information resource management (IRM), 187
  business orientation, 190
  conceptual problems, 189
  definitions of, 188–192
  differences in, 192
  emphasis on content of information, 188
  focus, 192–196
  goals and means necessary for attainment, 195–196
  interpretation, 196–201
  key activities, 199–200
  professional reaction, 196–201
  values of, 190–192

information resources shared meaning, 32
information retrieval (IR), 87–88, 175–182
  categorizing, 176–177
  change in emphasis in, 176–177
  cognitive science, 180–182
  computer science, 177–180
  computerized, 69
  contextual meaning, 87
  growth of, 68–69
  meaning, 87
  moves away from, 17
information science, 86–88, 155–157, 209
  antecedents, 157–158
  as social science, 167
  associating with scientific research, 12–13
  associations, 158–159
  bibliometrics, 170–175
  brute data, 167–168, 172
  changing paradigm, 169
  communicative potential, 103
  competing models, 88–89
  conception making sense to practitioners, 164
  confusion in definition of, 156–157
  connections with library science, 99
  definitions of, 159–162
  development, 157–158
  division between library science, 98–99
  documents, 168–169
  electronic version of, 102
  hermeneutics, 16
  inaccessibility of published research, 13
  incorporating experience of information scientists, 18
  independence, 163–164
  information retrieval (IR), 175–182
  interlocking levels of shared meanings, 89
  interpretation, 163–164
  interpretive approach, 1–2
  knowledge, 168–169
  lack of definition of, 7–8
  librarian view of, 156–157
  library tradition of, 167
  necessity of division of, 97–105
  needs of users, 174
  no polarity with librarianship, 104
  only part of librarian duties, 104
  primary focus of, 102

232 SUBJECT INDEX

   problems, 162–163
   professional preparation, 165–167
   publications, 158–159
   qualitative studies of information, 170–175
   reinterpretation, 2
   relating to epistemology, 12
   scientific character of, 160–161
   scientific method, 9–11
   shared concepts with library science, 102
   similarities to library science, 99–100
information scientists, 102
   organizing view of fields, 49
information society, 11, 58–60, 78, 171. See also information age
   communication problems, 71
   computers handling information, 62
   context of meaning, 62
   critically dependent on information, 60
   criticisms of, 70
   dangers inherent in, 71–75
   debate about, 66
   defining, 79–81
   determining language and interpretation, 62–63
   differing outcomes of, 70
   impact on man and society, 70
   impact on quality of life, 71
   inclusions and exclusions of members of, 81
   interpretation of economics, 63–66
   knowledge, 79
   maintenance or recovery of freedom, 73
   nature of, 80
   objections to idea of, 70
   polarization of segments of society, 71–72
   quality of life, 72–73
   shared meanings, 75
   technique, 75–76, 79
   technological system, 73–75
   technology, 59, 73
   world characterized by technical phenomena, 76
information specialist profile, 108
information studies, 2
   arguments about conceptions, 114–115
   as social science, 86–87
   aspects are historical data, 51

   barriers to development of confidence in, 14
   benefiting from association with social theory, 95
   bibliography closer to, 150
   classification schemes, 133
   communal knowledge, 130–133
   competing expressions of identification, 57
   complexity, 132
   computers, 78
   conceptions, 137–138
   conceptions constructed from historical data, 52
   conceptions of concept of, 49, 93–94
   context of meaning, 69, 114
   cumulative in knowledge, 49
   definition of, 89
   dependence on rules, 112–113
   describing and defining, 6–7
   educational function, 91
   examination of information culture, 20
   general discussions of, 115
   grounds for adopting interpretive approach, 94–96
   hermeneutic background, 2
   high-level theories, 6
   implications, 210–215
   information explosion, 171
   information society, 58–60
   interpretive approach, 16
   interpretive argument, 207–208
   lack of theoretical base, 85
   language development, 24
   language of perspicuous contrast, 94
   libraries and information research (IR), 214–215
   libraries and information theory, 213
   meaning and interpretation of practice, 1
   middle-range theories, 6
   need for hermeneutic, interpretive method, 34
   parallels with law, 42–43, 49
   past practices influencing present, 50
   phenomenological approach, 15–16
   philosophical reaction, 15
   practice or theory of practice, 90–94
   practices, 211–213
   principal requirement for hermeneutic science, 94–95

SUBJECT INDEX 233

propositions, 203
rules and development of theory, 113–114
scientific method, 9–11
sense or cohesion of, 94
shared interpretation and construction of solution, 95
shared meanings, 95–96
shortcomings of, 18
similarity to features in politics, 37
society, 211–213
suitability of interpretive approach, 85–86
theories, 211–213
uncomfortable aspects of epistemological situation, 8
view of information age, 57–58
work practices historical data, 51
information technology, 58, 77–78
　consequences of, 119–120
　influences and social impact, 1
　merging technologies, 77
　microcomputer revolution, 78
　practitioners and computers, 77–78
　social implications of, 59
　transforming economic life, 61
　transforming individual and social life, 61
insight, 30
intellectual technology, 67
interpretation, 8, 15, 21
　absence of interaction with those not sharing forms of expression, 47
　becoming essence, 135
　brute data, 26–27
　building knowledge, 25–29
　changes to, 55–56
　common language, 32–33
　completion, 135
　construct open to only one, 26
　constructive, 45–46, 129
　context of meaning, 55–57
　conversational, 45
　creative, 45, 129
　distinguishing between concepts and conceptions, 49
　economics of information society, 63–66
　experiential meaning, 29
　false ally, 31
　focusing, 135
　forms of, 45–46

gap between ours and others, 32–33
general justification for main elements of practice, 46
hermeneutics, 22–25
historical data, 51–53
historical dependence, 55–56
improved clarity, 29
information science, 163–164
information society determining, 62–63
internal technical arguments about, 48
interrelated layers, 29
intersubjective understanding, 23–24
judges and, 50
language crucial for, 56–57
law, 42–50
learning of, 23
meaning, 27–29
multiple in law, 49–50
new context of meaning and, 57
personal or external contributions to, 47
politics, 37–42
postinterpretive stage, 46
practical, 50
practices, 208
preinterpretive stage, 46
problems with language, 28
refilling, 135
scientific, 45
self-identity, 30
self-limitation, 135
self-reflection, 26
social practice, 44
social scientist being participant, 47
stages of, 46–47
striving to make object best it can be, 44
swerving, 135
validation, 29–33
what people do, 21–22
interpreters, 47
　limiting freedom of, 45
interpretive, 15
interpretive account, 31–32
interpretive approach, 1–2, 16, 19–20, 204
　brute data, 27, 34
　building from disparate sources, 19
　changes in practices, 121–122
　components of meaning, 205
　conditioning practice, 117–119

234 SUBJECT INDEX

conditions required for, 86–90
constructing clearer meanings, 26
distinction between meaning and embodiment of expression, 88
evidence, 19–20
experience, 19
field of objects, 88
finding and defining what librarians do, 31
grounds for adopting, 94–96
interpretation, 205–206
language of perspicuous contrast, 206
law, 47
linked to hermeneutics, 12
meaning, 27
meaning in relation to other meanings, 88
meanings dependent on source of improvement, 91
means of application, 90–94
no conception requirement, 114
objections to, 97–105
persons for whom meaning exists, 88
relationship of conceptions to technical skills, 116–117
requirements of hermeneutic science, 205
self-identity, 205–206
separate and incompatible expressions, 129
social sciences, 31, 85
suitability of, 85–86
testing, 133–134
theory and levels of theory, 127–128
validation, 30, 205
interpretive explanation method, 15
intersubjective understanding, 23–24

K
knowledge, 79, 168–169
vs. information, 64–65
objective, 168–169
postindustrial society, 67–68

L
language
common for interpretation, 32–33
complexity of, 125
crucial for interpretation, 56–57
ethnocentric, 33
forming and performing intentions, 56
historical data, 52–53
information society determining, 62–63
of perspicuous contrast, 40
practices, 124–125
problems with, 28
shared set of meanings, 26
used by users and librarians, 23–24
voting, 39
world made apparent by, 56
language of perspicuous contrast, 80, 94, 100
law
acceptable interpretation, 50
actions that serve purpose, 44
alternative conceptions of, 104
competing definitions of, 98
concepts and conceptions, 49
cumulative in knowledge, 49
dependence on social consent, 47–48
differing practices, 116–117
educational function, 91
formal interpretive body, 43
harmonizing internal and external views, 48
internal technical argument about interpretation, 48
interpretation, 42–50
judges and interpretation, 50, 134–135
knowledge-based construction, 42
multiple interpretations, 49–50
paradoxes in, 48
parallels with information studies, 42–43, 49
participating in social practice, 46
person interpreting social practice, 45
practice or theory of practice, 90–91
precedents conditioning interpretation, 48
problems with interpretation, 48
purpose as constraint, 48
shared meanings, 43–44
social practice, 44
sources of text, 92
theory altering practice, 48
work of average lawyer, 90
librarians, 5–7, 63
assessing quality, 171
complexity in interpretation of, 5
describing and defining, 5–7

SUBJECT INDEX 235

future of, 8
metainformation, 65
organizing view of fields, 49
relationship to text of books, 25
supplying information, 65
theory, research, and practice relationship, 6–7
librarianship
  barriers to development of confidence in, 14
  future of, 8
  human factor, 11
  inaccessibility of published research, 13
  interpretive account of, 103
  no polarity with information science, 104
  objective approach, 11
  principles of, 107–108
  relating to epistemology, 12
  scientific method, 9–11
  subjective approach, 11
libraries
  central resources for storage of knowledge, 68
  information research (IR), 214–215
  information theory, 213
  information work and, 63
  language used by users and librarians, 23–24
  meaning of, 89
  rules for cataloging, 49
  shared meaning, 32
library science
  attaining recognition as science, 9
  bibliography closer to, 150
  connections with information science, 99
  division with information science, 98–99
  necessity of division of, 97–105
  processes, 103
  scientific method, 9–11
  shared concepts with information science, 102
  similarities to information science, 99–100
library studies, 2
  as social science, 86–87
  complexity, 132
  computers, 78
  describing and defining, 6–7
  examination of information culture, 20
  general discussions of, 115
  language development, 24
  move away from paradigm, 17
  philosophical reaction, 15
  practice or theory of practice, 90–91
  propositions, 203
  scientific method, 9–11
  shared interpretation and construction of solution, 95
  shared meanings, 95–96
  suitability of interpretive approach, 85–86
  uncomfortable aspects of epistemological situation, 8
linguistic philosophy, 14
logical positivism, 12
  hermeneutics and, 33–35
  hypothetico-deductive, 33
  statistical-probabilistic, 33–34

M

meaning, 27–29, 87
  common, 31–32
  about something, 27
  relationship to other meanings, 27
  shared, 31–32
  structure and interpretation, 28–29
  subject, 27
merging technologies, 77
metainformation, 65
  not developing but handling, 68
metaknowledge, 133
methods
  anarchic claim, 14
  associating information science with scientific research, 12–13
  bibliographies, 146–147
  European philosophy, 13–14
  fusing of horizons, 14
  grand theory, 13
  hermeneutics, 12, 15, 18–19
  interpretive approach, 12, 16, 19–20
  linguistic philosophy, 14
  logical empiricism, 12
  logical positivism, 12
  phenomenological approach, 15–16
  positivism, 16–17

236 SUBJECT INDEX

rejection of, 14
symbolic interactionism, 45
microcomputer revolution, 78

N
nonarbitrary verification, 26

O
objective approach, 11
objective facts and historical data, 51
objective knowledge, 168, 169

P
paradigms and conceptions, 128–131
participants and nonprofessional users, 89
participation, defining, 45–46
phenomenological approach, 15–16, 95
phenomenological sociology, 23
philosophical reactions, 15
political science
  analysis of questionnaire data, 39
  attack on positivism, 37–40
  ethnocentrism of Western, 38
  individuals, 40–42
  language of voting, 39
  meanings attaching to brute data, 38
  searching for universalist base, 41
  societies, 40–42
  treatment of beliefs and attitudes as consensus, 41–42
politics
  attack on brute data, 38–40
  autonomous parties entering into contractual relationships, 40
  interpretation, 37–42
  practice or theory of practice, 90–91
  similarity to features of information studies, 37
  social science, 38
positivism, 1, 16
  hypothetico-deductive logical, 33
  inadequacy, 25–26
  logical, 33–35
  political science attack on, 37–40
  problems with, 17
  statements of fact, 16
  statements of logic and mathematics, 16
  statistical-probabilistic logical, 33–34
  theory neutral facts, 16
  verification, 29–30

postindustrial society, 67–68
power over knowledge, 130–133
  classification, 131–132
practical interpretation, 50
practical reason, 121–127
practices, 9, 35, 109–111, 121–127, 206–208, 215–216
  assessing, 106–111, 124
  author providing formal structure for all interpretive claims, 46
  bibliography, 146–147
  changes in, 123
  closest to shared meanings, 91–92
  complexity of, 124
  conceptions, 208–209
  current intentions of participants, 46
  definition of, 8, 122
  deriving from theory, 125–126
  differences in, 115
  disciplines, 117
  improvements in, 123
  interpretation, 208
  interpretive approach conditioning, 117–119
  interpreting, 210
  language, 124–125
  limiting, 111
  models of, 128
  practitioners, 121
  research, 102, 104
  rewards extending from, 122–123
  theory developed from, 100–101
  transforming conceptions, 210
practitioners, 121
  computers and, 77–78
  convictions of, 81
  definition of, 8
  development of theory, 100–101
  how good or bad at job, 106–107
  higher purposes motivating, 106
  information science conception making sense to, 164
  traditional techniques, 105–113
preinterpretive stage of interpretation, 46
procedures, 109–111
  rules for, 118
professional identity, 16
professional services, 66
psychologism approach, 95

Q

qualitative methods, 10
qualitative studies of information, 170–175
quality of life, 72–73
quantitative methods, 10

R

research, positivist or scientific models, 1
rules
　credibility of, 113
　dependence on, 112–113
　development of theory and, 113–114
　for procedures, 118
　shared set of, 118

S

scholarship and nonquantative terms, 172–173
science
　brute data, 26–27
　coherence of objects, 27
　correctness of rational assumptions about, 14
　distinguishing between meanings, 27–28
　hermeneutic requirements, 27–28
　incommensurability of theories, 129–130
　induction, 26
　nonarbitrary verification, 26
　nonquantitative terms, 172–173
　objective facts, 26
　related to technology, 67
　role of literature in, 170
　subject for whom meanings exists, 28
　technique preceding, 76
scientific interpretation, 45
scientific method, 9–11
　logical empiricism, 12
　logical positivism, 12
　positivism, 17
　social science research, 13
scientific research, 12–13, 15
scientific validity, 17
scientists, 171
self-identity, 30
self-reflection, 26
shared meanings, 31–32, 75, 95–96
　interlocking levels of, 89
　law, 43–44

social practice, 44–46
social sciences
　brute data, 172
　changing theories of, 31
　current thinking, 12
　epistemological problems, 13
　exactitude of brute data, 33
　explaining, 30
　false ally, 31
　historical accounts, 30
　historical in character, 51
　hypothetico-deductive logical positivism, 33
　information and library studies as, 86
　interpretive approach, 31, 85
　isolating human experience from external interference, 33
　neutral observations, 10
　politics, 38
　radical shift in thinking, 18
　reconciling hermeneutic and positivist traditions, 34
　research, 13
　statistical-probabilistic logical positivism, 34
　theory validation, 30–31
　universal empiricist, 33
social scientists, 45–47
societies, 40–42
　critically dependent on information, 60
sociology of texts, 149
statements of fact, 16
statements of logic and mathematics, 16
statistical-probabilistic logical positivism, 33–34
subjective approach, 11
symbolic interactionism, 27, 45, 95, 104

T

technical skill, 121–127
　not good measure of worker, 127
　not performing at this level, 126
　redefinition of importance of, 116–117
　relationship to conceptions, 116–117
techniques, 75–76, 79
　assessing, 106–107
　bibliography, 147
　efficiency, 76

how good or bad at job, 106–107
   immediate use, 76
   practices, 109–111
   preceding science, 76
   procedures, 109–111
   relationship to field, 107–108
   traditional, 105–113
technological system, 73–74
textual analysis, 23
theoretical knowledge, 67
theory, 127–128
   development of, 113–114
   levels of, 127–128
theory neutral facts, 16

U

understanding, 8, 21
users
   interpreting concepts, 112–113
   knowing rules, 111

V

validation, 29–33
   self-identity, 30
verification, 29–30
Verstehen, 8, 15, 21, 23

W

what people do, 21–22

www.ingramcontent.com/pod-product-compliance
Lightning Source LLC
Chambersburg PA
CBHW071351290426
44108CB00014B/1508